THE 16 AND 17TH PUBLICATION DESIGN ANNUAL

THANK YOU
Dennis Di Vincenzo & Rea Ackerman—Design and
Production of The Book

Howard Glenner and Typographic Communications, Inc.
—Credit Typography for Annual Sixteen

Sid Minson and Royal Composing Room—Credit
Typography for Annual Seventeen

U.S. Lithograph—Remaining Text and Lists

Interstate Book Manufacturers—Color Separations,
Text Printing and Binding

CONTENTS

DISTRIBUTION

Distributors to the Book Trade in the United
States
Robert Silver Associates
95 Madison Avenue
New York, New York 10016
(212) 686-5630

In Canada

General Publishing Co. Ltd.
30 Lesmil RD.
Don Mills, Ont. M3B 2T6

Distributed throughout
the rest of
the world by
Fleetbooks, S.A.
100 Park Avenue
New York, New York 10017 U.S.A.

LETTER FROM THE PRESIDENT:

The Society of Publication Designers is proud to publish the authoritative collection of the best publication design of 1980–81.

Chosen from more than five thousand entries in our international competition, these 701 innovative and exciting selections have been exhibited in New York and honored with Gold and Silver Awards of Excellence as well as Awards of Distinctive Merit—the highest awards for creativity that our industry affords.

Publications of every size, subject and paper stock are represented in this 336 page volume of dazzling and inspiring design solutions. And they are organized in categories that delineate the day-to-day creative challenges of publication design.

This book is an essential reference tool for design professionals and educators, corporate communications executive and artist, editor and publisher. It is the only comprehensive view of the state-of-the-art of publication design at a high point in its history.

Assembling and publishing this book was a herculean task and the Society gratefully acknowledges the invaluable assistance of Tom Lennon and Jerry Demoney without whose determined efforts, PUBLICATION DESIGN 16–17 wouldn't have been possible.

Myles Ludwig
President

Jerry Alten
TV Guide
Radnor, PA 19088

Elaine Anderson
Flowers &
2400 Compton Blvd.
Redondo Beach, CA 90278

Robert Barkin
Washington Post
Edit-New Art Dept.
1150-15th St. NW
Washington, DC 20071

Patrick Barney
Ford Motor Co.
P.O. Box 1509-13
Dearborn, MI 48121

Cheri L. Bayer
Jersey Journal
412-C Mayfair Blvd.
Columbus, OH 43213

Martin Bennett
North Chas. St. Des. Org.
222 W. Saratoga St.
Baltimore, MD 21201

John Bieniel
Bieniek Assoc.
2900 Wayne Turn.
Bensalem, PA 19020

Arline Bognar
1345 Haverston Rd.
Lyndhurst, OH 44124

Andrew Bornstein
1325-18th St. NW
Washington, DC 20036

Joseph Bowlby
1217 Main St.
Evanston, IL 60202

Michael Brock
11471 La Maida St.
N. Hollywood, CA 91601

Sandra Jean Brown
CDS Review
30 N. Michigan Ave.
Suite 1302
Chicago, IL 60602

Miles Burke
Powder Magazine
P.O. Box 1028
Dana Point, CA 92629

Larry Burkhart
The Register
P.O. Box 11626
625 N. Grand Ave.
Santa Ana, CA 92711

Ronn Campisi
The Boston Globe
135 Morrissey Blvd.
Boston, MA 02107

Judy Garlan
The Atlantic Monthly
8 Arlington St.
Boston, MA 02116

Robert Casebeer
312 Rear E. High Ave.
New Philadelphia, OH 44663

John B. Casey
3818 Davis Pl. NW 304
Washington, DC 20007

Paul A. Casper
Alexander Communications
212 W. Superior
Chicago, IL 60610

Jill Chen
Honolulu Magazine
828 Fort St. Mall
Suite 400
Honolulu, HI 96813

Mary T. Christoph
Broadcast Communications
4121 W. 83rd St., Suite 132
Prairie Village, KS 66208

M. J. Cody
Flowers &
518½ Clinton St.
Los Angeles, CA 90004

John H. Colville
Harrowsmith Magazine
Camden East
Ontario, Canada
K0K 1J0

Rich Conner
9333 N. Meridien
P.O. Box 80229
Indianapolis, IN 46240

Stan Corfman
Marathon World
539 S. Main St.
Findlay, OH 45840

Jim Darilek
Texas Monthly
P.O. Box 1569
Austin, TX 78767

Don Demaio
United Feature Syndicate, Inc.
1100 Central Trust Tower
Cincinnati, OH 45202

Jose L. Diaz De Villegas
Revista Asi
P.O. Box S 297
San Juan, PR 00902

Elizabeth G. Dixon
Wilson Quarterly
Smithsonian Inst. Bldg.
Washington, DC 20560

Daniel J. Driscoll
Dir. of Comm.
American Postal Worker
11903 Oakwood Dr.
Woodbridge, VA 22192

Steven Duckett
Florida Trend
440 First Ave. S
St. Petersburg, FL 33731

Gary Dykstra
2037 N. York
Dearborn, MI 48128

Henry Fien
Ford Motor Co.
P.O. Box 1509-B
Dearborn, MI 48121

Polly Friend
Director of Media
W. Bloomfield Schools
4500 Walnut Lake Rd.
W. Bloomfield, MI 48033

Sara Giovanitti
The Boston Globe
135 Morrissey Blvd.
Boston, MA 02107

Raymond Gibson
Harvest Publ.
7500 Old Oak Blvd.
Middleburgh Hgts., OH 44130

David Hale
Pitman Learning
530 University Ave.
Palo Alto, CA 94301

Stephen Hall
1175 Starks Bldg.
Louisville, KY 40202

Mike Hancock
Black Collegian
1240 S. Broad St.
New Orleans, LA 70125

Elizabeth J. Harding
2231 California St. NW
Washington, DC 20008

Charles Helmken
11 Du Pont Circle, NW
Suite 400
Washington, DC 20036

Florence Herman
Clarion-Ledger
6807 Vicksburg
New Orleans, LA 70124

Richard Hull
The Ensign
50 E. North Temple St.
Salt Lake City, UT 84150

Gail Hunt
6856 Eastern Ave., NW
Washington, DC 20012

Mary Inabnit
Houston Home & Garden
P.O. Box 25386
Houston, TX 77005

David Jendras
Amer. Bar Assoc.
33 W. Monroe St., 7th Fl.
Chicago, IL 60603

Jerald A. Johnson
Mutiable Publ.
1999 Shepard Rd.
St. Paul, MN 55116

Janice Keene
Amer. Guernsey Cattle Club
P.O. Box 27410
Columbus, OH 43227

Eric Keller
Art Director
1404 Commonwealth Bldg.
Detroit, MI 48226

Frank D. Kemper
904 Colfax
Evanston, IL 60201

Susan Kingsbury
Home Study Catalogue
1660 Stewart St.
Santa Monica, CA 90404

Ray Kohl
American Printer
300 W. Adams St.
Chicago, IL 60606

Louise Kollenbaum
Mother Jones Magazine
625 Third St.
San Francisco, CA 94107

Nancy Krueger
National Journal
1730 'M' St., NW
Washington, DC 20036

Mark Laurenson
Marriage & Family Living
St. Meinrad, IN 47577

Jack Lefkowitz
Industrial Launderer
Rt. 1, Box 307 E
Leesburg, VA 22075

Thomas G. Lewis
2900-4th St.
San Diego, CA 92103

Steven Liska
213 W. Institute Place
Chicago, IL 60610

Peggy Loeb
Simmons College
300 The Fenway
Boston, MA 02115

Jack Lund
Chicago-WFMT
500 N. Michigan Ave.
Chicago, IL 60611

John MacClellan
Richmond Lifestyle
701 E. Franklin St.
Suite 1100
Richmond, VA 23219

Fernando M. Martinez
Art Dir.
Designers West Magazine
8320 Melrose
Los Angeles, CA 90069

Lynda Maudlin
Envoy
620 Michigan Ave., NE
Washington, DC 20064

Ron McClellen
American College
Testing Program
P.O. Box 168
Iowa City, IA 52243

Meindl Graphics Inc.
435 Taft Ave.
Glen Ellyn, IL 60137

Donna Miller
Ranger Rick's Nature
1412-16th St., NW
Washington, DC 20036

Randy Miller
St. Louis Post Dispatch
900 N. Tucker
St. Louis, MO 63101

Bono Mitchell
Builder Magazine
15th & 'M' St., NW
Washington, DC 20005

Robert J. Moon
Stone In America
6902 N. High St.
Worthington, OH 43085

Suzanne Morin
Olin D'Oeil
100 Ave. Dresden
Ville Mont-Royal, Quebec
Canada H3P 2B6

Linda Fritts Moylan
Publication Design
18620 S.W. 88th Rd.
Miami, FL 33197

Judith Munro
Manuf Engineering
One SME Drive
Dearborn, MI 48128

Hilber Nelson
Nav Press
Discipleship Journal
3820 N. 30th St., C
Colorado Springs, CO 80934

William C. Newkirk
Malcolm Grear Designers
391 Eddy St.
Providence, RI 02906

Fino Ortiz
Interface Age
16704 Marquardt Ave.
Cerritos, CA 90701

Howard E. Paine
Natl. Geo. Society
17th & M Sts., NW
Washington, DC 20036

Arthur Paul
Playboy
919 N. Michigan Ave.
Chicago, IL 60611

Greg Paul
Plain Dealer Magazine
1801 Superior Ave.
Cleveland, OH 44114

Marty Petty
Kansas City Star-Times
1729 Grand
Kansas City, MO 64108

Jeffrey Pilarski
Chicago Magazine-WFMT
500 N. Michigan Ave.
Chicago, IL 60611

Jack Podell
American Bar Assoc.
1155 E. 60th St.
Chicago, IL 60637

Kerig Pope
Playboy
919 N. Michigan
Chicago, IL 60611

Dallas Powell
Dir.-Graph Comm.
R. J. Reynolds Indr., Inc.
World Headquarters Bldg.
Winston-Salem, NC 27102

Bill Prochnow
Sierra Club
530 Bush St.
San Francisco, CA 94108

Antonios Pronotis
Chaners Publications
1350 E. Touhy Ave.
P.O. Box 5080
Des Plaines, IL 60018

James H. Richardson
Modern Maturity
215 Long Beach Blvd.
Long Beach, CA 90803

Robyn Ricks
Pacific NW Magazine
222 Dexter Ave., N
Seattle, WA 98109

Leslie Riell
Mesa-Magazine of East Valley
2645 W. Ocaso Circle
Mesa, AZ 85202

Henry Robertz
Robertz Webb & Co.
111 E. Wacker Dr., No. 529
Chicago, IL 60601

Jill Roth
Maclean Hunter Publ. Co.
300 W. Adams St.
Chicago, IL 60606

Robert Miles Runyon & Assoc.
200 E. Culver Blvd.
Playa Del Rev, CA 90291

Mauren Ryan
MNPLS-St. Paul Magazine
512 Nicollet Mall
Minneapolis, MN 55410

B. F. Schmidt
Ford Motor Co.
P.O. Box 1509-B
Dearborn, MI 48121

Richard F. Shaw
P.O. Box 11848
Ft. Worth, TX 76109

Mr. Richard Shaw
99 S. Third St.
Apt. 7
Pensacola, FL 32507

Steven J. Shediyv
Credit Union Exec.
Box 431
Madison, WI 53701

Lanny Sherwin
Publisher
Gulfshore Publ. Co., Inc.
3620 N. Tamiami Trail
Naples, FL 33940

Art Smith
234 S. Marengo Ave.
Pasadena, CA 91101

Hal Smith
Private Practice
CCMS Publishers
P.O. Box 12489
Oklahoma City, OK 73157

Hal Smith
1109 Hunters Glen
Edmond, OK 73034

Kenneth Smith
13-30 Corp.
505 Market St.
Knoxville, TN 37902

Larry Smitherman
Smitherman Graphic Design
6448 Hwy. 290E D102
Austin, TX 78723

Tom Staebler
Playboy
919 N. Michigan Ave.
Chicago, IL 60611

Stephen Stanley
Stephen Stanley Design
251 Kearney St., No. 402
San Francisco, CA 94108

Allen Stebbins
AGRI-Marketing
AGRI-Finance
5520-G Touhy Ave.
Skokie, IL 60077

Dugald Stermer
1844 Union St.
San Francisco, CA 94123

Donna Tashjian
American Bar Assoc.
1155 E. 60th St.
Chicago, IL 60637

Pat Taylor
Construction Spec.
1150-17th St., NW
Washington, DC 20036

Hans Teensma
Rocky Mountain Magazine
1741 High St.
Denver, CO 80218

Al Trungale
Furniture Design
400 N. Michigan
Chicago, IL 60611

Victoria Valentine
American Film
JFK Center
Washington, DC 20566

Stephen F. Ward
Art Director
Down East Magazine
Box 679
Camden, ME 04843

Anne Wholf
Palm Beach Life
265 Royal Poinciana Way
Palm Beach, FL 33480

Shelley Williams
13-30 Corp.
505 Market St.
Knoxville, TN 37902

Burton Winnick
606 Stonegate Terr.
Glencoe, IL 60022

Ray Wong
The Clarion Ledger
311 E. Pearl St.
Jackson, MI 39205

Nelson Wright
Solar Age Magazine
Church Hill
Harrisville, NH 03450

Bob Zeni
Collector-Investor
740 N. Rush
Chicago, IL 60611

Austin Grandjean
Politiken
37 Raadhuspladsen
Copenhagen V 1585
Denmark

Cuneyt E. Koryurek
187-4 Cumhuriyet,
Elmadag I Istanbul
Turkey

Oswaldo Miranda
Joaquim Jose Pedrosa-856
Curitaba Parana
Brasil 80.00

Finn Nielsen
Politiken
37 Raadhuspladsen
Copenhagen V 1585
Denmark

Leslie Abney
Town & Country
1700 Broadway
New York, NY 10019

Rich Aloisio
145 E. 16th St., 7N
New York, NY 10003

Altemus
CBS Consumer Publishing
Family Weekly Magazine
641 Lexington Ave., 5 Fl.
New York, NY 10022

Art Directors Club
488 Madison Ave.
New York, NY 10022

Leon Auerbach
Astronauts & Aeronautics
1290 Ave. of Americas
New York, NY 10019

Jeff Babitz
110–37 Saultell Ave.
Corona, NY 11368

John Barban
Chemical Business
32 W. 40th St.
New York, NY 10018

Bob Barravecchia
Modern Plastics
1221 Ave. of Americas
New York, NY 10020

Ann Beckerman
50 W. 29th St.
New York, NY 10001

Murray Belsky
American Heritage
10 Rockefeller Pl.
New York, NY 10020

Milton Berwin
Lebhar–Friedman, Inc.
425 Park Ave. So.
New York, NY 10022

Robert Best
New York Magazine
755 Second Ave.
New York, NY 10017

Steven Black
Scientific American
415 Madison Ave.
New York, NY 10022

Bruce Blair
Money Magazine
1271 Ave. of Americas
New York, NY 10020

Ellen Blissman
Money Magazine
Time, Inc.
1271 6th Ave. 33rd Floor
New York, NY 10020

Amy Bogert
144 E. 37th St, 3C
New York, NY 10016

Carol Bokuniewicz
M & Co., Inc.
157 W. 57th St.
New York, NY 10019

Patricia Bradbury
New York Magazine
755 Second Ave.
New York, NY 10017

A. Braverman
Motor Boating & Sailing
959 Eighth Ave.
New York, NY 10019

Michael Brent
Art Director
Tennis Magazine
495 Westport Ave.
Norwalk, CT 06856

Carol Breslau
18 Woodlake Dr. E.
Woodbury, NY 11797

Joe Brooks
Penthouse
909 Third Ave.
New York, NY 10022

Alex Brown
Rd. 2 Wright Rd.
Cambridge, NY 12816

Kathie Brown
U.S. Lithograph, Inc.
853 Broadway
New York, NY 10003

Phyllis Busell
Diversion Mag. Assoc.
60 E. 42nd St.
New York, NY 10017

Bill Butt
400 E. 50th St., 2F
New York, NY 10022

Ed Buxbaum
Popular Electronics
1 Park Ave.
New York, NY 10016

Arline Campbell
61 Pierpont St.
Brooklyn, NY 11201

Ron Campbell
Fortune—Time
1271 Ave. of Americas
New York, NY 10020

Bryan Canniff
Ziff—Davis
Boating Magazine
1 Park Ave.
New York, NY 10016

Diane Cappadona
Diversion Mag. Assoc.
60 E. 42nd St.
New York, NY 10017

Tom Carnase, President
Carnase, Inc.
30 East 21st St.
New York, NY 10010

Barbara Carr
245 E. 40th St., 19D
New York, NY 10016

George Cawthorne
Sports Afield
250 W. 55th St.
New York, NY 10019

Barbara L. Chapman
40 Park Ave., 15E
New York, NY 10016

Traci Churchill
144 Sullivan St.
No. 21
New York, NY 10012

Seymour Chwast
Pushpin Lubalin—
Peckolick, Inc.
67 Irving Pl.
New York, NY 10003

Jennifer N. Clark
Lebhar—Friedman, Inc.
425 Park Ave. So.
New York, NY 10022

Mervyn Clay
Americana Magazine
29 W. 38th St.
New York, NY 10018

Robert Clive
New York Daily News
220 E. 42nd St.
New York, NY 10017

Victor J. Closi
Field & Stream
1515 Broadway
New York, NY 10036

George Coderre
Progressive Architecture
600 Summer St., Box 1361
Stamford, CT 06904

Robert A. Cohen
Boardroom Reports
500 Fifth Ave.
New York, NY 10036

John Conley
Exxon Corp.
1251 Ave. of Americas
Room 4692
New York, NY 10020

Alice Cooke
Scholastic Magazine
50 W. 44th St.
New York, NY 10036

Ms. Diane Coppandoa
50 East End Ave., 4D
New York, NY 10028

Susan Cotler
88 Lexington Ave.
New York, NY 10016

Louis Cruz
American Photographer
1515 Broadway
New York, NY 10036

Nancy Cutler
The Midnight Oil
309 W. 57th St.
New York, NY 10019

Mark Darlow
Cardinal Type Serv., Inc.
545 W. 45th St.
New York, NY 10036

Maxine Davidowitz
Redbook
230 Park Ave.
New York, NY 10017

Barrie Davidson
Venture Magazine
35 W. 45th St.
New York, NY 10036

Blair Davis
Weight Watchers Mag.
575 Lexington Ave.
New York, NY 10022

Joseph Davis
Housing Magazine
1221 Ave. of Americas
New York, NY 10020

Maida Davis
14 Washington Pl., 4M
New York, NY 10003

Paul T. Decker
Morgan Crampian
2 Park Ave.
New York, NY 10016

Jerry Demoney
Mobil Corp.
150 E. 42nd St.
New York, NY 10017

Joe Dizney
The American Lawyer
2 Park Ave.
New York, NY 10016

Chel Dong
Institutional Investor
488 Madison Ave.
New York, NY 10022

Robert M. Dougherty
Money Magazine
1271 Ave. of Americas
Room 2927
New York, NY 10020

Louis DuFault
American Inst. Chem. Eng.
345 E. 47th St.
New York, NY 10017

Nancy A. Englehardt
Conde Nast Publications
44 Abbott Drive
Huntington, NY 11743

Lois Erlacher
Emergency Medicine
280 Madison Ave.
New York, NY 10016

Robert Essman
63 E. 9th St.
New York, NY 10003

Judith Fendelman
Prime Time Magazine
1700 Broadway
New York, NY 10019

Robert Fillie
Graphiti Graphics
1515 Broadway, 39th Fl.
New York, NY 10036

Al Foti
MD Magazine
30 E. 60th St.
New York, NY 10022

Janet Froelich
480 Broome Street
New York, NY 10013

Len Fury
Corporate Annual Rept. Inc.
112 E. 31st St.
New York, NY 10016

Clifford Gardiner
Gruhner & Jahr
685 Third Ave.
New York, NY 10017

Nathan Garland
412 Orange St.
New Haven, CT 06511

Charles Glendinning
Amer. Teacher Magazine
11 DuPont Circle NW
Washington, DC 20036

Irwin Glusker
The Glusker Group
154 W. 57th St.
New York, NY 10019

Thomas Goddard
Xerox Educ. Publ.
245 Long Hill Rd.
Middletown, CT 06457

Jack Golden
555 Fifth Ave.
New York, NY 10017

Pegi Goodman
American Lawyer
27 W. 15th St., 1P
New York, NY 10011

Gary Gretter
Sports Afield
250 W. 55th St.
New York, NY 10019

Michael Grossman
Art Director
National Lampoon
635 Madison Ave.
New York, NY 10022

Everett Halvorsen
Forbes
60 Fifth Ave.
New York, NY 10011

Edward A. Hamilton
The Design Schools
200 Park Ave., E. Mezz.
Suite 256
New York, NY 10166

George Hartman
Glamour
350 Madison Ave.
New York, NY 10017

David Hauser
Popular Science
360 Madison Ave.
New York, NY 10017

Lesley—Hille
32 E. 21st St.
New York, NY 10010

Pam Hoffman
Modern Bride
1 Park Ave.
New York, NY 10016

Rudolph Hoglund
Time
Time-Life Bldg.
New York, NY 10020

Norman Hotz
Old Lyme Studio
110 Old Lyme Rd.
Chappaqua, NY 10514

Gino Ingrassia
J.W. Prendergast Assoc.
342 Madison Ave.
New York, NY 10017

Elaine Jaffee
67–87 Fleet St.
Forest Hills, NY 11375

Le Anne Jaffe
330 E. 63rd St., 4B
New York, NY 10021

Shaun Johnston
Wellcome Trends Inruology
15 Park Row
Room 2530
New York, NY 10038

Joe Kantorski
Progressive Grocer
1351 Washington Blvd.
Stamford, CT 06902

Florence Keller
Columbia University
303 Journalism
Columbia Magazine
New York, NY 10027

Scott C. Kelly
U.S. Lithograph, Inc.
853 Broadway
New York, NY 10003

David Kaestle
Pelligring & Kaestle, Inc.
16 E. 40th St.
New York, NY 10016

John Kalmes
Emergency Medicine
280 Madison Ave.
New York, NY 10016

Mindy Kombert
Mechanix Illustrated
1515 Broadway, 12 Flr.
New York, NY 10036

David Komitau
HBJ Publications
3rd Floor
757 Third Ave.
New York, NY 10017

Martin Kossoy
Marine Engineering
3 Maxwell Lane
Englishtown, NJ 07726

Greg Leeds
People—Life Bldg.,
Rm. 2920
Rockefeller Center
New York, NY 10020

Tom Lennon
460 James St.
New Milford, NJ 07646

Tom Lennon
Emergency Medicine
280 Madison Ave.
New York, NY 10016

Edward D. Libby
Chem. Engineering
1221 Ave. of Americas
New York, NY 10020

Bud Loader
Flying
1 Park Ave.
New York, NY 10016

Myles Ludwig
20 Waterside Plaza
New York, NY 10010

Noreen Mancini
c/o Families Magazine
Pleasantville, NY 10570

Mr. Robert Makowski
Journal of Metals
145 South Court R D 5
Mars, PA 16046

Carlos Mercado
Texasgulf, Inc.
Triangle
High Ridge Rd.
Stamford, CT 06904

Bonnie Meyer
Hayden Pub.
Computer Decisions
50 Essex St.
Rochelle Park, NJ 07662

Ron Meyerson
Newsweek
444 Madison Ave.
New York, NY 10022

Mr. Michael Miranda
The Shopper
Miranda Designs, Inc.
745 President St.
Brooklyn, NY 11215

Marion S. Mishkin
Marlowe Company
18–05 215th St.
Bayside, NY 11360

Orrin Mitch
Magazines for Indus., Inc.
747 Third Ave.
New York, NY 10017

Theresa Montvalo
Family Circle Mag.
488 Madison Ave.
New York, NY 10021

Dale Moyer
Scholastic Magazine
50 W. 44th St.
New York, NY 10036

Donald Mulligan
418 Central Park West
New York, NY 10025

Ginny Murphy-Hamill
United Tech. Publ.
645 Stewart Ave.
Garden City, NY 11530

Glenn Nakahara
Diversion Mag. Assoc.
60 E. 42nd St.
New York, NY 10017

Simon Nathan
Business Wide, Inc.
316 W. 79th St.
New York, NY 10024

John Noneman
Noneman & Noneman, Inc.
230 E. 18th St.
New York, NY 10003

Orit
Consumer Electronics
325 E. 75th St.
New York, NY 10021

Margaret Ottosen
Money Magazine
1271 6th Ave., 33rd Fl.
New York, NY 10020

Thomas Page
Museum of Nat. Hist.
79th St. & Central Pk. W.
New York, NY 10025

Brad Pallas
House Beautiful
1700 Broadway
New York, NY 10019

Alan Peckolick
67 Irving Pl.
New York, NY 10003

B. Martin Pederson
141 Lexington Ave.
New York, NY 10016

Joseph Perez
Family Circle
488 Madison Ave.
New York, NY 10022

Harold Perry
Motor Magazine
224 W. 57th St.
New York, NY 10019

Vicki Peslak
Seventeen Magazine
850 Third Ave.
New York, NY 10022

Thomas Phon
Electronic Design
50 Essex St.
Rochelle Park, NJ 07662

Robert Prestopino
Popular Magazine Group
CBS, 1515 Broadway
New York, NY 10036

Robert Priest
Esquire
2 Park Ave.
New York, NY 10016

Antonia Priola
Chemical Engineer
1221 Ave. of Americas
New York, NY 10020

Kerry Quigley
Emergency Medicine
280 Madison
New York, NY 10016

Brigid Quinn
Animal Kingdom Mag.
185th St. & Southern Bl.
Bronx, NY 10460

Alfons J. Reich
80 Park Ave, 17G
New York, NY 10016

Marilyn Reichstein
The Population Council
1 Dag Hammarskjold Plz.
New York, NY 10017

Edith Reimers
36 E. 38th St.
New York, NY 10016

Leonard L. Ringer
Graphic Communications
18 Wheeler Rd.
Kendall Park, NJ 08824

Philip Ritzenberg
New York News Magazine
220 E. 42nd St.
New York, NY 10017

Bennett Robinson
655 Third Ave.
New York, NY 10017

Herbert Rogalski
Rogalski Associates
186 Lincoln St.
Boston, MA 02111

Richard Rogers
Richard Rogers, Inc.
300 E. 33rd St.
New York, NY 10016

Marilyn Rose
Nautical Quarterly
373 Park Ave. So., Lo. Fl.
New York, NY 10016

Mary Rosen
Town & Country
1700 Broadway
New York, NY 10019

Frank Rothmann
Science Digest
959 Eighth Ave.
New York, NY 10019

Elton Robinson
Att: The Lamp
Exxon Corp.
1221 Ave. of Americas
New York, NY 10020

Thomas P. Ruis
New York News Magazine
220 E. 42nd St.
New York, NY 10017

Robin Rule
Lebhar-Friedman, Inc.
425 Park Ave. So.
New York, NY 10022

Anthony Rutka
Rutka Weadock
1627 E. Baltimore St.
Baltimore, MD 21231

Renee Santhouse
The Population Council
1 Dag Hammarskjold Plz.
New York, NY 10017

Stephen Saxe
1100 Madison Ave.
New York, NY 10028

Nina Scerbo
Art Director
Working Mother Magazine
230 Park Ave., Rm. 747
New York, NY 10017

Richard Schemm, Owner
Amer. Hairdresser Salon
100 Park Ave.
Suite 1000
New York, NY 10017

Tamara Schneider
Ladies Home Journal
641 Lexington Ave.
New York, NY 10017

Eileen H. Schultz
Good Housekeeping
Eighth Ave. & 57th St.
New York, NY 10019

James Sebastian
Design Frame, Inc.
1 Union Sq.
New York, NY 10003

Greg Sharko
103-56 103rd St.
Ozone Park, NY 11417

Joan Shearer
Hearst Publications
645 Steward Ave.
Garden City, NY 11530

Mitch Sholstak
P C Magazine
1 Park Ave., 7th Fl.
New York, NY 10016

Ira Silberlicht
210 W. 70th St.
New York, NY 10023

Louis Silverstein
New York Times
229 W. 43rd St.
New York, NY 10036

Rosemary Simmons
Woman's Day Super Spcls.
1515 Broadway
New York, NY 10036

Milt Simpson
49 Bleecker St.
Newark, NJ 07102

Bill Slavicsek
The Torch
St. John's Univ.
Jamaica, NY 11439

Kathy Smith
Assoc. A D
c/o Morgan-Grampian
2 Park Ave.
New York, NY 10016

Miriam Smith
Newsday
Melville, NY 11747

Mark Snyder
Mechanical Engineering
22 Farmstead Lane
Brookville, NY 11545

Society of Publication
Designers
555 Fifth Ave.
New York, NY 10017

Sandra Starr
Starr Graphic Prods.
1357 Washington St.
West Newton, MA 02165

Byron Steele
Review & Herald Pub. Assn.
6856 Eastern Ave., NW
Washington, DC 20012

Karen H. Steffaro
Exxon
1251 Ave. of Americas
New York, NY 10019

Vera Steiner
Printgraphics
435 E. 79th St. 11H
New York, NY 10021

Alex Stillano
Architechtural Record
1221 Ave. of Americas
New York, NY 10020

Phillip Sykstra
Cliggot Publishing
500 W. Putnam Ave.
Greenwich, CT 06830

Dave Talbot
Cuisine Magazine
1515 Broadway, 17th Fl.
New York, NY 10036

Wendy Talve
World Tennis
1515 Broadway
New York, NY 10036

Melissa Tardiff
Town & Country
1700 Broadway
New York, NY 10019

Melcon Tashian
Design Dir.
Museum Magazine
260 Madison Ave.
New York, NY 10016

Adrian Taylor
American Express Publng.
1120 Ave. of the Americas
New York, NY 10036

Elizabeth M. Thayer
Art Director
Bride's Magazine
350 Madison Ave.
New York, NY 10017

Shin Tora
Popular Photography
1 Park Ave.
New York, NY 10016

James Udell
40 Park Ave.
New York, NY 10016

Holland Utley
House Beautiful
Hearst Publications
1700 Broadway
New York, NY 10019

Linda Vessup
Black Enterprise
295 Madison Ave.
New York, NY 10017

Clifford W. Vincent, Jr.
Horwitt Publ. & Adv.
Appetizingly Yours
58 Boston St.
Guilford, CT 06437

Jim Walsh
Emergency Medicine
280 Madison Ave.
New York, NY 10016

Jessica Weber
Book-of-the-Month Club
485 Lexington Ave.
New York, NY 10017

Noel Werret
222 Central Park South
Apt. 18
New York, NY 10019

Jan White
Architectural Record
213 Wilton Rd.
Westport, CT 06880

Loretta White
New York Times
229 W. 43rd St.
New York, NY 10036

Victor Wong
Young Miss
685 Third Ave.
New York, NY 10017

John Workman
Heavy Metal
635 Madison Ave.
New York, NY 10022

Barbara Yacono
Morgan Grampian
2 Park Ave.-4th Floor
New York, NY 10016

Susan Yip
Public Relations Society
of America Journal
843 3rd Ave.
New York, NY 10022

Ira Yoffee
Parade Magazine
750 Third Ave.
New York, NY 10017

Carmille Zaino
Newsweek
444 Madison Ave.
New York, NY 10022

Roger Zapke
Forbes Magazine
60 Fifth Ave.
New York, NY 10011

Lloyd Ziff
House & Garden
350 Madison Ave.
New York, NY 10017

Mary Zisk
640 Harmon Cove Twrs.
Secaucus, NJ 07094

Russell Zolan
Science Digest
Hearst Corp.
888 Seventh Ave.
New York, NY 10019

AWARDS
PUBLICATION
DESIGN 16

Dennis DiVincenzo

1

Publication   **Jardin des Modes**
Art Director   **bill butt**
Designer   **bill butt, Bulle Chabalier,**
   Nicole Esperance, Frederique Schott
Publisher   **Vercingetorix International Publications**

Silver 1

2,3

Publication   **Pratt Institute Annual Report/1979-80**
Art Director   **Michael McGinn**
Designer   **Michael McGinn**
Illustrator   **Steven Bennett, Sharon Gresh, Judy Pensky, Scott Menchin**
Photographer   **Jeanne Strongin, Marc Weinstein, Douglas Wonders**
Publisher   **Pratt Institute**

Silver 2

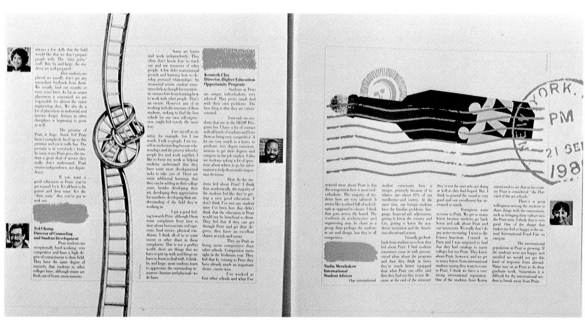

Silver 3

4

Publication	Nautical Quarterly
Art Director	B. Martin Pederson
Designer	B. Martin Pederson
Photographer	Allen Weitz
Publisher	Nautical Quarterly

5

Publication	Nautical Quarterly
Art Director	B. Martin Pederson
Designer	B. Martin Pederson
Photographer	Ted Spiegel, David Barnes
Publisher	Nautical Quarterly

Gold 4

Silver 5

6,7

Publication	**Rolling Stone**
Art Director	**Christopher Austopchuk,**
	Mary Shanahan, Dave Wilder
Designer	**Christopher Austopchuk,**
	Mary Shanahan, Dave Wilder
Publisher	**Straight Arrow Publishers**

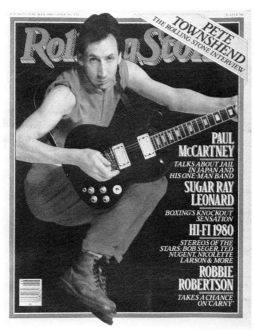

Silver 6

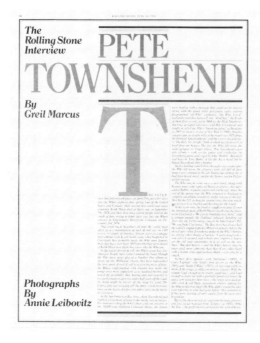

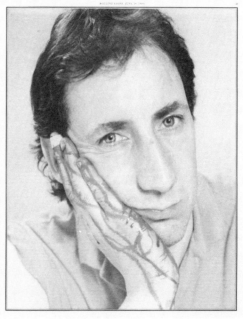

Silver 7

8–11
Publication   **U & lc**
Art Director   **Herb Lubalin**
Designer   **Herb Lubalin**
Illustrator   **Cover art by Wally Neibart;**
                  inside art by various artists
Publisher   **International**
                  Typeface Corp.

Gold 8

Gold 9

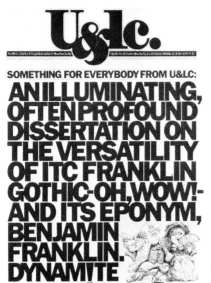

Silver 10

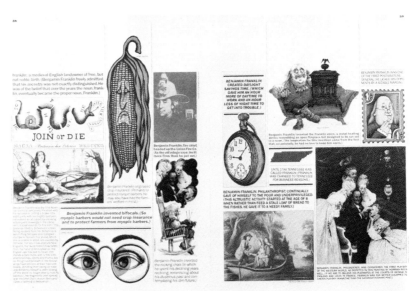

Silver 11

21

12

Publication	**The Printing Salesman's Herald/Book 43**
Art Director	**James Sebastian**
Designer	**James Sebastian, Michael Lauretano,**
	Kathleen Lee, Margaret Popper
Illustrator	**Max Waldman,**
	Harry Callahan, Phil Koenig
Publisher	**Champion International Corporation,**
	Paper Division

Silver 12

13
Publication   Emergency Medicine
Art Director   Tom Lennon
Designer   Cheun Chiang
Photographer   Jon Fisher
Publisher   Fischer Medical Publications, Inc.

14
Publication   Emergency Medicine
Art Director   Tom Lennon
Designer   Cheun Chiang
Illustrator   Nick Aristovulos
Photographer   Shig Ikeda
Publisher   Fischer Medical Publications, Inc.

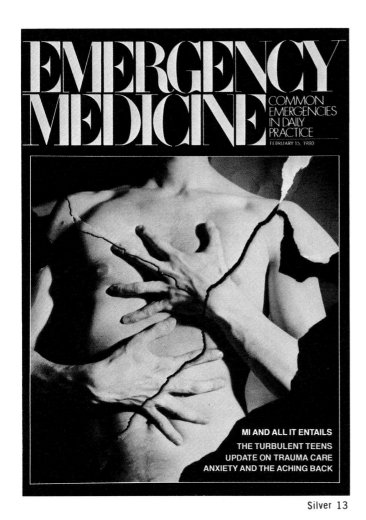

Silver 13

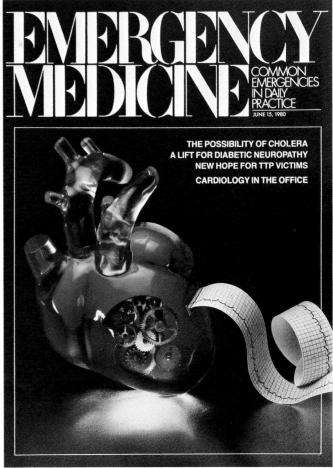

Silver 14

15
Publication **Postgraduate Medicine**
Art Director **Tina Adamek**
Illustrator **John Collier**
Publisher **McGraw-Hill, Inc.**

MARCH 1980   A McGraw-Hill Publication

The Journal of
Applied Medicine
for the Primary Care
Physician

Postgraduate Medicine

EDITORIAL
Side effects'
side effect

ARTICLES/Complete contents beginning page 5

Pediatric abdominal examination: How to make it
more productive

Modern treatment of intracranial aneurysms

Gonococcal arthritis syndromes—an update

The primary care physician and sleep disorders

Cholesterol, triglyceride, and lipoprotein studies:
Strategies for clinical use

Allergic disease
and its diagnosis:
Focus on a
billion dollar
disorder

Silver 15

24

16
Publication **Long Lines**
Art Director **Bob Eichinger**
Designer **Bob Eichinger**
Illustrator **Ed Soyka**
Publisher **American Telephone &
Telegraph Company**

17
Publication **Postgraduate Medicine**
Art Director **Tina Adamek**
Illustrator **Alan Cober**
Publisher **McGraw-Hill, Inc.**

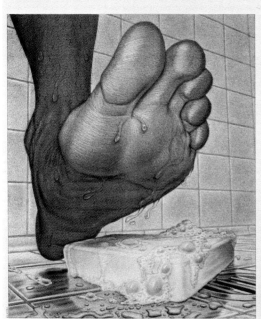

Silver 16

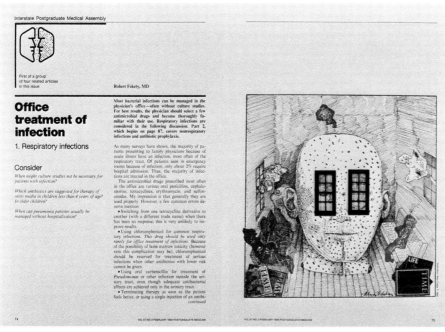

Silver 17

18
Publication **The Wharton Magazine**
Art Director **Mitch Shostak**
Designer **Mitch Stostak**
Illustrator **Ed Soyka**
Publisher **University of Pennsylvania**

19
Publication **Playboy**
Art Director **Arthur Paul, Tom Staebler**
Designer **Len Willis**
Illustrator **Thomas Ingham**
Publisher **Playboy Enterprises, Inc.**

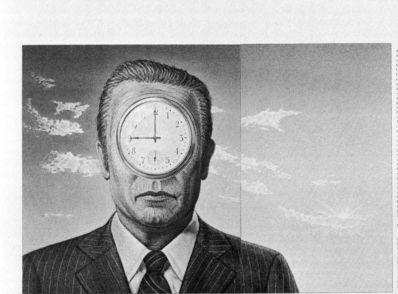

Silver 18

THE AMERICAN JAMES BOND: A TRUE STORY

Silver 19

20

Publication   **Postgraduate Medicine**
Art Director   **Tina Adamek**
Illustrator   **Geoffrey Moss**
Publisher   **McGraw-Hill, Inc.**

Illustration: Geoffrey Moss © 1980

VOL 67/NO 4/APRIL 1980/POSTGRADUATE MEDICINE • **OLFACTORY DIAGNOSIS**   111

21

Publication	**Rolling Stone**
Art Director	**Christopher Austopchuk, Mary Shanahan, Dave Wilder**
Designer	**Christopher Austopchuk, Mary Shanahan, Dave Wilder**
Publisher	**Straight Arrow Publishers**

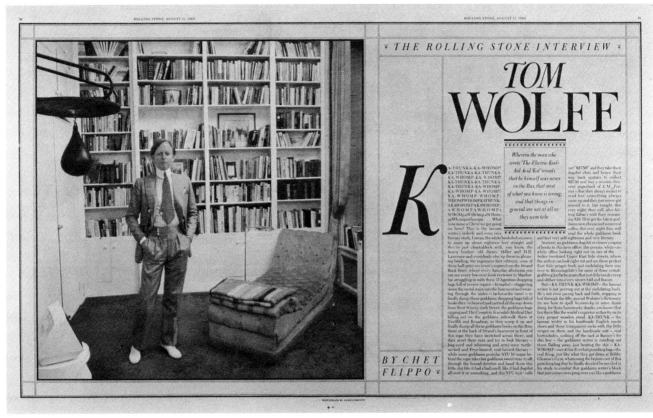

Silver 21

22

Publication **Industry Week**
Art Director **Nickolas Dankovich**
Designer **Nickolas Dankovich**
Photographer **Robert Holcepl**

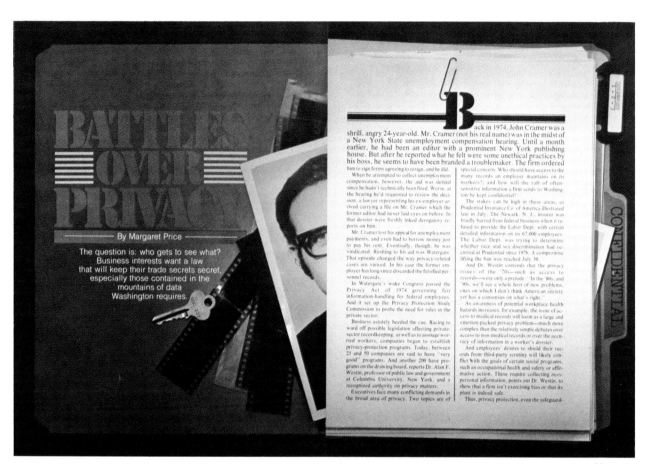

Silver 22

23,24
Publication   **Nautical Quarterly**
Art Director **B. Martin Pederson**
Designer   **B. Martin Pederson**
Illustrator   **Ted Spiegel**
Photographer **Ted Spiegel, B. Martin Pederson,
              Universitetet I Oslo**
Publisher   **Nautical Quarterly**

Silver 23

Silver 24

25

Publication	**Nautical Quarterly**
Art Director	**B. Martin Pederson**
Designer	**B. Martin Pederson**
Photographer	**Sam Abell**
Publisher	**Nautical Quarterly**

NAUTICAL QUARTERLY

NEWFOUNDLAND

PHOTOGRAPHS BY SAM ABELL

Photographs like these are rare, although their images are not. If there is any message in the photographs on the following nine pages beyond their quality of exquisite simplicity, it may be one appropriately rich and simple: that our eyes see things like them every day. But our eyes see without holding; they are active and distracted, tools for our minds, focusing a moment and then moving on. The camera holds the image, and in the holding makes it something else. The something else is a moment frozen and made classic, a more profound kind of seeing than our active eyes normally deliver. These are seacoast photographs, classic images of the kinds of things that flavor small-boat cruising: men working at the fishing trade, fog and gannets, shapes and colors of boats and buildings. In cruising we see things like these in passing, and in the fast cuts of recollection we see them again in a romantic tumble, a nostalgia that makes us smile and plan for next year. A good cruise. Photographs like these make plain the hard beauty of the world. It is a beauty worth the eye and mind seeing and recalling the way the camera does, worth concentrating a minute's attention on the look of a beached whaleboat, the white-blue-green of clouds-water-grass, whenever we cruise along a coast.

These photographs were made by Sam Abell on a trip to the island of Newfoundland. A young and largely self-taught photographer, Abell was born in Sylvania, Ohio, in 1945 and graduated from the University of Kentucky in 1969 with a degree in English. He has been a contract photographer for National Geographic since 1970. He says of these Newfoundland photographs: "Some photographers I know seem to absorb aspects of their assignments like actors from the roles they play; this happens especially early in our careers, and eventually it helps shape our seeing. The island of Newfoundland, austere at first and lyrical at last, was that place for me. From it I took a directness and simplicity of seeing I had not brought with me, and if in the interplay of light and line and color there is a notion of mystery it is because I look for just that."

Gold 25

26
Publication **Rocky Mountain Magazine**
Art Director **Hans Teensma**
Designer **Nancy Butkus**
Photographer **Jayme Odgers**
Publisher **Rocky Mountain Magazine**

27
Publication **Life**
Art Director **Bob Ciano**
Designer **Mary K. Baumann**
Photographer **Eve Arnold, MAGNUM**
Publisher **Time-Life**

Silver 26

Silver 27

PUBLICATION DESIGN 16

POINT SIZE

13   15

INCHES

1 — 1

2 — 2

3 — 3

28–31
Publication **Jardin des Modes**
Art Director **bill butt**
Designer **bill butt, Bulle Chabalier, Nicole Esperance, Frederique Schott**
Photographer **Dick Ballarian, Thomas Brandau, Erica Lennard, et al.**
Publisher **Vercingetorix International Publications**

28

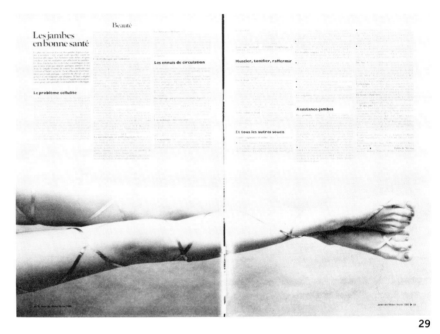

29

30

31

32–35
Publication **American Photographer**
Art Director **Will Hopkins**
Designer **Louis F. Cruz**
Publisher **CBS Publications**

32

33

34

35

36—39
Publication   Smithsonian Magazine
Art Director   (Picture Editor) Caroline Despard
Publisher   Smithsonian

36

37

38

39

40–42
Publication **U & lc**
Art Director **Herb Lubalin**
Designer **Herb Lubalin**
Publisher **International Typeface Corporation**

40

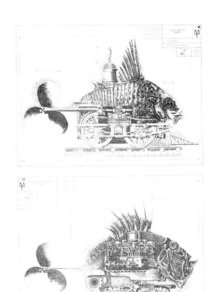

41

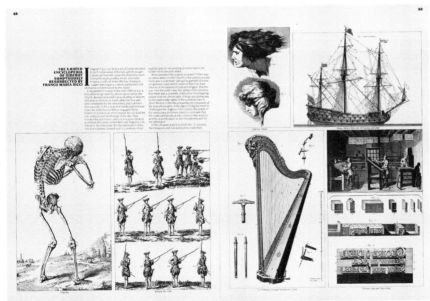

42

43,44
Publication   **L.I. Magazine/Newsday**
Art Director   **Miriam Smith**
Designer   **Miriam Smith**
Photographer   **Don Jacobsen, Ken Spencer**
Publisher   **Newsday**

45
Publication   **Touche Ross Life**
Art Director   **Bernhardt Fudyma Design Group**
Photographer   **Touche Ross and Company**

43

44

45

46,47
Publication   **Books & Arts**
Art Director   **Corbin Gwaltney, Gaal Shepherd, Ted Weidlein**
Photographer   **John C. Phillips**
Publisher   **The Chronicle of Higher Education**

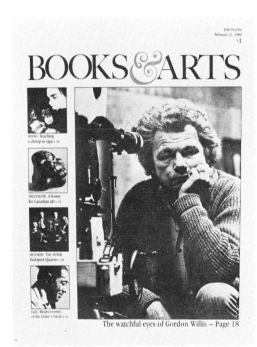

46

47

48,49

Publication **The New York Times**
Art Director **Louis Silverstein, Bob Eisner**
Designer **Louis Silverstein, Bob Eisner**
Publisher **The New York Times**

50

50,51

Publication	**Esquire**
Art Director	**Robert Priest**
Designer	**April Silver, Stephen Doyle, Vincent Winter**
Publisher	**Esquire Publishing, Inc.**

THESE Are a Few of My Favorite Things

by John Simon

Over the years this controversial critic has applied the acid test of his wit and intelligence to theater, film, music, art, and literature. He is so famous for his hatred of the mediocre that people often ask, "Doesn't he like *anything?*" Here, in reply, are brief tributes to nine modern artists or works of art that he not only likes but also loves.

PRIMA BALLERINA SUZANNE FARRELL, IN 1980

SUZANNE FARRELL
Ballerina

SUZANNE Farrell (1945—) is not only in possession of flawless technique and supreme artistry—other prima ballerinas have that, too. She may be prettier than most, with that half-ironic, half-come-hither look on her gamine face, with her long, slender but not curveless body, and with legs that seem to stretch on and on and to add an extra something to whatever they do, she is certainly sexier than any. But it goes beyond that: there is the personal signature to everything she does. Let's say she appeared masked in a ballet; within a few seconds you would know it was Farrell. Only she can so blend precision with a certain languor, be so impishly childlike even when doing mature, womanly parts or executing some difficult piece of perfectly geometrical abstraction. Always, mysteriously, she is both Farrell *and* the part she is dancing; the slight, teasing discrepancy redounds to the glory of both. And her performances are technically seamless; transitions are invisible, each step or leap has been executed effortlessly but also as an inextricable part of a sequence: flow is everywhere.

Farrell owns nine cats (that's eighty-one additional lives) and is, surely, herself the Queen of the Cats. There is the litheness, independence, inscrutability, unpredictableness of cats, of the essence of felineness, about her; yet she does exactly what the choreographer prescribes and should not, as we mentally cheer her on for the hundredth time in that role, surprise us. Yet surprise us she does, moment after moment. And she holds us, from entrance to exit, entranced and exhilarated: the stage, the audience, the dance belong to her, without her indulging in the least scene-stealing. Cats are always filled with grace; and they always, always have their way with us.

FREDRIC MARCH
Actor

A GREAT actor can either make a role disappear into himself or make himself disappear into the role. I have nothing but esteem for those intelligent and graceful actors—Cary Grant, say, and Robert Redford—who absorb every part completely and emerge bigger than the sum of their parts. But I reserve my greatest admiration for actors who become, body and soul, what they are playing, so that you do not say X is doing a wonderful job as Macbeth, Susan B. Anthony, or Charles Foster Kane, but "My God, this really *was* Macbeth; I hardly recognized X in the part." Such a performer was Fredric March (1897–1975), in my opinion the greatest American stage and screen actor between the Thirties and the Seventies. And one who, though generally respected, has yet to receive his full due.

There is no role that, touched by Fredric March, did not turn to gold—well, maybe he was not quite ethnic enough for *Death of a Salesman* and *Middle of the Night*. Who, however, can forget his Jekyll and Hyde (surpassing those of the actor he himself most regarded, Spencer Tracy), his Robert Browning and Mark Twain, his Vronsky and Jean Valjean, and, at the very end, his Harry Hope? Or, onstage, his George Antrobus and James Tyrone? No actor ever wore his great good looks more lightly; none made less fuss over his acting. "I do the things the guy who wrote the play has written," he told Lilian Ross and Helen Ross. "There's so much mumbo-jumbo about acting.... Little girls, particularly, know what it's all about. They do Method acting naturally." And this often-bypassed bit of wisdom: "It's a mistake, I think, to go for parts, as some actors do, instead of for the play as a whole."

March understood beautifully that less is more, that one must relax into the role even when—perhaps especially when—great intensity is required. That is the paradox of acting. Most important, March had no discernible mannerisms, vocal, facial, or gestural. He simply—but this is no easy simplicity—poured himself into the role until the role said "When." Whether in romantic leads (e.g., as Bothwell in *Mary of Scotland* or as Anthony Adverse) or in modern dress (as in *Death Takes a Holiday* or *A Star Is Born*—the *good* version), March was easefully, manfully in command. He could invest sentimental twaddle such as *Smilin' Through* and *The Dark Angel* with heartbreaking authenticity; in a good part (as in *Nothing Sacred* or *Inherit the Wind*), whether comic or dramatic, he was magisterial. He made the transitions from juvenile to leading man to character actor with elegant facility and was just as

FREDRIC MARCH WITH (LEFT) GARBO IN *ANNA KARENINA* (1935)

52—55

Publication **Travel & Leisure**
Art Director **Adrian Taylor**
Designer **Adrian Taylor**
Illustrator **Jean Michael Folon**
Photographer **Ron Schwerin, Arnold Newman**
Publisher **American Express Publishing Corporation**

WHEN NIGHT FALLS

52

53

54

55

56–59

Publication **AIA Journal**

Art Director **Carole Palmer, Suzy Thomas**

Designer **Carole Palmer**

Publisher **The American Institute of Architects**

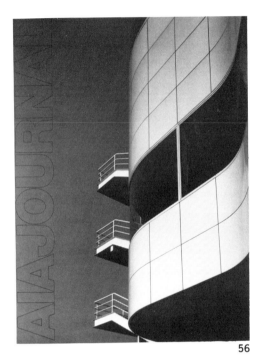

56

57

Exercise in 'Competence and Confidence'

Roche/Dinkeloo's Helen Bonfils Theater, Denver. By S.A.

58

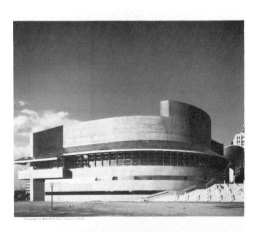

59

60–63
Publication   **American Fabrics & Fashions**
Art Director   **Bill Bonnell**
Designer   **Bill Bonnell**
Publisher   **Doric Publishing Company, Inc.**

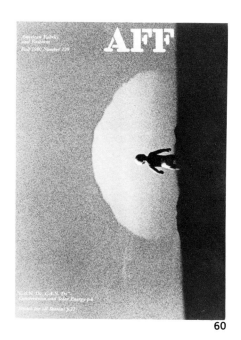

60

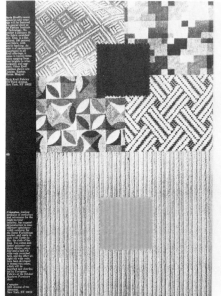

61

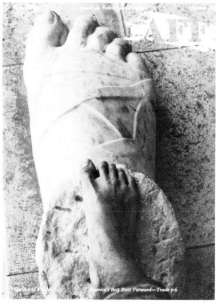

62

63

64,65

Publication   **Uncommon Characters**
Art Director   **Richard Wilde**
Designer   **Laura Goodman, Roberto Klachky**
Publisher   **School of Visual Arts Press, Ltd.**

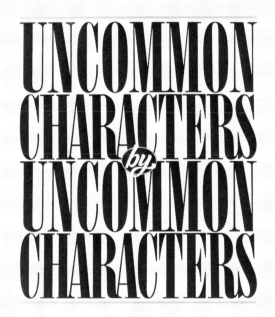

64

TERRY MUI

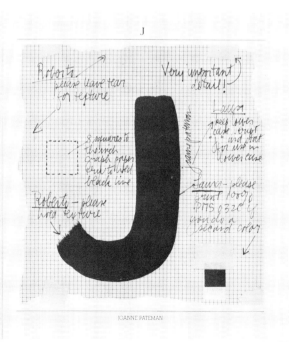

JOANNE PATEMAN

65

66,67

Publication **Shield**
Art Director **Edyce Hall**
Designer **Edyce Hall**
Illustrator **James Pegram**
Publisher **Del Monte Corporation**

68,69

Publication **Sea-Land Facilities Book**
Art Director **John Cernak**
Designer **John Cernak**
Illustrator **Tim Bruce**
Photographer **Ron Appelbe**
Publisher **R.J. Reynolds Industries, Inc.**

66

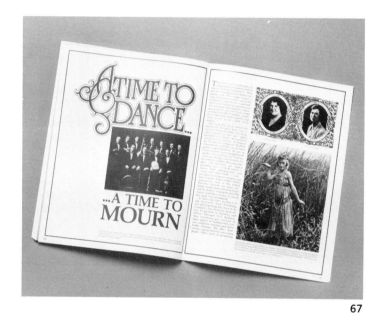

67

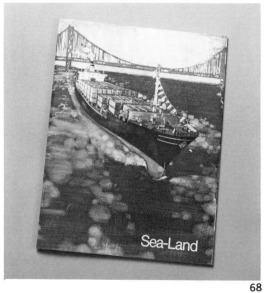

68

69

70,71
Publication **Assets**
Art Director **Kit Hinrichs/Jonson, Pederson, Hinrichs & Shakery**
Designer **Kit Hinrichs, Barbara Vick**
Illustrator **Morgan, Kit Hinrichs, Barbara Vick**
Photographer **Tom Tracy, Suzanne Estel, John Benson**
Publisher **Crocker Bank**

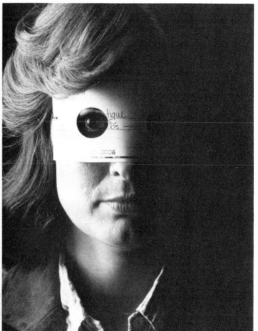

70

71

72,73

Publication **Rolling Stone**
Art Director **Christopher Austopchuk, Mary Shanahan, Dave Wilder**
Designer **Christopher Austopchuk, Mary Shanahan, Dave Wilder**
Publisher **Straight Arrow Publishers**

72

73

74
Publication   **L.I. Magazine/Newsday**
Art Director   **Miriam Smith**
Designer   **Miriam Smith**
Photographer   **Don Jacobsen, Ken Spencer**
Publisher   **Newsday**

75 – 76
Publication   **Long Island Newsday**
Art Director   **Miriam Smith**
Designer   **Miriam Smith**
Publisher   **Newsday**

74

75

76

77
Publication **The Clarion Ledger "The Delta"**
Art Director **Ray Wong**
Designer **Ray Wong**
Photographer **Paul Beaver**
Publisher **The Clarion Ledger/Mississippi Publishers**

78
Publication **The Kansas City Star**
Art Director **Marty Petty**
Designer **Marty Petty**
Photographer **Jim McTaggart**
Publisher **The Kansas City Star Company**

77

78

79

80

79,80

Publication   **The New York Times Magazine Section**
Art Director   **Michael Todd**
Designer   **Michael Todd**
Photographer   **Paccione**
Publisher   **The New York Times**

81

Publication   **The New York Times Book Review**
Art Director   **Steve Heller**
Designer   **Steve Heller**
Illustrator   **Randall Enos**
Publisher   **The New York Times**

81

82,83
Publication **Multibank Annual Report/1979**
Art Director **Bob Newman**
Designer **Bob Newman**
Photographer **Clint Clemens**
Publisher **Hill & Knowlton, Inc.**

84
Publication **Nabisco Report to Employees/1979**
Art Director **Len Fury**
Designer **Len Fury**
Illustrator **D. Bazzel**
Publisher **Corpcom Services, Inc.**

82

83

84

85,86
Publication **Revlon Annual Report**
Art Director **Ken Resen**
Designer **Ken Resen**
Photographer **Hiro**
Publisher **Revlon, Inc.**

87
Publication **International Center of Photography/6th Year Report**
Art Director **Peter Rauch**
Designer **Janice Hildebrand**
Publisher **International Center of Photography**

85

86

87

88,89

Publication **Technicolor Inc., Annual Report/1980**
Art Director **Robert Miles Runyon/Jim Berte**
Designer **Jim Berte**
Photographer **Steve Kahn**

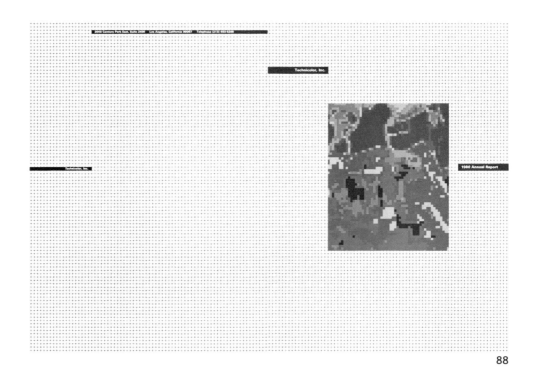

88

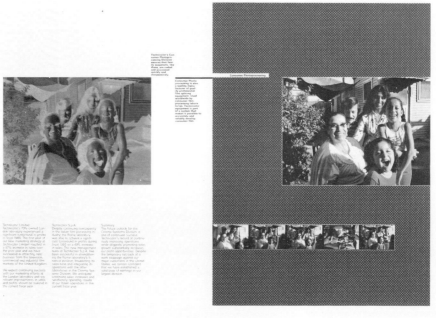

89

90,91
Publication **Pratt Institute Annual Report/1978-79**
Art Director **Michael McGinn**
Designer **Michael McGinn**
Photographer **Douglas Wonders, Marc Weinstein**
Publisher **Pratt Institute**

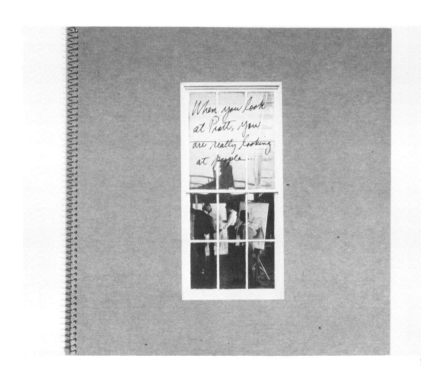

90

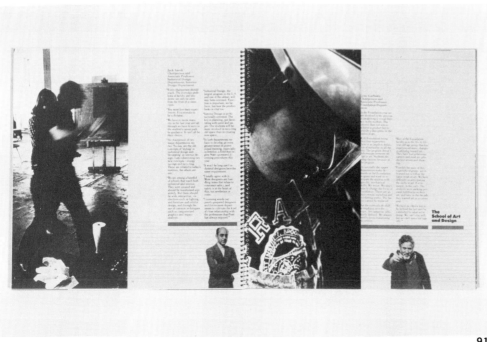

91

92,93
Publication **Warner Communications Inc., Annual Report/1979**
Art Director **Neil Shakery**
Designer **Neil Shakery**
Photographer **Burt Glinn**

94
Publication **Grupo Industrial Alfa Annual Report/1979**
Art Director **Alan Peckolick**
Designer **Alan Peckolick**
Photographer **Frank Moscati**
Publisher **Grupo Industrial Alfa**

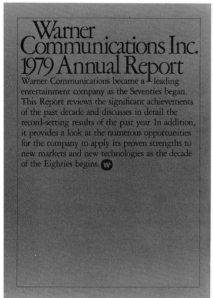

92

93

94

95,96
Publication   **Filmways Inc., Annual Report/1980**
Art Director   **Kit Hinrichs**
Designer   **Kit Hinrichs, Arlene Finger**
Photographer   **Tom Tracy**
Publisher   **Jonson, Pederson, Hinrichs & Shakery**

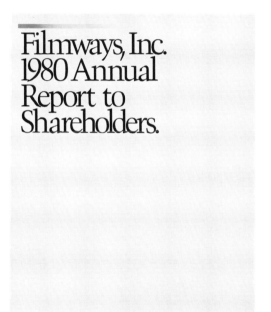

Filmways, Inc.
1980 Annual
Report to
Shareholders.

95

96

97,98
Publication **Castle & Cooke, Inc., Annual Report/1979**
Art Director **Kit Hinrichs**
Designer **Kit Hinrichs, Arlene Finger**
Photographer **Tom Tracy**
Publisher **Jonson, Pederson, Hinrichs & Shakery**

97

Processed Pineapple
Castle & Cooke's processed pineapple operations continued in 1979 to be the largest contributor to corporate earnings as operating income about equaled the level of 1978. However, higher interest charges caused net income for 1979 to be slightly below 1978. In spite of the strongest competitive market experienced in the last five years, sales volumes reached record levels in almost all markets.

The intensified competition, resulting largely from increased shipments of low-cost foreign product into the North American market, hampered sales of Dole® consumer-size solid-pack pineapple. However, private-label consumer sales increased substantially during the year. Furthermore, Dole® retail pineapple juice products continued to increase their profit contribution.

Record sales and earnings were achieved in the Company's foodservice-industrial market during the year. That performance resulted from increased shipments of solid-pack, juice and juice concentrate products.

International processed pineapple earnings remained at their 1978 level despite increased costs. Development of a new marketing program for Europe, begun in the latter half of 1979 in West Germany, is expected in the years ahead to enhance consumer knowledge of the Dole® brand quality and to increase European market share.

Production facilities in all three processed pineapple divisions—Hawaii, the Philippines and Thailand—operated near capacity levels throughout the year, and the Philippine and Thai output reached new peaks. However, all operations were hard hit by a variety of inflationary factors, particularly substantial cost increases for packaging materials, fuel and fuel-related supplies, and by higher labor costs in the Far East.

To help offset the inflationary spiral, the Company embarked in 1979 on a new ocean shipping program that has converted all processed pineapple shipments from the Far East to a completely containerized freight service. The new service replaces the traditional break-bulk method of shipping and is greatly reducing the costly in-transit product damage that had occurred in the past. Savings resulting from the new program will be fully realized beginning in 1980.

While competition in the marketplace increased in 1979, it did not reach the level anticipated earlier when forecasts of world pineapple production indicated a major surplus of product. Adverse weather plus the economics of the processed pineapple business have acted to curtail expanding production. A better balance in world supplies presently exists than had been expected a year ago.

During 1979, the Company launched a major effort to protect the Dole® label. Two serious instances of label infringement were halted through out-of-court settlements.

The Company's fruit and vegetable cannery in Salem, Oregon, reported a satisfactory level of earnings as reduced volumes of shipments were largely offset by improved profit

margins. Green bean shipments were lower as a result of competitive pressures in the marketplace, and pear shipments were reduced from the prior year's level because of a temporary lack of raw product. The cannery packs products grown in the Pacific Northwest for sale primarily to the private-label retail market and to the foodservice industry.

Fresh Pineapple
Operating earnings from fresh pineapple activities slipped slightly below their 1978 performance, although the volume of shipments remained about the same. The Far Eastern market, supplied from the Philippines, continued its uninterrupted growth in volume and profitability. However, this improvement was unable to offset a decline in operating earnings in the U.S. market, supplied from Hawaii and Honduras.

Prices in the U.S. market were depressed throughout much of 1979 by intensified competition from other sources of supply. In addition, the lengthy United Air Lines strike, followed by the temporary grounding of the nation's DC-10 aircraft, severely disrupted the Hawaii "Jet-Fresh" pineapple program, further aggravating U.S. marketing results.

98

99,100
Publication   Crocker National Corp., Annual Report/1979
Art Director Kit Hinrichs
Designer   Kit Hinrichs
Illustrator   Philippe Weisbecker, Baron Story, Robert Pryor
Photographer John Blaustein
Publisher   Jonson, Pederson, Hinrichs & Shakery

101,102
Publication   Touche Ross Annual Report/1980
Art Director Ernie Smith
Designer   Ernie Smith
Publisher   Touche Ross & Co.

99

100

101

102

61

	103		**104**
Publication	**Life**	Publication	**Jardin des Modes**
Art Director	**Bob Ciano**	Art Director	**bill butt**
Designer	**Bob Ciano, Lou Valentino**	Designer	**bill butt, Frederique Schott**
Photographer	**Douglas Whitney Collection**	Photographer	**Michel Momy**
Publisher	**Time-Life**	Publisher	**Vercingetorix International Publications**

103

104

105
Publication **Sports Afield**
Art Director **Gary Gretter**
Designer **Gary Gretter**
Illustrator **N.C. Wyeth**
Publisher **Hearst Magazines, Inc.**

106
Publication **Science Digest**
Art Director **Frank Rothmann, Mary Zisk**
Designer **Frank Rothmann, Mary Zisk**
Illustrator **Nick Aristovulos**
Photographer **Shig Ikeda**
Publisher **Hearst Magazines, Inc.**

105

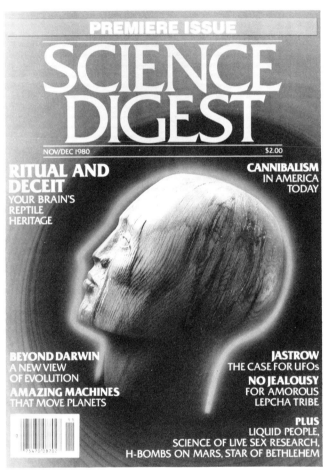

106

107

Publication **Cuisine Magazine**
Art Director **David Talbot**
Photographer **Lynn St. John**
Publisher **Cuisine Magazine, Inc.**

THE MAGAZINE OF FINE FOOD AND CREATIVE LIVING   JANUARY/FEBRUARY 1981 • $1.50

CUISINE

Oaxaca: A Traveler's Feast • Kitchen Design • Armagnac • Lentils

Poached Pear in Orange Sauce

108
Publication **National Lampoon Magazine**
Art Director **Skip Johnston**
Illustrator **Eraldo Carugati**
Publisher **National Lampoon, Inc.**

109
Publication **The Dial**
Art Director **Susan Reinhardt,
Henry Wolf**
Designer **Susan Reinhardt,
Henry Wolf**
Illustrator **Henry Wolf**
Publisher **Public
Broadcasting
Communications, Inc.**

110
Publication **Four Winds**
Art Director **Larry Smitherman**
Designer **Larry Smitherman**
Photographer **Laura Gilpin**
Publisher **Smitherman
Graphic Design
& Illustration, Inc.**

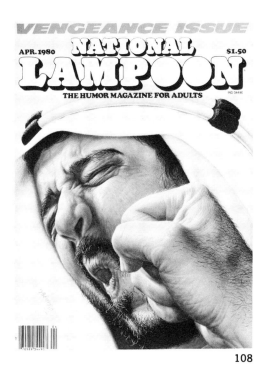

108

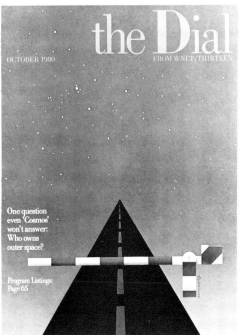

109

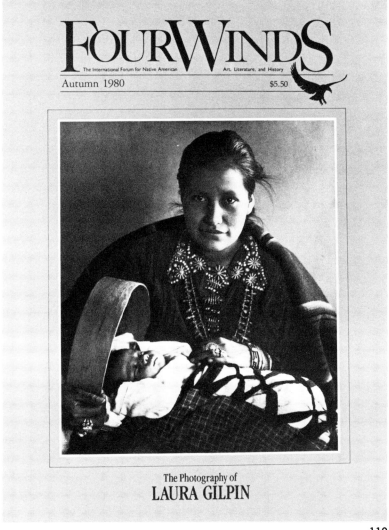

The Photography of
LAURA GILPIN

110

111

Publication **Comedy**
Art Director **Carol Bokuniewicz, Tibor Kalman**
Designer **Larry Kazal**
Illustrator **M & Co.**
Photographer **Gary Cumiskey**
Publisher **Trite Expectations, Inc.**

112

Publication **American Photographer Magazine**
Art Director **Will Hopkins**
Designer **Louis F. Cruz**
Photographer **Arthur Elgort**
Publisher **CBS Publications**

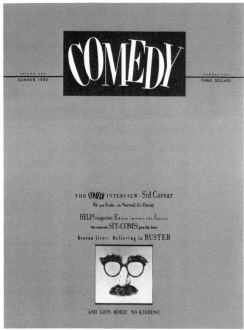

111

112

113

Publication **Travel & Leisure**
Art Director **Adrian Taylor**
Designer **Adrian Taylor**
Photographer **Charles Weckler**
Publisher **American Express Publishing Corporation**

114

Publication **Esquire**
Art Director **Robert Priest**
Designer **Robert Priest, Vincent Winter**
Illustrator **Sally Slight**
Publisher **Esquire Publishing, Inc.**

113

114

115

Publication	**Rocky Mountain Magazine**
Art Director	**Hans Teensma**
Designer	**Howard Klein**
Photographer	**William Albert Allard**
Publisher	**Rocky Mountain Magazine**

116

Publication	**Industry Week**
Art Director	**Nickolas Dankovich**
Designer	**Nickolas Dankovich**
Illustrator	**(Retoucher) Paul Dzuroff**
Photographer	**Andrew Russetti**
Publisher	**Penton-IPC**

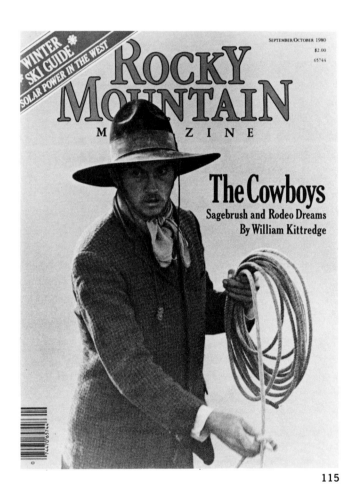

115

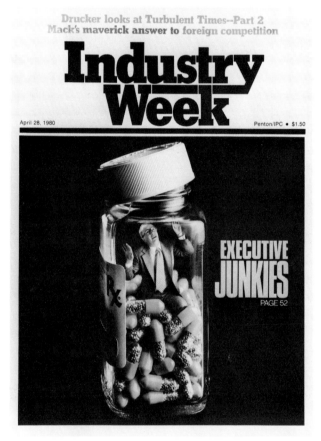

116

117
Publication **Texaco Marketer** ³/₈₀
Art Director **David Kaestle**
Designer **Ted Williams**
Illustrator **Dick Frank**
Publisher **Pellegrini & Kaestle, Inc.**

118
Publication **Folio**
Designer **Steve Phillips Design, Inc.**
Publisher **Folio Magazine**

117

118

119
Publication **Postgraduate Medicine**
Art Director **Tina Adamek**
Illustrator **Sandra Filippucci**
Publisher **McGraw-Hill, Inc.**

120
Publication **Industrial Launderer**
Art Director **Jack Lefkowitz**
Designer **Jack Lefkowitz**
Illustrator **Jeff Davis**
Publisher **Institute of Industrial Launderers, Inc.**

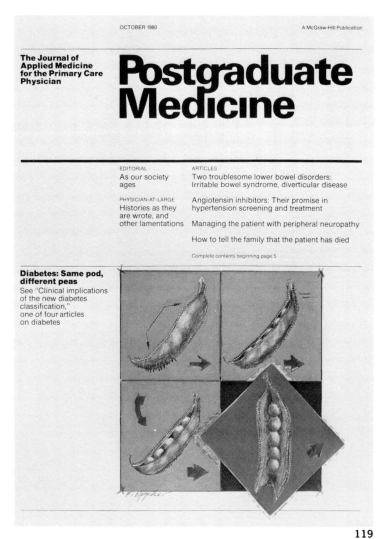

119

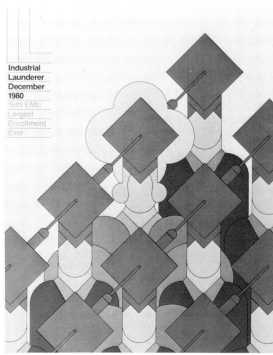

120

121
Publication   **Today's Art and Graphics**
Art Director   **Harvey Bernstein**
Designer   **Harvey Bernstein, Michelle Kolb**
Illustrator   **Lorraine Epstein**
Publisher   **Syndicate Magazines, Inc.**

Illustration and Drawing   **Vacation Tools**

Today's Art and Graphics

Volume 28 Number 6

121

122
Publication **Builder**
Art Director **Bono Mitchell**
Photographer **Kaz Tsurta**
Publisher **National Association
of Home Builders**

123
Publication   **RN Magazine**
Art Director   **Hector W. Marrero**
Designer   **Hector W. Marrero**
Illustrator   **Rick McCollum**
Publisher   **Medical Economis
                 Company**

124
Publication   **Footwear News
                 Magazine**
Art Director   **Traci Churchill**
Designer   **Traci Churchill**
Illustrator   **Andrea Pfister**
Publisher   **Fairchild Publications**

125
Publication   **MD Magazines**
Art Director   **Al Foti**
Designer   **Al Foti**
Photographer   **Four by Five Agency**
Publisher   **MD Publications, Inc.**

123

125

124

126
Publication **Flowers &**
Art Director **M.J. Cody**
Designer **Dugald Stermer**
Photographer **Jerry Fruchtman**
Publisher **Teleflora, Inc.**

127
Publication **Restaurant Business Magazine**
Art Director **Joan Dworkin**
Illustrator **Joan Dworkin**
Photographer **Don Kushnick**
Publisher **Bill Communications, Inc.**

126

127

128
Publication | **Progressive Grocer**
Art Director | **Mitch Shostak**
Designer | **Mitch Shostak**
Photographer | **John Bean**
Publisher | **Maclean Hunter Media**

129
Publication | **The Wharton Magazine**
Art Director | **Mitch Shostak**
Designer | **Mitch Shostak**
Illustrator | **Teresa Fasolino**
Publisher | **University of Pennsylvania**

128

129

130
Publication **Contemporary OB/GYN**
Art Director **Barbara P. Silbert**
Designer **Barbara P. Silbert**
Illustrator **Barbara P. Silbert**
Publisher **Medical Economics Company, Inc.**

131
Publication **Behavioral Medicine**
Art Director **Paul Nemesure**
Designer **Paul Nemesure**
Photographer **Paul Nemesure**
Publisher **Magazines for Medicine, Inc.**

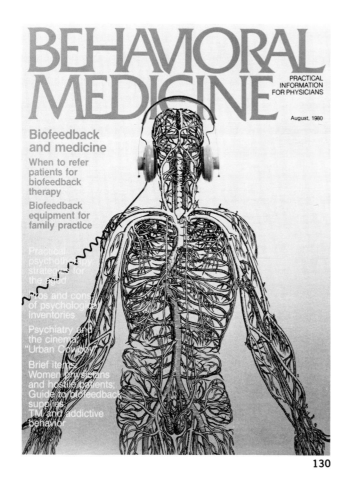

130

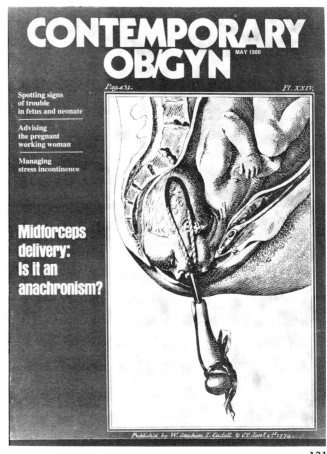

131

132
Publication **Convenience Stores**
Art Director **Mitch Shostak**
Designer **Magda Malachowski**
Illustrator **Teresa Fasolino**
Publisher **Maclean Hunter Media**

133
Publication **Medical Laboratory Observer**
Art Director **Barbara P. Silbert**
Designer **Barbara P. Silbert**
Illustrator **Don Brautigam**
Publisher **Medical Economics Company, Inc.**

132

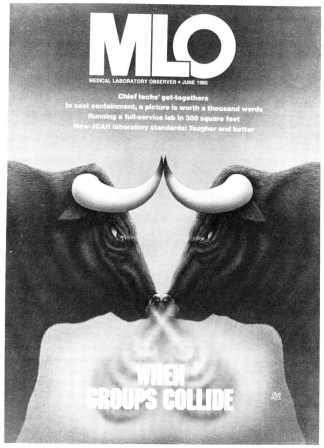

133

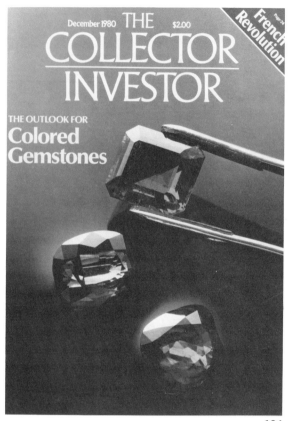

134

135

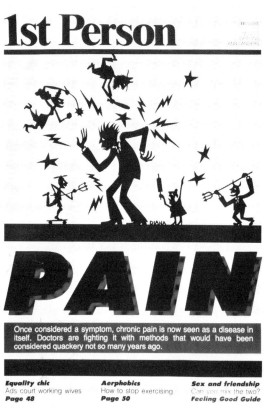

136

137

136

Publication	**First Person**
Art Director	**Andrew J. Epstein, Phil Ritzenberg**
Designer	**Andrew J. Epstein**
Illustrator	**Diana Bryan**
Publisher	**New York Daily News**

137

Publication	**The Boston Globe Magazine**
Art Director	**Ronn Campisi**
Designer	**Ronn Campisi**
Illustrator	**Catherine Aldrich**
Photographer	**Charles E. Feinberg Collection**
Publisher	**The Boston Globe**

138
Publication   **The Plain Dealer Magazine**
Art Director   **Greg Paul**
Designer   **Greg Paul**
Photographer   **Corson Hirschfeld**
Publisher   **The Plain Dealer**

139
Publication   **Star Magazine/Kansas City Star**
Art Director   **Tom Strongman**
Illustrator   **Tom Dolphens**
Photographer   **Roy Inman**
Publisher   **Kansas City Star**

138

139

140

Publication	**ARTnews**
Art Director	**Mary Mullin**
Designer	**Mary Mullin**
Illustrator	**(Calligrapher) Mary Mullin**
Photographer	**Michael Halsband**
Publisher	**ARTnews Associates**

Publication	**Horizon**
Art Director	**Will Hopkins, Ira Friedlander**
Designer	**Will Hopkins, Ira Friedlander**
Illustrator	**Arnold Roth**
Publisher	**Horizon Publishers, Inc.**

141

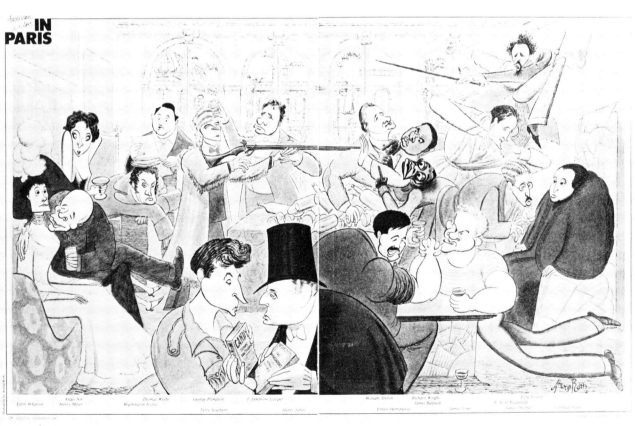

141

142
Publication   **Jardin des Modes**
Art Director   **bill butt**
Designer   **bill butt, Frederique Schott**
Photographer   **Dominique Issermann**
Publisher   **Vercingetorix International Publications**

Coiffes
D'UN PAYS APPELÉ MARIAGE

Un voyage qui ne dure qu'un jour, dans une contrée très étrangère, où les habitants sont toujours en fête, mais où les mères ont la larme à l'œil et où les pères toussent dans leur mouchoir. Un pays où la reine est souvent toute de blanc vêtue.

Mais le plus curieux de leur costume est leur couronne. Les couronnes de la reine du mariage sont des coiffes très typiques, hors du temps, hors des modes, qui semblent sorties d'un folklore plus sentimental que géographique.

Le bandeau 1930

La demi-couronne

La garlande de leurres

La couronne à l'ancienne. Explications page suivante

142

143

Publication **Seventeen**
Art Director **Tamara Schneider**
Designer **Tamara Schneider**
Photographer **Michael Tcherevkoff**
Publisher **Triangle Communications**

144

Publication **Life**
Art Director **Bob Ciano**
Designer **Mary K. Baumann**
Photographer **Heinz Kluetmeier**
Publisher **Time-Life**

143

144

145

146

147
Publication **National Lampoon Magazine**
Art Director **Skip Johnston**
Illustrator **Larry Williams**
Publisher **National Lampoon, Inc.**

148
Publication **Oui**
Art Director **Michael Brock**
Designer **Michael Brock**
Photographer **Gary Heery**
Publisher **Playboy Enterprises, Inc.**

147

148

149
Publication **Christmas Ideas**
Art Director **Jon Snyder, Rudy Evans**
Designer **Rudy Evans**
Photographer **William N. Hopkins**
Publisher **Better Homes & Gardens/
Special Interest Publications**

150
Publication **Esquire**
Art Director **Robert Priest**
Designer **April Silver**
Photographer **Dmitri Kasterine**
Publisher **Esquire Publishing, Inc.**

149

150

151
Publication **Food & Wine**
Art Director **Jessica M. Weber**
Designer **Jessica M. Weber**
Photographer **Larry Couzens**
Publisher **The International Review of Food & Wine Associations**

152
Publication **Mother Jones**
Art Director **Louise Kollenbaum**
Designer **Dian-Aziza Ooka**
Photographer **Elizabeth Marshall**
Publisher **Foundation for National Progress**

151

152

153

Publication   **Boating Magazine**
Art Director   **Shelley Heller**
Designer   **Shelley Heller**
Photographer   **Bob Gelberg**
Publisher   **Ziff-Davis**
   Publishing Company

Boating Boards

She doesn't look like a raceboat for nothing. The
only question is are you man enough to handle her?

MAGNUM
45 SPORT
BY DEX HART

The 44 Magnum revolver is the most powerful handgun made; it's
also costly to buy and operate. The Magnum 45 Sport has similar
characteristics. I don't want to stretch the comparison too thin, but
both products are a real handful. *Two* handfuls, in fact. In a libber's
world, the 44 Magnum and the Magnum 45 are strictly male hard-
ware, Betty Cook notwithstanding. Available also as a hardtop and a
flying bridge model, the 45
Sport is an open runabout in
style, although it sports a
roomy saloon/galley and
owner's cabin beneath that
parking-lot-sized
foredeck.

*continued on
page 510*

Master stateroom has double bed, head with bidet.

153

	154		155
Publication	**Nautical Quarterly**	Publication	**Nautical Quarterly**
Art Director	**B. Martin Pederson**	Art Director	**B. Martin Pederson**
Designer	**B. Martin Pederson**	Designer	**B. Martin Pederson**
Photographer	**Allan Weitz**	Photographer	**Andrew Unangst**
Publisher	**Nautical Quarterly**	Publisher	**Nautical Quarterly**

154

155

156
Publication **Footwear News Magazine**
Art Director **Traci Churchill**
Designer **Traci Churchill**
Illustrator **Traci Churchill**
Photographer **Tobi Seftel**
Publisher **Fairchild Publications**

157
Publication **MD Magazine**
Art Director **Al Foti**
Designer **Al Foti**
Photographer **Ted H. Funk**
Publisher **MD Publications, Inc.**

158
Publication **RN Magazine**
Art Director **Hector W. Marrero**
Designer **Hector W. Marrero,
Kiaran O'Brien**
Illustrator **Lou Bory**
Publisher **Medical Economics
Company**

156

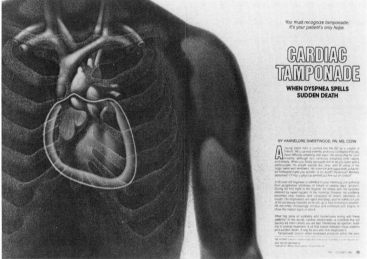

157

158

159

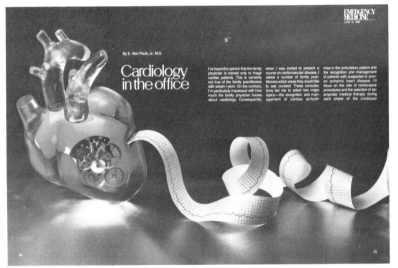

160

161

159
Publication **The (Army) Times Magazine**
Art Director **Robert St. John**
Designer **Robert St. John**
Photographer **Joseph Matera**
Publisher **Army Times Publishing Company**

160
Publication **Emergency Medicine**
Art Director **Tom Lennon**
Designer **Cheun Chiang**
Illustrator **Nick Aristovulos**
Photographer **Shig Ikeda**
Publisher **Fischer Medical Publications, Inc.**

161
Publication **Industry Week**
Art Director **Nickolas Dankovich**
Designer **Nickolas Dankovich**
Photographer **Andrew Russetti**
Publisher **Penton-IPC**

162
Publication **Radford Magazine**
Art Director **Bernice A. Thiebolt**
Designer **Martin F. Bennett**
Photographer **Doug Barber**
Publisher **North Charles Street Design Organization**

163
Publication **Rolling Stone**
Art Director **Christopher Austopchuk, Mary Shanahan**
Designer **Christopher Austopchuk**
Photographer **Annie Leibovitz**
Publisher **Straight Arrow Publishers**

164
Publication **Rolling Stone**
Art Director **Christopher Austopchuk**
Designer **Christopher Austopchuk**
Illustrator **Victor Juhasz**
Publisher **Straight Arrow Publishers**

162

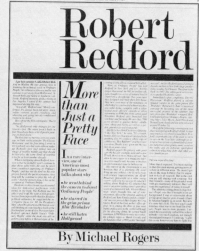

163

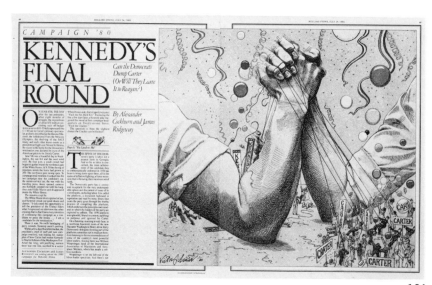

164

165

Publication	**The Plain Dealer Magazine**
Art Director	**Greg Paul**
Designer	**Greg Paul**
Illustrator	**Tom Curry**
Publisher	**The Plain Dealer**

166

Publication	**The Plain Dealer Magazine**
Art Director	**Greg Paul**
Designer	**Greg Paul**
Illustrator	**Mark Spangler**
Publisher	**The Plain Dealer**

165

166

167

168

Publication	The Washington Post
Art Director	Bob Barken
Designer	Carol Porter
Illustrator	Jim Owens
Photographer	Dick Darcey
Publisher	The Washington Post

170

Publication	The Plain Dealer Magazine
Art Director	Sam Capuano
Designer	Sam Capuano
Illustrator	Gary Kelley
Publisher	The Plain Dealer

169

170

95

171,172
Publication **American Photographer**
Art Director **Will Hopkins**
Designer **Louis F. Cruz**
Photographer **Steichen, Hoynungen-Huene, Blumenfeld, Penn, Avedon, Newton, Turbeville, Elgort**
Publisher **CBS Publications**

173,174
Publication **American Photographer**
Art Director **Will Hopkins**
Designer **Louis F. Cruz**
Photographer **Steve McCurry**
Publisher **CBS Publications**

171

172

173

174

175–177
Publication   **Jardin des Modes**
Art Director   **bill butt**
Designer   **bill butt, Frederique Schott**
Photographer   **Sacha**
Publisher   **Vercingetorix International Publications**

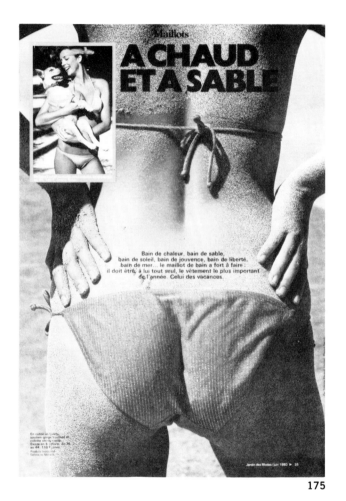

175

176

177

178,179

Publication	McCall's
Art Director	Al Grossman
Designer	Kit Hinrichs/Jonson, Pederson, Hinrichs & Shakery
Illustrator	Lynne Dennis, Ellen Blonder, Kit Hinrichs
Photographer	Dennis Bettencourt
Publisher	McCall's

178

179

	180,181		182,183
Publication	**Life**	Publication	**Life**
Art Director	**Bob Ciano**	Art Director	**Bob Ciano**
Designer	**Bob Ciano**	Designer	**Bob Ciano**
Photographer	**Greg Heisler**	Photographer	**Gjon Mili**
Publisher	**Time-Life**	Publisher	**Time-Life**

180

181

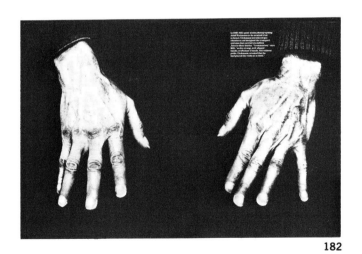

182

183

184,185

Publication	**Town & Country**
Art Director	**Melissa Tardiff**
Designer	**Mark Borden**
Photographer	**Klaus Lucka**
Publisher	**The Hearst Corporation**

184

185

100

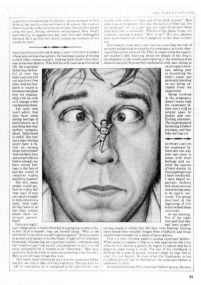

186

187

186,187

Publication	**Pre-Parent Adviser**
Art Director	**Vincent Winter, Shelley Williams**
Designer	**Vincent Winter**
Illustrator	**Ed Soyka**
Publisher	**13-30 Corporation**

188,189

Publication	**Gardener's Handbook**
Art Director	**Jon Snyder, Karen Huber**
Designer	**Karen Huber**
Illustrator	**Steve Schindler**
Publisher	**Meredith Corporation**

188   189

190–192

Publication   **Rocky Mountain Magazine**
Art Director   **Hans Teensma**
Designer   **Hans Teensma, Howard Klein**
Publisher   **Rocky Mountain Magazine**

190

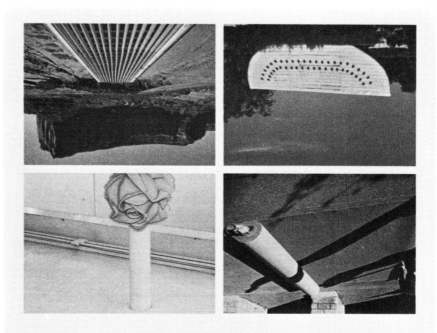

191

Craig Pozzi, Salt Lake City, Utah. "These photographs are from a work in progress entitled *Living in Utah: Things and Beings*. I am interested in man's relationship with his surroundings and his alterations of both the natural and built environment. Further, I am curious about his artifacts and how they reflect his values." Craig Pozzi is a graduate of Brown University, the Brooks Institute and the California Institute of the Arts. His work has been widely exhibited, and he is the editor of the exhibition catalog, *Living in the Salt Lake Valley*, Salt Lake Art Center, 1980.

CRAIG POZZI

192

193,194

Publication **New York Magazine**
Art Director **Roger Black**
Designer **Robert Best**
Photographer **Bert Stern**
Publisher **News Group Publications, Inc.**

193

Fall Fashions: Everything Goes

By John Duka • Photographed by Bert Stern

DON'T look for any order to inform the latest fall clothes for women. There is none. And don't look for one overriding theme. There are many. In fact, the new season's fashions represent the most eclectic assortment of styles since the mid-seventies. Perhaps the designers decided to be exceptionally thoughtful, each one filling his line with a little something for everyone. Or, more likely, they are just as scared as everyone else about the recession and are hedging their bets.

Whatever the reason, there is a surfeit of styles to choose from: sweater sets and winter whites. Knickers and kilts. Capes and greatcoats. Argyles and plaids from just about everyone. And enough angora and mohair to keep us in lint for a lifetime.

To bring visual order to all this diversity, we asked Bert Stern to photograph the clothes for us. Stern, the quintessential photographer, hero and the last photographer to work with Marilyn Monroe, had, since 1971, put aside fashion photography. But we convinced him to return to shoot two of New York's most beautiful models—Rosie Vela (right) and Iman (next page). Stern's lighting, as always, was perfect.

194

195,196
Publication **Nautical Quarterly**
Art Director **B. Martin Pederson**
Designer **B. Martin Pederson**
Photographer **Sam Abell**
Publisher **Nautical Quarterly**

197,198
Publication **Nautical Quarterly**
Art Director **B. Martin Pederson**
Designer **B. Martin Pederson**
Photographer **Allen Weitz**
Publisher **Nautical Quarterly**

195

196

197

198

THE DIET

A SELF-PORTRAIT BY BOB ADELMAN

IN WHICH OUR HERO LOSES 115 POUNDS, IS TRANSFORMED FROM HUMAN BALLOON TO STANDARD MODEL, AND LEARNS THAT THE HARD WAY CAN BE THE BEST WAY

I was an obsessive eater—whenever there was food around, I'd eat it. Whether psychologically or genetically (both my parents were very fat), I was programmed to eat. I often didn't even taste food, I'd be gobbling so fast. Feeling full was pleasant, and I was a cheery sort of person because I was always gratifying my desires. A lot of people found me comforting and supportive and reassuring to be around.

305 lbs.

199–201
Publication **Esquire**
Art Director **Robert Priest**
Designer **Robert Priest**
Photographer **Bob Adelman**
Publisher **Esquire Publishing, Inc.**

199

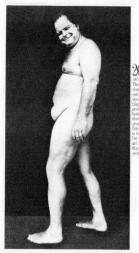

260 lbs.

220 lbs.

200

190 lbs.

201

202,203

Publication	**Professional Builder**
Art Director	**Ingeborg Jakobson**
Designer	**Ingeborg Jakobson**
Illustrator	**Roger Jadown**
Publisher	**Cahners Publishing Company**

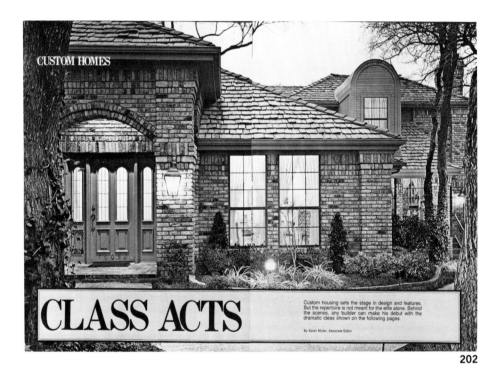

202

203

204,205

Publication **Builder**
Art Director **Bono Mitchell**
Designer **Pat Taylor**
Publisher **National Association of Home Builders**

2 WEST GERMAN MANUFACTURERS ENTER MARKET

German designers make every inch in a kitchen count. They have to — German kitchens are small: about half as large as American kitchens.

And German houses and apartments are sold or rented without kitchen appliances and cabinets. Germans either buy new appliances and cabinets or bring with them what they had in their previous homes.

For these reasons German kitchen design has had to respond to a demanding market: one that wants function, flexibility and good looks.

As homes — and kitchens — in this country become more compact, the demands of the American market will be much like those of the German market.

The cabinets and appliances shown on these four pages illustrate how German designers have met market demands. All these products are available in the U.S.

Because the cabinets are made to be moved from one home to another, with the possibility of additions and rearrangement they are modular in order to maintain strict tolerances.

the boxes usually are made of particleboard, which warps less than wood. The particleboard is covered on both sides with plastic laminate.

The homeowner can satisfy the taste and pocketbook with a choice of door fronts and storage options. According to Dieter Rosenberger, kitchen designer at Häggenpohl USA, the German products cost about 15 percent more than their American counterparts. But German manufacturers believe that if you offer customers everything they want, they will pay for it.

TRADITIONAL STYLED OAK CABINETRY COMES IN MORE THAN 250 DIFFERENT UNITS.

WITHOUT DOORS, YOU CAN SEE THE INNER WORKINGS OF THESE CABINETS - PULL-OUT DRAWERS FOR BOTTLE TRAY, FOOD BINS AND POP-UP MEAT SLICER, CORNER SPIN SHELF AND ICE-SPACE DRAWER.

2 WEST GERMAN KITCHEN PRODUCTS

PLASTIC LAMINATE DOOR FRONTS IN SOLID OAK APRONS AND HANDLES AMONG THE OPTIONS OPEN OAK SHELVING

204

1 BREAK BARRIERS TO OPEN KITCHENS TO THE HOME

BREAKFAST BAR SEPARATES THE KITCHEN FROM THE LIVING AREA AND PROVIDES A CONVENIENT SPOT FOR CASUAL DINING. PASS-THROUGH WET BAR TO DINING ROOM ON LEFT.

KITCHEN IS OPEN TO THE INSIDE AS WELL AS THE OUTSIDE TILE, COPPER AND WOOD FINISHES ARE OF PEAK QUALITY

HALF WALL OPENS A SMALL GALLEY KITCHEN TO THE FAMILY ROOM, CREATING A COMFORTABLE LIVING ENVIRONMENT.

ONLY AN ISLAND SEPARATES THE KITCHEN FROM AN INFORMAL LIVING AREA. DROPPED CEILING GIVES THE ISLAND MORE IMPACT. LIGHTED CEILING UNIFIES SPACE.

CLAY PAVERS EMPHASIZE THE LINK BETWEEN THE BREAKFAST ROOM, KITCHEN AND FAMILY ROOM. PLENTY OF CIRCULATION SPACE THROUGH THIS SPACIOUS OPEN AREA.

205

206,207

Publication	**Texaco Marketer**
Art Director	**David Kaestle**
Designer	**Ted Williams**
Illustrator	**Dick Frank**
Publisher	**Pellegrini and Kaestle, Inc.**

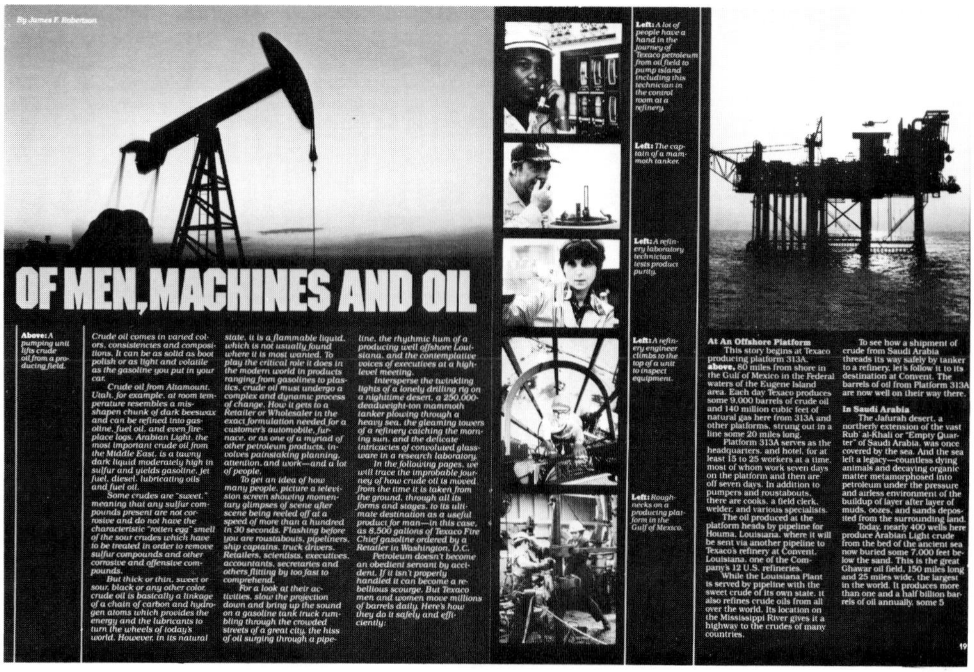

206

OF MEN, MACHINES AND OIL

207

208

Publication   **Learning**
Art Director   **David Hale**
Designer   **David Hale**
Publisher   **Pitman Learning, Inc.**

209

Publication   **Progress Number One/1980**
Art Director   **Dominic Arbitrio**
Designer   **Stephen Ferrari**
Illustrator   **Daniel Tybaert**
Publisher   **Combustion Engineering**

208

209

210–212
Publication   **The Plain Dealer Magazine**
Art Director   **Greg Paul**
Designer   **Greg Paul**
Photographer   **Robert E. Dorksen**
Publisher   **The Plain Dealer**

210

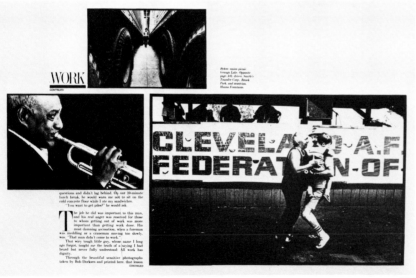

211

212

213,214

Publication	**Rolling Stone**
Art Director	**Christopher Austopchuk, Mary Shanahan**
Designer	**Christopher Austopchuk**
Photographer	**Bonnie Schiffman**
Publisher	**Straight Arrow Publishers**

213

214

215
Publication **TV Guide**
Art Director **Jerry Alten**
Designer **Jerry Alten**
Illustrator **Richard Amsel**
Publisher **Triangle Communications**

216
Publication **Time**
Art Director **Walter Bernard, Rudolph Hoglund**
Illustrator **Guy Billout**
Publisher **Time, Inc.**

217
Publication **Time**
Art Director **Walter Bernard**
Illustrator **Edward Sorel**
Publisher **Time, Inc.**

218
Publication **Time**
Art Director **Walter Bernard**
Illustrator **Stanislaw Zagorski**
Publisher **Time, Inc.**

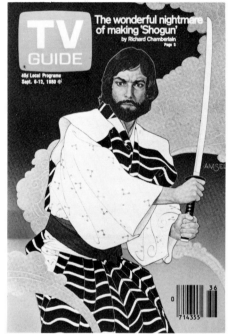

215

217

216

218

219

Publication **Psychology Today**
Art Director **Carveth Kramer**
Designer **Carveth Kramer**
Illustrator **Robert Grossman**
Publisher **Ziff-Davis**
Publishing Company

220

Publication **Emergency Medicine**
Art Director **Tom Lennon**
Designer **James T. Walsh**
Illustrator **Edwin Herder**
Publisher **Fischer Medical**
Publications, Inc.

221

Publication **Forbes**
Art Director **Everett**
Halvorsen
Designer **Roger Zapke**
Illustrator **Kinuko Craft**
Publisher **Forbes**

222

Publication **Emergency**
Medicine
Art Director **Tom Lennon**
Designer **Cheun Chiang**
Illustrator **Joan Hall**
Publisher **Fischer**
Medical
Publications,
Inc.

219

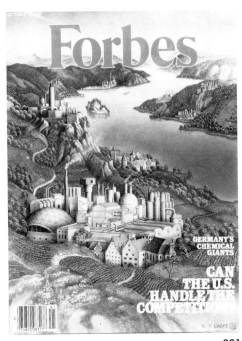

221

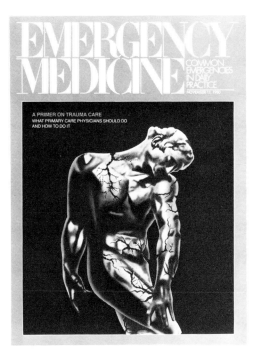

220

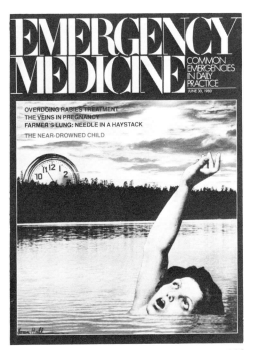

222

223
Publication **The Plain Dealer Magazine**
Art Director **Greg Paul**
Designer **Greg Paul**
Illustrator **Mark Andresen**
Publisher **The Plain Dealer**

224
Publication **The Wharton Magazine**
Art Director **Mitch Shostak**
Designer **Mitch Shostak**
Illustrator **Ed Soyka**
Publisher **University of Pennsylvania**

223

224

	225			**226**
Publication	**Flowers &**		Publication	**The Kansas City Star**
Art Director	**M.J. Cody**		Art Director	**Marty Petty**
Designer	**Dugald Stermer**		Designer	**Marty Petty**
Illustrator	**Mary Rubin**		Illustrator	**Tom Dolphens**
Publisher	**Teleflora, Inc.**		Publisher	**The Kansas City Star Company**

225

226

227
Publication **Oui**
Art Director **Michael Brock**
Designer **James Kiehle**
Illustrator **Robert Rodriquez**
Publisher **Playboy Enterprises, Inc.**

228
Publication **Oui**
Art Director **Michael Brock**
Designer **Michael Brock**
Illustrator **Haruo Miyauchi**
Publisher **Playboy Enterprises, Inc.**

229
Publication **Rocky Mountain Magazine**
Art Director **Hans Teensma**
Designer **Hans Teensma**
Illustrator **Brad Holland**
Publisher **Rocky Mountain Magazine**

227

228

229

THE PUBLIC DISTRUST

BY PHILLIP SHAVER

"We can attribute much of the 'crisis in confidence' to unrealistic expectations of leaders, a kind of adolescent rebellion encouraged by leaders themselves."

230

RISKY ASSUMPTIONS

BY PAUL SLOVIC, BARUCH FISCHHOFF,
AND SARAH LICHTENSTEIN

Asked to rate the risk of death from 30 possible causes, people tend to inflate some fears and deflate others. Often, experts are no more accurate. Psychological studies help explain how perceptions come to be so distorted.

231

THE PROMISCUOUS WOMAN
"Sandy was the first in a series of people I was to encounter again and again in my interviews—women who, like her, had become promiscuous in a frantic effort to ward off feelings of isolation, abandonment, and depression."

BY MAGGIE SCARF

232

230

Publication **Psychology Today**
Art Director **Carveth Kramer**
Designer **Carveth Kramer**
Illustrator **Bernard Bonhomme**
Publisher **Ziff-Davis Publishing Company**

231

Publication **Psychology Today**
Art Director **Carveth Kramer**
Designer **Carveth Kramer**
Illustrator **Carlos Aguirre**
Publisher **Ziff-Davis Publishing Company**

232

Publication **Psychology Today**
Art Director **Carveth Kramer**
Designer **Carveth Kramer**
Illustrator **Joan Hall**
Publisher **Ziff-Davis Publishing Company**

233

Publication	**Science Digest**
Art Director	**Frank Rothmann, Mary Zisk**
Designer	**Mary Zisk**
Illustrator	**Alan Cober**
Publisher	**Hearst Magazines, Inc.**

234

Publication	**Science Digest**
Art Director	**Frank Rothmann, Mary Zisk**
Designer	**Frank Rothmann, Mary Zisk**
Illustrator	**Chris Spollen**
Publisher	**Hearst Magazines, Inc.**

235

Publication	**Science Digest**
Art Director	**Frank Rothmann**
Designer	**Frank Rothmann**
Illustrator	**Carol Wald**
Publisher	**Hearst Magazines, Inc.**

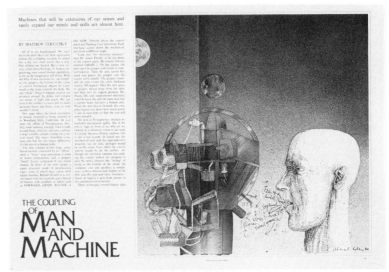

233

234

235

236

Publication **National Lampoon Magazine**
Art Director **Skip Johnston**
Illustrator **Ron Barrett**
Photographers **Bill Dolce, Steve Dolce**
Publisher **National Lampoon, Inc.**

237

Publication **Mother Jones**
Art Director **Louise Kollenbaum**
Designer **Dian-Aziza Ooka**
Illustrator **Brad Holland**
Publisher **Foundation for National Progress**

236

MISSION IMPROBABLE

How Mother Jones Joined The Ruling Class

By Eve Pell and Mark Dowie

Illustration by Brad Holland

Editor's note: *Somewhere in Texas a few months ago, a temporary office worker picked up an invitation intended only for a high-level executive and rerouted it to Mother Jones. "A Corporate Strategy for the '80s," the brochure promised: a four-day, shirt-sleeves, working seminar in Palm Springs, California, with former President Gerald R. Ford, General Alexander Haig, Nixon economist Alan Greenspan, former CIA chief William Colby and a selection of top executives from America's leading corporations. The topics of discussion included: "U.S. Military Preparedness Around the World—What It Means to Corporate Interests," "Government Regulations in the '80s—How to Survive the Bureaucracy" and "Political Unrest in the '80s—Countries Safe and Unsafe for Corporate Expansion." The invitation added: "Due to the volatile nature of the subjects to be discussed, members of the press will not be permitted to attend."*

How could we resist?

All this was offered by something called Corporate Seminars Inc. for only $1,750 registration (transportation and the price of a room in a posh Palm Springs hotel not included). And so MJ publisher Mark Dowie, as treasurer of

the FNP Corporation (not too great a stretch of the truth, for Dowie is treasurer of MJ's parent organization, the Foundation for National Progress), accepted the invitation. Since speakers could attend at no extra charge, Treasurer Dowie brought along Mrs. Dowie —his wife, freelance journalist Eve Pell. Here is their report on how big business views the '80s.

PALM SPRINGS is a white city. White cars (Mercedes-Benzes mostly), white houses that look like mausoleums, white sand, white sunlight undimmed by smog and mostly white people dressed mainly in white. The Canyon Racquet & Golf Resort, where about 85 of America's top echelon executives met last October, is a white hotel. White reflects the heat.

They came like pilgrims from companies large and small—Boeing, Shell Oil, Martin-Marietta, Transcontinental Oil, Minnesota Rubber and Dato-Paper Bags—to this desert city of golf courses, pale flat houses, carefully manicured shrubs and Westinghouse Security signs. Palm Springs is where the superrich and the superfamous go out to pasture: Walter Annenberg, Bob Hope, Gerald Ford and Liberace all live here, among anonymous corporate retirees and a gaggle of Mafia has-beens. We drove in from an airport packed with rows of corporate jets, wondering how we would fit in.

SINCE WE HAD grown up with executive fathers, we thought we knew what to expect: a gathering of well-groomed, gray-sideburned corporate leaders exuding the confidence that comes with wealth and power. In fact, had we both lived the lives our parents had mapped out for us, we might have been attending this conference as a genuine executive and his wife instead of as reporters in semidisguise. We were playing ourselves as we might have become had we not been changed by political and social currents of the 1960s.

We arrived resplendent in a three-piece suit and smartly tailored black dress, looking as executive as we could manage, with borrowed suitcases, new shoes and expensive haircuts. We wondered anxiously whether Corporate Seminars Inc. or the Secret Service had checked anxiously whether Corporate checked out the FNP Corporation. Would they whisk us aside before we even checked in? Not at all.

237

238,239
Publication   **Playboy Magazine (Germany)**
Art Director   **Rainer Wortmann**
Designer   **Rainer Wortmann**
Illustrator   **Kinuko Y. Craft**
Publisher   **Heinrich Bauer Verlag, Munchen**

KU-KLUX-KLAN: HINTER DER MASKE...

238

...DIE BRAVEN KOMPLIZEN DES TERRORS

Wer sich mit den Kapuzenmännern einläßt, muß lebensmüde sein. Amerikas biedere Bürger machen nicht nur Neger fertig. Porträt eines Geheimbundes von
PATSY SIMS

239

240
Publication   **McCall's/Working Mother**
Art Director   **Nina Scerbo**
Designer   **Nina Scerbo**
Illustrator   **Dagmar Frinta**
Publisher   **McCall's**

241
Publication   **Runner Magazine**
Art Director   **Rita Milos**
Designer   **Steve Phillips**
Illustrator   **Daniel Maffia**
Publisher   **Ziff-Davis Publication Company**

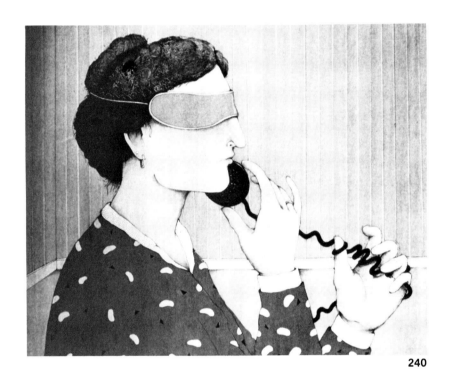

240

241

121

242
Publication **Playboy**
Art Director **Arthur Paul, Tom Staebler**
Designer **Bob Post**
Illustrator **Joann Daley**
Publisher **Playboy Enterprises, Inc.**

243
Publication **Playboy**
Art Director **Arthur Paul, Tom Staebler**
Designer **Theo Kouvatsos**
Illustrator **Tom Gala**
Publisher **Playboy Enterprises, Inc.**

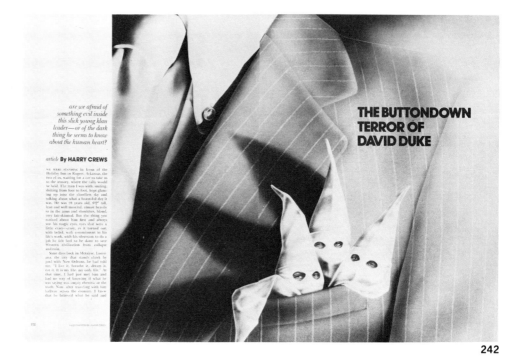

242

243

244

Publication   **Senior Scholastic**
Art Director   **Dale Moyer, Audrey Perella**
Designer   **Geoffrey Moss**
Publisher   **Scholastic Magazines**

245

Publication   **Esquire**
Art Director   **Robert Priest**
Designer   **April Silver**
Illustrator   **Ed Soyka**
Publisher   **Esquire Publishing, Inc.**

244

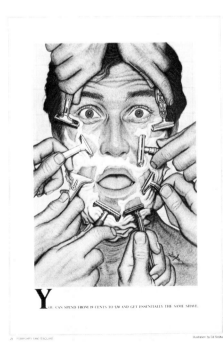

245

123

246
Publication **Time**
Art Director **Irene Ramp**
Illustrator **Eugene Mihaesco**
Publisher **Time, Inc.**

247
Publication **Nautical Quarterly**
Art Director **B. Martin Pederson**
Designer **B. Martin Pederson**
Illustrator **R.O. Blechman**
Publisher **Nautical Quarterly**

246

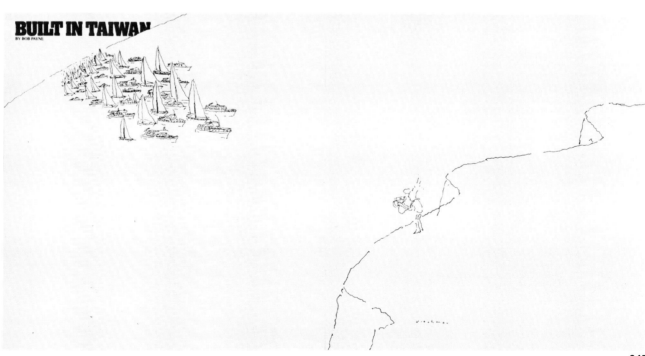

247

248

Publication **Oceans**
Art Director **Dugald Stermer**
Designer **Dugald Stermer**
Illustrator **Dugald Stermer**
Publisher **The Oceanic Society**

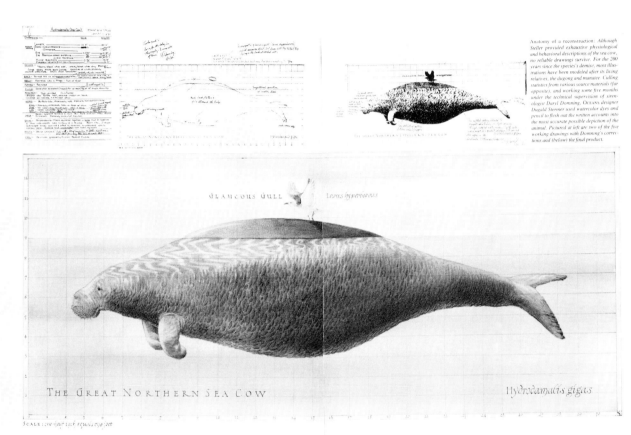

Anatomy of a reconstruction: Although Steller provided exhaustive physiological and behavioral descriptions of the sea cow, no reliable drawings survive. For the 200 years since the species's demise, most illustrations have been modeled after its living relatives, the dugong and manatee. Culling statistics from various source materials (far opposite), and working some five months under the technical supervision of sirenologist Daryl Domning, OCEANS designer Dugald Stermer used watercolor dyes and pencil to flesh out the written accounts into the most accurate possible depiction of the animal. Pictured at left are two of the five working drawings with Domning's corrections and (below) the final product.

248

125

249

Publication **Postgraduate Medicine**
Art Director **Tina Adamek**
Illustrator **Richard Sparks**
Publisher **McGraw-Hill, Inc.**

250

Publication **Postgraduate Medicine**
Art Director **Tina Adamek**
Illustrator **Bart Forbes**
Publisher **McGraw-Hill, Inc.**

Second of a group
of three related articles
in this issue

David G. Sherman, MD
J. Donald Easton, MD

Cerebral edema in stroke

A common, often fatal
complication

Consider

*What are the various types of cerebral edema?
What determines which type will predominate?*

*Which clinical sign of ischemic cerebral edema
is most common?*

*What have experimental studies shown about
the usefulness of dimethyl sulfoxide or of
pentoxifylline in preventing or treating cerebral
edema?*

In stroke, the brain undergoes a complex sequence of events resulting from ischemia, necrosis, and edema. Maintenance of normotension and avoidance of hypoxia, hyperthermia, and probably hypercapnia are the cornerstones of therapy. Any of a variety of agents, including corticosteroids, glycerol, and diuretics, may prove beneficial.

Stroke is a major cause of death and disability in the US and beyond.

Classification of cerebral edema

Cerebral edema increases the brain's volume by increasing its water content.

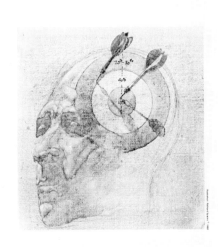

Interstate Postgraduate Medical Assembly

First of a group
of three related articles
in this issue

Antonio C. de Leon, Jr, MD

Mitral valve prolapse

Etiology, diagnosis, and
management

Consider

*What abnormalities can cause mitral valve
prolapse?*

*With what other conditions might mitral valve
prolapse be confused? Why? How can it be
differentiated?*

What is the proper course of management?

Mitral valve prolapse, known by a variety of names, is characterized by the auscultatory finding of systolic clicks and murmurs of mitral origin. It is often asymptomatic and accompanied by a benign clinical course, but it can cause a variety of symptoms and, rarely, even sudden death.

One of the most frequent forms of cardiac anomalies seen in clinical practice today is mitral valve prolapse.

251
Publication **Physician and Sportsmedicine**
Art Director **Tina Adamek**
Designer **Steve Blom**
Illustrator **Leland Klanderman**
Publisher **McGraw-Hill, Inc.**

252
Publication **Chief Executive Magazine**
Art Director **Rusti Esmont**
Designer **Rusti Esmont, Frank Bozzo**
Illustrator **Frank Bozzo**
Publisher **Chief Executive Magazine, Inc.**

253
Publication **The Wharton Magazine**
Art Director **Mitch Shostak**
Designer **Mitch Shostak**
Illustrator **Alan E. Cober**
Publisher **University of Pennsylvania**

251

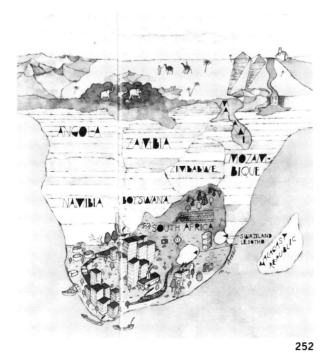

252

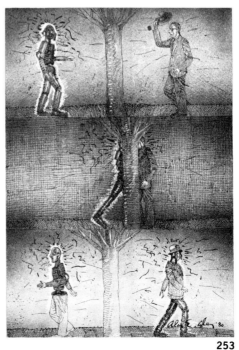

253

254

Publication   **Emergency Medicine**
Art Director   **Tom Lennon**
Designer   **James T. Walsh**
Illustrator   **Alan Cober**
Publisher   **Fischer Medical
Publications, Inc.**

255

Publication   **Emergency Medicine**
Art Director   **Tom Lennon**
Designer   **Cheun Chiang**
Illustrator   **Joan Hall**
Publisher   **Fischer Medical
Publications, Inc.**

256

Publication   **Emergency Medicine**
Art Director   **Tom Lennon**
Designer   **Tom Lennon**
Illustrator   **Edwin Herder**
Publisher   **Fischer Medical
Publications, Inc.**

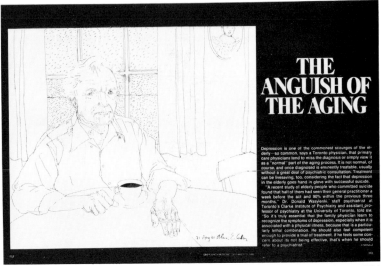

254

255

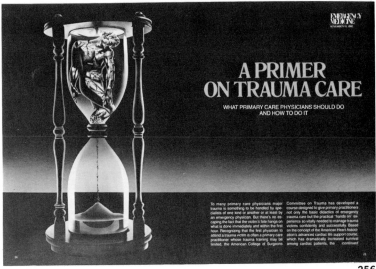

256

NEW ROSE HYBRIDS

Roses have bloomed both in the wild and in gardens for centuries, but until the 1800s, rose hybridization was left completely up to Mother Nature. Then, in 1804, the Empress Josephine, wife of Napoleon Bonaparte, began to cultivate her famous rose gardens at Malmaison. Collectors from all over the world sent her more than 250 specimens, some from as far away as China. When these new varieties were crossed with old roses, the end result was our modern hybrid tea. Today, the process of hybridization continues as specialists search for

40

even stronger, hardier, longer-lasting and more unusually colored varieties. Hybridizers cross-pollinate thousands of likely prospects, discarding all but a few which are then developed for years before marketing. Some of their work is illustrated by the new hybrids pictured above, which are described more fully on the next page. With such beautiful examples of the rose breeder's art already on the market, why do hybridizers continue producing new varieties of roses each year? Perhaps because even the perfect flower isn't perfect enough — yet.   41

257

Capturing Commercial Accounts

by Steve Stearns

They're out there — large and money-spending — just waiting to be trapped. But you've got to have the right bait.

18

LEGIONS OF BUSINESSMEN go forth every day and sell their products or services to other businesses. Should more florists be making the same effort? Some industry marketing specialists insist on the alternative, saying that commercial accounts offer the best opportunity of all for increasing florists' sales.

Today, when "commercial accounts" are mentioned, the discussion is apt to focus on plantscaping, which deals with the installation and maintenance of greenery in offices on a rental or purchase plus maintenance contract plan. While there are exciting opportunities in this field, it is a separate business entirely for a flower shop. To do this, a florist must have a crew that can go out every week and service the plants and a supervisor to oversee the work, performed away from the shop. Not all florists desire to spread out this far from the more traditional sources of shop income.

There's another side of selling to businesses, however, that is right up every florist's alley. Companies like to remember or thank people, to promote their images, decorate their reception areas with flowers, celebrate anniversaries and so on. In this respect, the needs of businesses are much like those of individuals, multiplied by the sizes of the firms and the scope of their activities.

A lot of floriculture products are being used today by commercial establishments, but very few florists have actually gone out and tried to build this market. They often assume that the only value of business accounts is being able to sell an extra 50 poinsettias at Christmas for employee gifts. But this is only the start.

Ralph Null, horticulture professor at Mississippi State University, stresses this point: "If you correctly promote flower purchasing to a company, say, with 40 or 50 employees, it's *totally* awesome. The worst thing you can do is to ask companies just for Christmas orders, because this is when you are already strapped to get things done. Rather, if you talk about flowers as company gifts for many purposes, that spreads out your business. You could sell those same poinsettias one by one elsewhere, if you work at it. But when there are few individual customers buying in June, July and August, this is when you need that $150 or $200 monthly commercial account."

Charley Kremp of Kremp's Flower and Plant Shop in Philadelphia, Pennsylvania, estimates that 20 percent of his shop's revenue is from commercial accounts. One company in particular orders 30 arrangements every week to place on

all the secretaries' desks. "In these times we are supposed to be holding up the production of our employees," says Kremp, "and the only way our shop can do that is to concentrate our efforts in the areas we know best. This type of order fits right in with our other daily work."

Besides helping to keep shop work flowing from month to month, Kremp finds that commercial orders are often larger unit sales. "Some of our biggest orders have been from companies sending baby novelties to employees in the maternity ward. Then there are company openings, when an account wants a big, splashy decoration to make an impression. Sometimes they say, 'I just want it to be nice — can you give me something for $100?' Their only requirement is for a showy piece, and that's really easy to do!"

The latter observation points up another advantage of commercial accounts, according to Kremp's experience. He often finds that private individuals are more exacting about their needs than companies, which only want to know if the shop can supply them with a nice gift that is representative of their business. "They usually leave the selection a little more open," says Kremp, "and this gives our designers more leeway."

It Takes Commitment

One high-volume shop makes up more than 100 arrangements every Monday morning for commercial businesses. Then on Wednesday afternoon all the arrangements are packed up and reworked for delivery again on Thursday. The business accounts represent only a part of the total activity, but they are the key to the success of the entire operation. All other customers also benefit from the shop's ability to consistently purchase a diversity of products. This brings the people in.

Florists who realize such advantages, however, also recognize the necessity of making a commitment to their commercial accounts. The shop in this example arranges to employ extra help on the two peak days so the commercial orders can be handled properly and placed in the offices early in the morning, as expected.

Ralph Null talks about another florist who delivers a decoration for a company's reception desk every Monday morning, and the arrangement is seen daily by throngs of people who walk through the doors. Although the account spends a set amount regardless of what is sent, the florist always pays special attention to selecting flowers that will look good for five days. He states that complacency is the quickest way to lose an account.   19

258

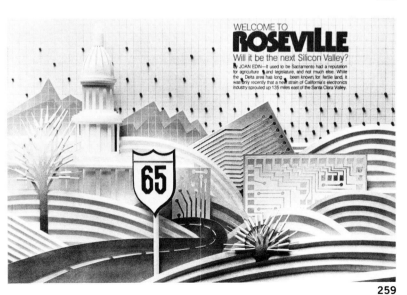

259

257
Publication	**Flowers &**
Art Director	**M.J. Cody**
Designer	**Dugald Stermer**
Illustrator	**Royce Wood**
Publisher	**Teleflora, Inc.**

258
Publication	**Flowers &**
Art Director	**M.J. Cody**
Designer	**Dugald Stermer**
Illustrator	**Gary Lund**
Publisher	**Teleflora, Inc.**

259
Publication	**California Business**
Art Director	**Ray Yee Graphics**
Designer	**Ray Yee**
Illustrator	**Leo Monahan**
Publisher	**California Business News, Inc.**

260
Publication **The Plain Truth**
Art Director **Randall Cole**
Designer **Randall Cole**
Illustrator **Jeffrey J. Smith**
Publisher **Ambassador College**

261
Publication **L.I. Magazine/Newsday**
Art Director **Miriam Smith**
Designer **Lee Hill**
Illustrator **Gary Viskupic**
Publisher **Newsday**

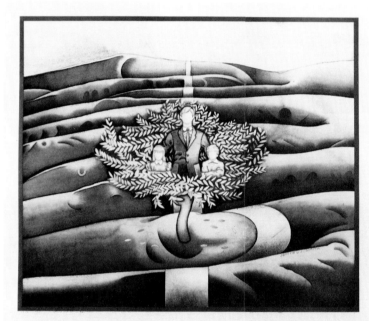

A revolution in American society threatens the foundations of the Free World.

THE WOMEN'S MOVEMENT—
Where Is It Leading?

by Ruth E. Walter

NEVER BEFORE in history has there been such an abundance of books, words and pictures on the subject of the "fair sex," marriage and sexuality.

A visit to any library or bookstore (and especially our large university facilities) will reveal an array of titles to pique your curiosity: *The Feminine Mystique, Woman in a Man-Made World, The Second Sex, The New Feminism in Twentieth Century America, On Being Female, Beyond Sex Role Stereotypes* to name a few.

But it's not necessary to go any farther than the local grocery store to find the same subject matter displayed prominently on magazine covers. Or for that matter if you just stay home and listen to the radio, watch television or read the daily newspaper you will probably learn of organized attempts to help abused wives, of ways to counteract sex-role stereotyping and of new lifestyles and opportunities opening up for women.

Many view this flood of information and exposure as the means of helping us all down the simple path of equal rights and justice. Others see the movement as a threat to the stability of society.

Where is the Women's Movement ultimately leading? Who are the leaders? What are the real issues? Will feminist goals affect the fabric of society? Above all, what does God say about it?

The issues at first seem so complex that it may appear difficult to "get a handle" on cause-and-effect relationships. Is the Women's Movement responsible for increasing divorce and child crime as critics charge? Is the constant harping by feminists on the "tyranny of men" driving a wedge between the sexes?

These questions need to be answered because

25

260

Why It's Okay to Be

FAT

Being overweight is not necessarily unhealthy, says this writer, and fat people should not have to be defensive about their excess poundage.

By Erich Goode
Illustration by Gary Viskupic

I'm looking at a poster that is sold in one of our Long Island supermarkets. The headline reads: "How to Rate Girls!" The subtitle claims to be "your guide to luscious loves and horrendous hags." On the left side of the poster is a photograph of a slender young woman clad in a bikini, perched atop high heels. On the right side is a fat young woman, also in a skimpy bathing suit, shod in sneakers.

Lines direct our attention to various portions of the anatomy of each one. The fat woman's hair? "Shampoos yearly but faithfully replaces her flea collar each month. Contains more oil than Saudia Arabia." Her breasts: "Two watermelons on a downhill race. If she burned her bra the energy crisis would be solved." Her waist: "Even King Kong couldn't wrap his arms around this." Her sneakers earn the final insult: "When walking, sets off earthquake warnings in Hong Kong. Responsible for most Bigfoot rumors."

While feminists would point out that the poster is insulting to all women, both of the women depicted on the poster are dissected solely on the basis of their appearance, and no fat woman could walk away from this poster without feeling the stigma that comes with being fat in this society.

As a result, mammoth efforts are made by "overweight" men and women (especially women) to lose five, 10, or 15 pounds, when actually such a level of "overweight" poses

Erich Goode, who is an associate professor of sociology at the State University at Stony Brook, is 5 feet, 3 inches tall and weighs 160 pounds.

no threat to their health at all. Many women who torture themselves by existing on spartan diets do so solely for cosmetic reasons. They are not, by "objective" standards, overweight—they just don't look like they stepped out of the pages of *Vogue.* In fact, the very group that is most concerned about its weight—affluent, urban, upper-middle class women—is, in reality, the group that is "objectively" the thinnest.

No doubt about it: Thin is in—and its appeal extends even to products advertised and sold on the market: thin watches, thin electronic calculators, thin cigarettes, thin mint candies, even "thin" makeup. But most of all, thin people. Our society is gripped by a virtual mania concerning fat and thin. Everybody is "on a diet"; everyone feels overweight and feels guilty because of it. Women aren't go to the beach in skimpy bathing suits until they've lost that midriff bulge. Advertisements claim that the way housewives can win back their husbands' affections is to "take it off."

There is some immutable law, emblazoned on the firmament, that says "fat is ugly"? There have been times and places where thin was ugly, and fat a sign of abundance, affluence, and beauty. Nineteenth-Century beauties such as Lillian Russell and Lily Langtree would be called, charitably, voluptuous today. A 19th-Century promoter named Billy Watson managed a chorus line of women, nicknamed "the Beef Trust," each one of which weighed at least 200 pounds.

Look at art work of the past, paintings and statuary depicting instances of female beauty. The Venus de Milo measures 37-27-38, which—if that is 22 inches around, and an upper arm that is 13 inches around. The beauties in Ingres' "The Turkish Bath" are chubby by contemporary standards, and a Rubens model weighed in at close to 200 pounds.

Overweight American tourists, visiting the Polynesian Islands and some areas of Africa, find themselves the object of male attention to a degree they never experienced in the States.

In other words, standards of beauty, with regard to weight, are relative to time and place. There is nothing intrinsically beautiful about sunken eyes and protruding ribs. And standards that vary, and have been changed, can be changed again. Admiration of thin women (and men—again, our sexist standards dictate that it is a greater sin for women to be fat than men) is what might be called a public salute—it's what gets expressed in the open, to others. Admiring overweight women (or men) is still a bit "closet" phenomenon—if one does it, one doesn't admit it. And yet, there are "closet fat admirers" everywhere—men and women for whom overweight is not a consideration, or for whom voluptuousness is actually a turn-on.

No one has put this sentiment so persuasively in print as Llewellyn Louderback, in his book, *Fat Power,*, a virtual Declaration of Independence for the overweight. Louderback writes of the "polarization of two separate nations—one thin, one fat." American culture, he says, has become "so completely permeated with anti-fat prejudice, that the fat themselves have been infected by it. They suffer other fat people, hate themselves when they are fat and will risk anything—even their lives—in an attempt to get thin." It is, in other words, a process of colluding in one's own oppression, exactly the same as if blacks smiled and laughed every time they encountered a racial slur. The stigma associated with obesity

starts early in life. In the late 1950s several sociologists and social psychologists, including Stony Brook professor Norman Goodman, made a study of the attitudes of eight different samples of 10- and 11-year-old boys and girls. The youngsters in the experiment were asked to look at six drawings of children. One of the drawings was of a "normal" child, four were of physically handicapped children and one was of an obese child. The experimenter then said: "Tell me which boys (or girl) you like best." This was done sequentially until the last drawing remained. Almost without exception, the drawing of the fat child was chosen last. The authors concluded that there was a "remarkable uniformity" in the children's hierarchy of preferences. In other words, the stigma of obesity is as pervasive as it is powerful.

The stigma of obesity is so powerful that it extends even to men and women of average weight who associate with fat people. In fact, I interviewed fat people who, at one or another time of their lives refused to associate with other fat people because of this social stigma. And the most intimate the association, the greater the stigma—and this applies, obviously, most directly to romantic and sexual relationships.

Even the right to be educated is influenced by one's size. In a study conducted by Dr. Jean Mayer, former Harvard University physiologist, presidential consultant on nutrition, author of the book *Overweight,* and current president of Tufts University, the applications of fat and average-sized high school seniors to the nation's most prestigious and selective colleges and universities were compared. While the obese high school students had the same grades, IQs, aptitude test scores and health records, they were accepted

261

130

262
Publication **The New York Times Magazine**
Art Director **Ruth Ansel**
Designer **Ruth Ansel**
Illustrator **Richard Hess**
Publisher **The New York Times**

263
Publication **Rolling Stone**
Art Director **Christopher Austopchuk**
Designer **Christopher Austopchuk**
Illustrator **Dagmar Frinta**
Publisher **Straight Arrow Publishers**

262

263

ILLUSTRATION—STORY PRESENTATION

264
Publication **Golf Digest**
Art Director **Pete Libby**
Illustrator **Walter Spitzmiller**
Publisher **The New York Times**

265
Publication **Sports Afield**
Art Director **Gary Gretter**
Designer **Gary Gretter**
Illustrator **Walter Spitzmiller**
Publisher **Hearst Magazines, Inc.**

264

North America's Big Five

This quintet of deer—whitetails, mulies, caribou, elk and moose—abounds with a wealth of challenging antlered trophies.
by Dave Bowring

The biggest and most impressive North American trophy I ever saw rode by me in pieces atop a packtrain in the San Juan mountains of southern Colorado. Our party of elk hunters had paused to eat some sandwiches alongside little Goose Creek when the packtrain, tack rings jangling and mule shoes ringing on trail rocks, passed by at a fast walk. I remember a great black-bearded outfitter on the lead horse, followed by a trio of hunters and half a dozen mules loaded with bundles of canvas, panniers of food boxes—and the biggest damned set of elk antlers I'd ever seen.

The rack was unbelievably massive. Gnarled and looking as hard as flint, each antler's beam was larger than the calf of my leg. Bone tines—my guide later called them dog killers, their Indian name—extended fully 20 inches out from the main beams, curving up at the ivory-white tips. The main network of antlers dwarfed the mule packing it, the tips swept well behind the animal's tail. I was able to count seven points on each side of the rack before the packtrain jogged noisily around a bend in the spruce-lined trail. I continued staring after the trophy, my mouth full of half-chewed sandwich, a thermos jug of coffee forgotten on a flat rock at my elbow. To a big-game hunter like me, it had seemed a magical moment. The fact that these mountains, the very ones our party of four guns and three guides was hunting, contained such a brute of a trophy, silenced us until, a few moments later, we rediscovered the food in our mouths. Still, we had trouble finding words to describe what we'd just seen. What must the bull have looked like to the incredibly fortunate hunter at the very moment it stepped from a stand of quaking aspen, the sun gleaming on that awesome rack of antler? Had the hunter realized the size of the animal at first sight, and had his hands shaken more than a little when he tried to settle crosshairs where shoulder met chest? All three men had been smiling when they rode past us, and one had turned in our direction long enough to wave. I like to think he was the trophy hunter whose den wall is now graced with what must be the trophy of a lifetime. Had it been me, I would have done more than wave. I would have shouted, done somersaults through the spruces, whooped loud enough to be heard in Denver.

For true trophies do that to people who seek them in the mountains of the West, the tundras of Alaska and the Yukon, or the hardwooded and brushy ridges of the East and Midwest. Trophies—true, mas-

Come winter snows, mulies band together, bucks and does. With the spring thaw, however, they separate, males usually traveling in groups of six or more, females in twos or threes.

Sports Afield August 1980   *Sports Afield August 1980*

265

266,267
Publication **Fortune**
Art Director **Ron Campbell**
Designer **Ron Campbell**
Illustrator **Nicholas Solovioff**
Publisher **Time, Inc.**

MONUMENTAL
RELICS
OF ABANDONED
TECHNOLOGY

A Fortune Portfolio

266

MONUMENTAL RELICS

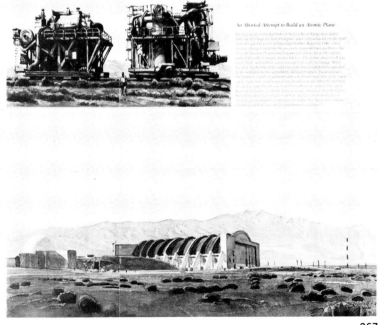

An Aborted Attempt to Build an Atomic Plane

S cattered around the United States, in places with names such as Jackass Flats and Sugar Grove, are monuments to a level of high technology a shattered decades or close to our time and complexity, the wilderness-temples and pyramids of abused civilizations. Some of the abandoned projects memorialize Americans' attempts to fly rather higher and further in all-noted means of transport, while others testify to the country's determination to defend itself, or to spy on potential enemies, with the assistance of sophisticated electronics.

Among the most spectacular of the relics is the one shown on the preceding pages. It is a giant hangar built at Moffett Field near San Francisco in the early 1930's to house the Macon, one of the U.S. Navy's balloon-tfilled airships. The hangar, rising to stories high and 1,130 feet long, already was lost to the vast Houston's Astrodome. But the Macon perished in a disaster in 1935, two years before the Hindenburg crash brought the short-lived age of the rigid dirigible to an end. Today, the hangar accommodates Navy repair shops, classrooms, and antisubmarine planes.

In contrast, as each and as technologically minded as the U.S., it is perhaps most exhibit that some grand designs have turned into failures, that is hangars, to abandoned over case the nation was simply responding to politics and military pressures of the moment. When that "moment" passed, so did the projects, forcingly. It is, how, some of the greatest and engineering concepts may to have over been, to these projects are not enough at all, but the ground themselves gained design on the things.

Paintings by Nicholas Solovioff

267

133

268–270
Publication **Playboy**
Art Director **Arthur Paul, Tom Staebler**
Designer **Bruce Hansen**
Illustrator **Martin Hoffman**
Publisher **Playboy Enterprises, Inc.**

BIRTH OF A NOTION

*just for us— five
manhattan designers
interpret the eighties*

268

269

270

134

271,272

Publication	**Chicago Magazine**
Art Director	**Charles A. Thomas**
Designer	**Charles A. Thomas**
Illustrator	**Laurie Rubin**
Publisher	**WFMT, Inc.**

12 CHAIRS

Hot seats that won't grow cold

by Judith Neisser

Illustrations by Laurie Rubin

Master chair designer Charles Eames put it nicely: "Furniture is architecture in miniature." Like good architecture, fine furniture reflects the society, the art, and the technology of its day. When you buy an important chair, you are acquiring not only an object to sit on, but also a historical benchmark that will look just as good, if not better, 50 or 100 years from now. And modern, mass-produced chairs of real quality are no exception.

Since the mid-19th century, chair design, along with technology, has changed radically. From a basic wooden form, usually consisting of a plain or upholstered seat and back and four legs (more or less straight), seating has been redefined in arresting new shapes and in such 20th-century materials as plastic and steel, not to mention the more traditional woods, canes, and leathers. Today you find wooden "scroll" chairs, plastic pedestal "tulip" chairs, leather and chrome "cube" chairs, even fiber-glass "womb" chairs. Many of these styles, startling when new, have survived the vagaries of fashion to attain the status of classics.

As with all good ideas, the most popular designs may be the victims of knock-off artists who offer cheaper copies ranging from the shoddy to the quite clever impersonation. According to designer Ward Bennett, "even the closest copy can't measure up to the original [built to the designer's exact specifications]. The cheaper version inevitably sacrifices quality of line, materials, and craftsmanship."

While the cleverest impostor may be a tempting bargain, it really pays to go first class. And who knows? In future years, when these chairs are no longer made, an authentic Breuer or Eames may command the same reverence and price that seating by Hepplewhite or Sheraton does today.

The chairs on these pages already have a secure place in the history of modern furniture design. They are all available new from the manufacturers listed and are sold through major department stores and furniture retailers, as well as through architects and designers. (The Rietveld and Mackintosh chairs can also be bought at a special member's discount at the Museum of Contemporary Art Store.)

Vienna Cafe Chair #18. Thonet Brothers, 1876. Michael Thonet, with the invention in 1840 of the bentwood process, created a more durable, lighter chair than the handmade solid-wood pieces of his day. From Thonet.

Oval backrail chair for Argyle Tearooms. Charles Rennie Mackintosh, 1897. This chair—made of ebonized oak and upholstered in checkered horsehair—had a far-reaching effect on the Modern movement. From Atelier International.

Wassily chair. Marcel Breuer, 1925. Breuer named this chair after the artist Wassily Kandinsky and used it in the furnishings of Kandinsky's house on the Bauhaus campus in Dessau, Germany. Inspired by bicycle handlebars, he was the first designer to fabricate a chair with chrome-plated steel tubing. From Knoll International.

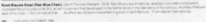

Rood Blauwe Stoel (Red-Blue Chair). Gerrit Thomas Rietveld, 1918. Red-Blue's asymmetrical, abstract concrete composition illustrates the principles of De Stijl, an art movement that developed in the Netherlands in the late teens of this century. Architect Rietveld said of this chair, "I did not realize that ... its effect would be so overwhelming even in architecture." From Atelier International.

MR chair (also called the Mies chair or Loop chair). Mies van der Rohe, 1926. One of the first designs to use the cantilever principle for metal-frame chairs, this handsome piece, crafted of hand-woven cane and chrome-plated tubular steel, reiterates Mies's philosophy that "God is in the details." From Stendig.

271

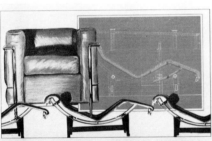

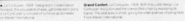

Chaise Longue. Le Corbusier, 1928. Designed in collaboration with Charlotte Perriand, this adjustable chaise, upholstered in pony skin, epitomizes Le Corbusier's concept of furniture as domestic equipment. From Atelier International.

Grand Confort. Le Corbusier, 1928. With this cube design, Le Corbusier revolutionized the overstuffed chair by exposing its frame. The seat area is small, giving the sitter a sense of being held. From Atelier International.

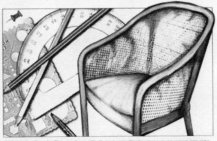

Lounge Chair 670. Charles Eames, 1956. According to Robert Black (a design consultant and former vice-president of design, Herman Miller), this chair sprang from Eames's question to himself, What ever happened to the leather chair in the Eiko clubs? Eames's equally comfortable version combines old and new materials—soft leather cushions and molded rosewood veneer. From Herman Miller.

Plia folding chair. Giancarlo Piretti, 1968. Space-saving and lightweight, the Plia, made of transparent plastic and aluminum, is just the old wooden folding chair elegantly refined. From Castelli.

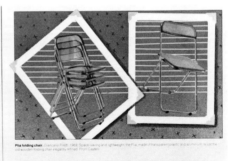

Scroll chair. Alvar Aalto, 1929. Aalto has been dubbed by historians the greatest inventor in wood furniture since Michael Thonet. Using the bentwood technique, he molded flat pieces of birch plywood to create a wonderfully flowing yet functional design with minimal parts. From International Contract Furnishings.

1073 Carved Wood Frame Arm Chair. Ward Bennett, 1964. "My chair," explains Ward Bennett, "is a natural bucket seat. The bucket is the natural form of the human back and of the buttocks and is the height of the arm. If you dig a hole in the soil it is wide enough to fit your hips, then dig it a little more around, you can create the same bucket kind of pitch." From Brickel Associates.

Soriana chair. Afra and Tobia Scarpa, 1970. This luxurious form of seating, a squishier, organic version of Le Corbusier's Grand Confort chair, has a soft body resting on a minimal polyurethane and is folded into its anatomical form by an external skeleton of chrome-plated steel-wire clips. From Atelier International.

272

273,274

Publication **Texas Monthly**
Art Director **Jim Darilek, Sybil Broyles**
Designer **Jim Darilek, Sybil Broyles**
Illustrator **Jack Unruh**
Publisher **Mediatex Communications Corporation**

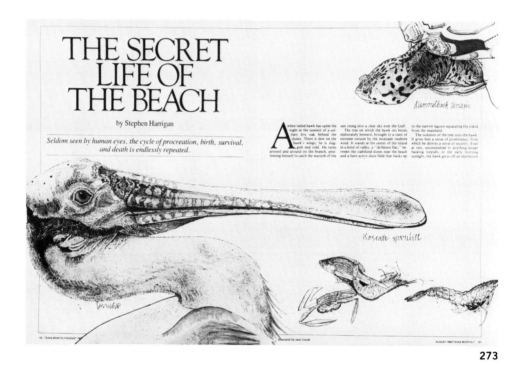

273

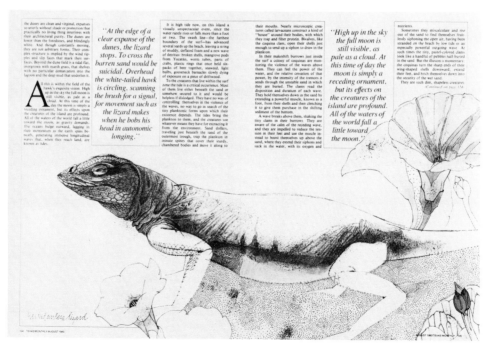

274

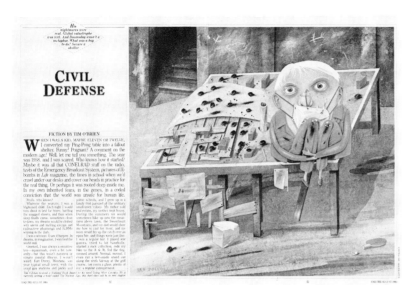

275

276

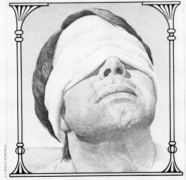

277

275

Publication	**Esquire**
Art Director	**Robert Priest**
Designer	**Robert Priest**
Illustrator	**Ian Pollock**
Publisher	**Esquire Publishing, Inc.**

276

Publication	**Esquire**
Art Director	**Robert Priest**
Designer	**Stephen Doyle**
Illustrator	**Wolf Erlbruch**
Publisher	**Esquire Publishing, Inc.**

277

Publication	**Esquire**
Art Director	**Robert Priest**
Designer	**April Silver,**
	Stephen Doyle
Illustrator	**Ralph Steadman,**
	Blair Drawson,
	Bernie Maissner,
	Peter Knock,
	Georganne Deen,
	Madelon Vriesendorf
Publisher	**Esquire Publishing, Inc.**

	278
Publication	**U & lc**
Art Director	**Herb Lubalin**
Designer	**Herb Lubalin**
Illustrator	**Wally Neibart, Rhoda Sparber,**
	Lionel Kalish, Jason Calfo
Publisher	**International**
	Typeface Corporation

	279
Publication	**U & lc**
Art Director	**Herb Lubalin**
Designer	**Herb Lubalin**
Illustrator	**Jason Calfo**
Photographer	**Francois Robert**
Publisher	**International**
	Typeface Corporation

	280
Publication	**Minneapolis Tribune/Picture**
Art Director	**Michael Carroll**
Illustrator	**John R. Miller**
Publisher	**Minneapolis Star**
	& Tribune Company

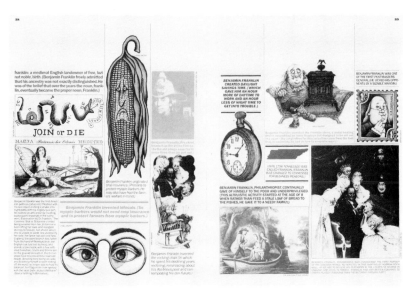

278

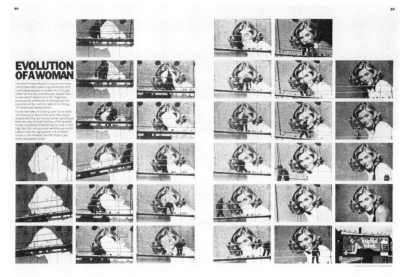

279

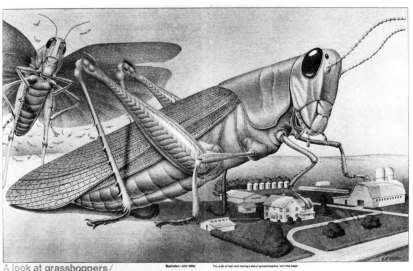

280

281
Publication **Travel & Leisure**
Art Director **Adrian Taylor**
Designer **Adrian Taylor**
Photographer **Renee Burri, MAGNUM**
Publisher **American Express Publishing Corporation**

281

282

283
Publication **Time**
Art Director **Rudolph Hoglund**
Photographer **Raul Vega**
Publisher **Time, Inc.**

284
Publication **California Business**
Art Director **Chris Mossman Design**
Designer **Chris Mossman**
Photographer **Tim Hine**
Publisher **California Business News, Inc.**

283

284

285

Publication — **Emergency Medicine**
Art Director — **Tom Lennon**
Designer — **James T. Walsh**
Photographer — **Shig Ikeda**
Publisher — **Fischer Medical Publications, Inc.**

286

Publication — **Emergency Medicine**
Art Director — **Tom Lennon**
Designer — **Cheun Chiang**
Photographer — **Benn Mitchell**
Publisher — **Fischer Medical Publications, Inc.**

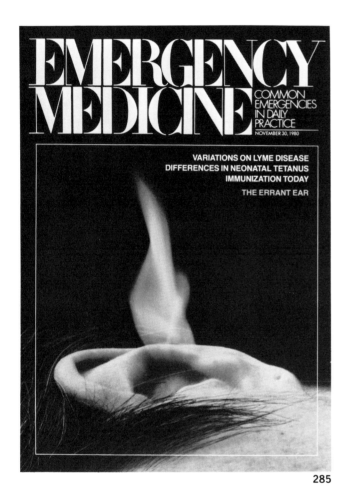

285

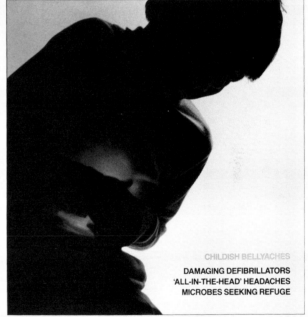

286

287
Publication **Flowers &**
Art Director **M.J. Cody**
Designer **Dugald Stermer**
Photographer **Jerry Fruchtman**
Publisher **Teleflora, Inc.**

288
Publication **Flowers &**
Art Director **M.J. Cody**
Designer **Dugald Stermer**
Photographer **Light Language**
Publisher **Teleflora, Inc.**

287

288

142

289
Publication   Animal Kingdom Magazine
Art Director   Brigid Quinn
Designer   Brigid Quinn
Photographer   Julie O'Neil
Publisher   The New York Zoological Society

290
Publication   Contemporary OB/GYN
Art Director   Barbara P. Silbert
Designer   Barbara P. Silbert
Illustrator   Nick Aristovulos
Photographer   Shig Ikeda
Publisher   Medical Economics
               Company, Inc.

291
Publication   Oceans
Art Director   Dugald Stermer
Designer   Dugald Stermer
Photographer   Pat Morris
Publisher   The Oceanic Society

289

290

291

292
Publication **Diagnostic Medicine**
Art Director **Cristine Hafner Wong**
Designer **Cristine Hafner Wong**
Photographer **David A. Wagner**
Publisher **Medical Economics Company**

293
Publication **Learning**
Art Director **David Hale, Penny Carlick**
Designer **Penny Carlick**
Photographer **Bill Arbogast**
Publisher **Pitman Learning, Inc.**

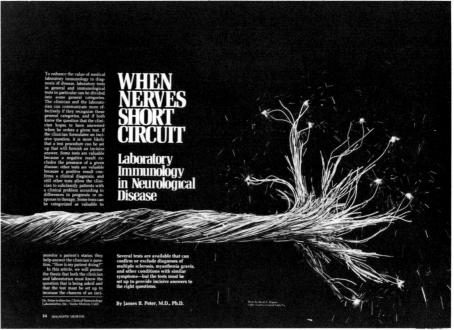

292

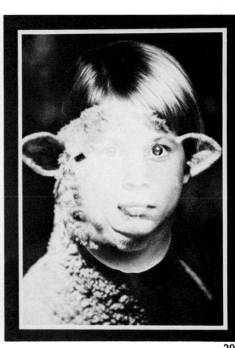

293

294
Publication **California Business**
Art Director **Ray Yee Graphics**
Designer **Ray Yee**
Photographer **Tom Myers**
Publisher **California Business News, Inc.**

295
Publication **Town & Country**
Art Director **Melissa Tardiff**
Designer **Mark Borden**
Photographer **Skrebneski**
Publisher **The Hearst Corporation**

294

295

296,297
Publication   **Flowers &**
Art Director   **M.J. Cody**
Designer   **Dugald Stermer**
Photographer   **Jerry Fruchtman**
Publisher   **Teleflora, Inc.**

296

297

299

Publication	**AIA Journal**
Art Director	**Suzy Thomas**
Designer	**Suzy Thomas**
Photographer	**David Muench**
Publisher	**The American Institute of Architects**

300

Publication	**Animal Kingdom Magazine**
Art Director	**Brigid Quinn**
Designer	**Brigid Quinn**
Photographer	**John Gibbons**
Publisher	**The New York Zoological Society**

299

First photos of a new species!

Discovery of the Crested Iguana

Photographs by John Gibbons

After eight months of incubation young crested iguanas (left) emerge from their ping-pong-ball-sized eggs. A close-up (above) shows the well-defined crest of spines that gives this lizard its common name.

IMAGINE THE THRILL of a nineteenth-century biologist—the young Charles Darwin, perhaps—when he first spied a spectacular new animal species. In the heyday of wildlife discoveries, his whirling mind would have envisioned instant acclaim, peer recognition, and, above all, a thoroughly unknown creature to study. Today the odds against such good fortune are staggering. But on January 4, 1979, it came to Dr. John Gibbons, a member of the teaching staff at the University of the South Pacific in Suva, the capital of Fiji.

For six months Gibbons had been on the trail of a rare and elusive lizard—the banded iguana, *Brachylophus fasciatus*, of the Fiji and Tonga islands. He had heard the local people's tales of this strikingly attractive lizard and had followed each lead they provided.

By the onset of 1979 too many fruitless days in the field and nearly depleted funds had left the herpetologist demoralized. Still, one last lead held promise: Yaduataba, a remote and uninhabited 173-acre island owned by Ratu Meli and his brother Ratu Alifereti.

December/January 23

300

301
Publication **RN Magazine**
Art Director **Barbara P. Silbert**
Designer **Barbara P. Silbert,**
Kiaran O'Brien
Photographer **Lennart Nilsson**
Publisher **Medical Economics**
Company

302
Publication **Physician and**
Sportsmedicine
Art Director **Tina Adamek**
Designer **Steve Blom**
Illustrator **Mike Pearson**
Photographer **Nancy Bundt Linzer**
Publisher **McGraw-Hill, Inc.**

303
Publication **Postgraduate**
Medicine
Art Director **Tina Adamek**
Photographer **Ed Gallucci**
Publisher **McGraw-Hill, Inc.**

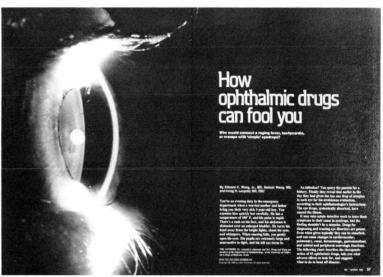

301

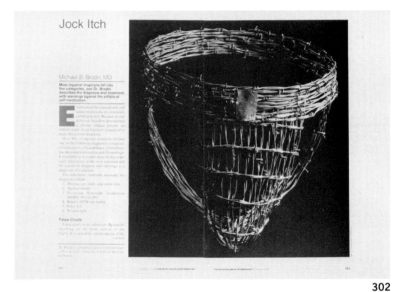

302

303

304

Publication	**Emergency Medicine**
Art Director	**Tom Lennon**
Designer	**James T. Walsh**
Illustrator	**(Calligrapher) Robert A. Mullen**
Photographer	**James Gilmour**
Publisher	**Fischer Medical Publications, Inc.**

EMERGENCY MEDICINE VOLUME 12 1980

EMERGENCY MEDICINE DECEMBER 15 1980

304

305, 306

Publication	**Psychology Today**
Art Director	**Carveth Kramer**
Designer	**Carveth Kramer**
Photographer	**Fred Burrell**
Publisher	**Ziff-Davis Publishing Company**

A traveler in Jerusalem in the year 30 A.D. would have thought the tomb that was sealed at the beginning of Passover had finished the meteoric career of the young Galilean rabbi. So many other powerful preachers and teachers had come down from the north only to be eliminated by either Jewish or Roman authorities or both. This one exited rather peacefully, taking none of his followers to the grave with him and fighting no bloody battles with the political leadership of the land.

The survival of Jesus after death is a matter on which social science, as such, can make no judgment, though the social scientist himself will find it hard not to. It is a measure of how wrong the obvious prognostications about the oblivion of the Galilean rabbi were that hardly anyone who hears of him today can scarcely avoid making some kind of judgment, some kind of decision.

Whatever is to be said of the resurrection of Jesus, the phenomenon of his continued importance and continued challenge is, in itself, marvelous if not miraculous, that phenomenon has always fascinated those who analyze political and social behavior. With the emergence of social science as a distinctive human enterprise, the question of the possibility of a sociological explanation for the origins of Christianity became a matter high on the agenda of many social as well as religious researchers.

Two recent examples of this genre are being widely discussed in religious circles. Both *The Gnostic Gospels* by historian Elaine Pagels of Columbia University and *The Community of the Beloved Disciple* by Raymond E. Brown of Union Theological Seminary describe the role of a dissident faction in early Christianity. Each of the books constructs the era in its own way. Of the two, Brown's is more cautious and seeks to work with sophisticated biblical methodology. Pagels's work is engaging, but will provoke sensational exaggeration. For a sociologist, the data for such reconstructions are inadequate, even if the results are impressive.

The more controversial book is *The Gnostic Gospels*, in which author Pagels has attempted to find in a collection of recently (1945) rediscovered early Christian books a hint of how social and political factors affected both the shape of the early Christian church and the doctrinal emphases in Christianity today. The Gnostics were a faction within primitive Christianity who sought the hidden or "se-

cret" meaning behind the more obvious stories and teachings of Jesus and his immediate followers. They were mystics, influenced by Eastern esoteric traditions and possibly, as Pagels observes, by Indian occult beliefs and practices. They were, by their own admission, a minority faction, strongly opposed by the emerging institutional church. Nevertheless, they persisted within the boundaries of the church for at least the first two centuries and then seemed to have vanished—suppressed, it Pagels is to be believed, by the orthodox Christian church structure.

The discovery of many of the gospels and other writings of this Christian faction ("sect" would imply more organization than they had) buried in the earth near the town of Nag Hammadi in upper Egypt has provided an opportunity for scholars to see the Gnostics from their own perspective instead of that of their enemies. Many of their positions seem startlingly modern—they put a "spiritual" interpretation on the resurrection of Jesus, they believed in the equality of men and women, they thought that God existed within the self and that knowledge of the self led to knowledge of God. They favored religious individualism over and against the insti-

RELIGION'S OLDEST SCOOP

BY ANDREW M. GREELEY

The Gnostics were a small group of early Christians who claimed to have a monopoly on a secret. A controversial new book—*The Gnostic Gospels*—suggests they were startlingly modern in some of their positions. Why the Gnostics died out may provide a parable for today's religious cults.

FACE READING
The Persistence of Physiognomy

BY ANTHONY BRANDT

"The face at rest, with no expression, cannot be 'read' scientifically. But its very impassivity awakens ancient, deep-seated fears. The study of physiognomy has always tried—however inaccurately—to see through the mask and allay those fears."

The face is a weak guarantee; yet it deserves some consideration.
—MONTAIGNE

The instinctive propensity to read faces has been an object of curiosity to scientists at least since Darwin wrote *The Expression of Emotions in Man and Animals*. Psychologists have discovered that the emotional language of the face is more or less universal among people in Japan, Argentina, England, and other civilized countries, as well as primitive tribes in New Guinea, all interpret a smile, a frown, or a look of amazement in pretty much the same way. Neuropsychologists have recently been studying the asymmetry of expression between the two sides of the face, while students of the perceptual process have become increasingly interested in how we recognize faces, how out of millions of people we have so little trouble in identifying Cousin Arnold, or even the girl who used to live down the street eight or nine years ago. But all this work together and our might, without exaggeration, speak of a science of the face.

Such a science would not, however, be new. Few of us may realize it, but

for several thousand years there has existed a systematic, widely practiced, and, at least until the last 100 years or so, respected science of face reading. This science—we would now call it a pseudoscience—is physiognomy, the reading of "character and disposition," as the Oxford English Dictionary defines it, "from the features of the face or the form and lineaments of the body generally." It is so old that references to it have been found in Assyrian texts, and it was once so highly regarded that an early treatise on the subject was for centuries attributed to Aristotle.

Plato and Aristotle both apparently gave some credence to physiognomy in fact, and a story circulated in ancient times that Socrates had his character read by one of the first professional physiognomists, a man known as Zopyrus. Zopyrus described Socrates, that wisest of men, as "stupid and thick-witted because he had not got hollows in the neck above the collarbone" and added that he was, among other vices, addicted to women—at which Alcibiades, Socrates' male lover, "is said to have given a loud guffaw." To the surprise of Alcibiades and the rest of his followers, however, Socrates acknowledged the truth of

307

Publication	**Motor Boating & Sailing**
Art Director	**Al Braverman**
Designer	**Stewart Siskind**
Photographer	**Roy Attaway**
Publisher	**Hearst Magazines, Inc.**

308

Publication	**Science Digest**
Art Director	**Frank Rothmann**
Designer	**Frank Rothmann**
Photographer	**Howard Sochurek**
Publisher	**Hearst Magazines, Inc.**

307

308

309
Publication **Motor Boating & Sailing**
Art Director **Frank Rothmann**
Designer **Frank Rothmann, Stewart Siskind**
Photographer **Larry Dunmire**
Publisher **Hearst Magazines, Inc.**

310
Publication **Sports Afield**
Art Director **Gary Gretter**
Designer **Gary Gretter**
Photographer **Leonard Kamsler**
Publisher **Hearst Magazines, Inc.**

309

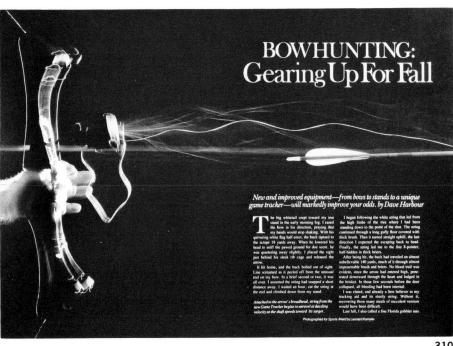

310

311
Publication **Mother Jones**
Art Director **Louise Kollenbaum**
Designer **Dian-Aziza Ooka**
Photographer **Abbas, GAMMA-LIAISON**
Publisher **Foundation for National Progress**

312
Publication **New York Magazine**
Art Director **Roger Black**
Designer **Karen Mullarkey**
Photographer **E.J. Camp**
Publisher **News Group Publications, Inc.**

IN THE FINAL DAYS

While South Africa's Whites Indulge In Health Foods And Scientology, What May Be A 20-Year Civil War Has Begun

By Adam Hochschild

Photograph by Abbas/Gamma-Liaison

311

Dress White

312

313

Publication **Travel & Leisure**
Art Director **Adrian Taylor**
Designer **Adrian Taylor**
Photographer **David Muench**
Publisher **American Express Publishing Corporation**

314

Publication **Esquire**
Art Director **Robert Priest**
Designer **Vincent Winter**
Photographer **Neil Selkirk**
Publisher **Esquire Publishing Inc.**

AH, WILDERNESS!

313

It's the archaic joint,
the weak link,
the pivotal hinge for the
modern athlete

The Knee

*by
Rick
Telander*

The fabled knees of E. J. Holub, a dozen operations later.

314

FROM 'BLUE LAGOON' TO BLUE ADS FOR BLUE JEANS, NOTHING IS COMING BETWEEN HER AND SUCCESS

On Madison Avenue it's been gospel for years. Sex sells. And sells. But nobody has proved it better, or younger, than nubile 15-year-old Brooke Shields. Stepping out of her image as the girl in the *Blue Lagoon* loincloth, she squeezed into a pair of undersized Calvin Klein jeans ("Comfortably, I wear size seven—these were five"), aimed herself at Richard Avedon's camera and inquired huskily, "You know what comes between me and my Calvins? Nothing." Nothing, that is, until a growing number of outraged viewers persuaded TV stations to ban the 30-second spot. Brooke, for one, is bewildered. "She doesn't pick up double meanings and she has no idea what's causing all the uproar," says Lila Wisdom, her godmother and vice-president of Brooke Shields and Co. In fact, Brooke knew nothing of the controversy until clued in by classmates at her New Jersey private school. "I didn't think anything was wrong," she says. "If people complain, it makes me wonder what's in their minds."

Presumably the same thing that was in the mind of designer Klein, whose sales jumped after the Shields campaign debuted last summer. "Brooke is the most beautiful girl in the world," he says. "She can portray many characters, from a teenager to a very sophisticated woman." But in real life Brooke remains a typical kid, with a 10 o'clock curfew. Director Franco

Zaffirelli stopped work for a week on her eighth and latest film, *Endless Love*, so that she could take exams. No movie challenge has seemed more momentous to her than her tryout for the high school cheerleading squad (she made it). Her idea of a swinging time includes a mocha chocolate chip ice cream binge and a giggly overnight with her girlfriends. In her heart of hearts, boys still run second to horses.

"Brooke will be a very happy adult," predicts Lila Wisdom. "She wants to go to college, get married and have children." Meanwhile her manager mother, Teri Shields, keeps angling to make her little (5'10½") girl richer. She has signed Brooke on as the first teen model for Wella Balsam. Teri is also reviewing three "very promising" screenplays for the actress who just leaped ahead of Tatum O'Neal and made the top 10 box office list of actresses. "If I ever get an award, it will be for the kid who has been in show business longest," sighs Brooke, an Ivory Snow baby at 11 months. "But I don't feel exploited. I love my life."

315

315

Publication	**People**
Art Director	**Robert N. Essman**
Designer	**Robert N. Essman**
Photographer	**Francesco Scavullo**
Publisher	**Time, Inc.**

316

Publication	**Nautical Quarterly**
Art Director	**B. Martin Pederson**
Designer	**B. Martin Pederson**
Photographer	**B. Martin Pederson**
Publisher	**Nautical Quarterly**

316

PHOTOGRAPHY—STORY PRESENTATION

317,318

Publication	**Oui**
Art Director	**Michael Brock**
Designer	**Michael Brock**
Photographer	**Lucien Clergue**
Publisher	**Playboy Enterprises, Inc.**

319

Publication	**Oui**
Art Director	**Michael Brock**
Designer	**Michael Brock**
Photographer	**Phillip Dixon**
Publisher	**Playboy Enterprises, Inc.**

317

318

319

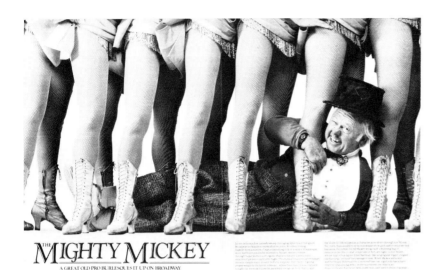

THE MIGHTY MICKEY

A GREAT OLD PRO BURLESQUES IT UP ON BROADWAY

320

320
Publication **Life**
Art Director **Bob Ciano**
Designer **Carla Barr**
Photographer **Greg Heisler**
Publisher **Time-Life**

321,322
Publication **Fortune**
Art Director **Ron Campbell**
Designer **Leonard Wolfe,**
Maureen Duffy Benziger
Photographer **Enrico Ferorelli**
Publisher **Time-Life**

THINGS TO DO, THINGS TO SEE

321

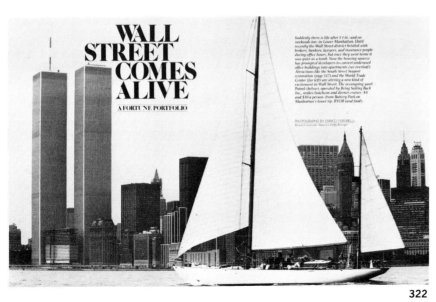

WALL STREET COMES ALIVE

A FORTUNE PORTFOLIO

322

323,324
Publication **Popular Photography**
Art Director **Shinichiro Tora**
Designer **Shinichiro Tora**
Photographer **Bruce Davidson**
Publisher **Ziff-Davis Publishing Company**

323

324

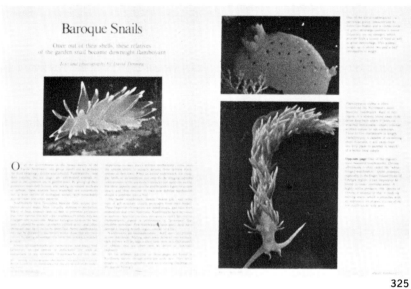

325

326

325–327
Publication   **Pacific Northwest Magazine**
Art Director   **Robyn Ricks, Peter Potterfield**
Designer   **Robyn Ricks**
Photographer   **David Denning**
Publisher   **Pacific Search Publications**

327

328–330

Publication **Photography Annual/ 1980-81**

Art Director **Brenda Suler**

Designer **Brenda Suler**

Photographer **Serge Lutens**

Publisher **Ziff-Davis Publishing Company**

328

329

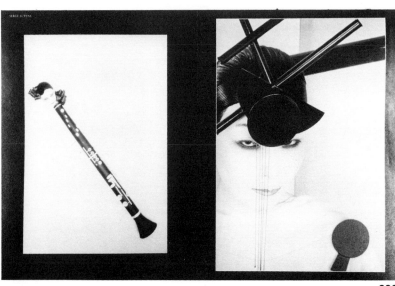

330

331

331,332

Publication   **Weight Watchers Magazine**
Art Director   **Jeanne Dzienciol**
Designer   **Jeanne Dzienciol**
Photographer   **Michel Tcherevkoff**
Publisher   **Twentyfirst Corporation**

332

333,334

Publication **Texas Monthly**
Art Director **Jim Darilek, Sybil Broyles**
Designer **Jim Darilek, Sybil Broyles**
Photographer **Robert A. Widdicombe**
Publisher **Mediatex Communications Corporation**

In the Still Of the
NIGHT

Photography by Robert A. Widdicombe

Darkness, illuminated by a flash, reveals mysteries unknown by day.

Bob Widdicombe takes photos about people. Not *of* people, but about them. Specifically, he takes photos about the people of the Southwestern towns he has lived in, of Albuquerque and Austin and points in between.

Because it makes him unhappy to disrupt people's privacy with his lights and lenses, Widdicombe has learned to see people through their surroundings. To his eye, human beings reveal themselves in the icons and detritus they leave behind them, in—literally—the writing on the wall. So he prowls behind Texas' glittering facades, through alleyways, back rooms, and border towns, seeking out secret colors and hidden vitality.

The photos on these pages were all taken at dusk, a special time for Widdicombe. He penetrates its mysteries with his flash but shows his respect for its subtleties by leaving his lens open for several seconds afterward, letting the lingering twilight soften and blur his images. The arresting results, like the subject matter, repay close examination. ♦

*Pink facade
Nuevo Laredo
Spring 1980*

*Garage
Albuquerque
Fall 1978*

*Alley
Albuquerque
Fall 1978*

335,336

Publication **New York Magazine**
Art Director **Roger Black**
Designer **Karen Mullarkey, Jordan Schaps**
Photographer **Elizabeth Lennard**
Publisher **News Group Publications, Inc.**

PAINTING THE TOWN

Photographs by Elizabeth Lennard

EMPIRE STATE NIGHT. "NEW YORK HAS AN ACCIDENTAL, INCIDENTAL BEAUTY."

MARCH 24, 1980/NEW YORK   41

335

CORNER OF PARK AND 18TH STREET. "I'VE REDISCOVERED DOWNTOWN."

COMES A HORSEMAN, 41ND STREET. "I PHOTOGRAPH SCENES BECAUSE I WANT TO COLOR THEM."

NEW YORK is arguably the most photographed city in the world—from the Depression-era Realphotographie of Berenice Abbott to the window world of Ruth Orkin. Twenty-seven-year-old photographer Elizabeth Lennard's New York comes alive in her studio, where she paints her black-and-white compositions in oil glazes. Result: "The city as I want to see it."

CHINESE KITCHEN. "I'M ALMOST ALWAYS AN OUTSIDER."

42   NEW YORK/MARCH 24, 1980

MARCH 24, 1980/NEW YORK   43

336

163

337,338
Publication **Nautical Quarterly**
Art Director **B. Martin Pederson**
Designer **B. Martin Pederson**
Photographer **Dudley Whitney, Laura Rosen**
Publisher **Nautical Quarterly**

337

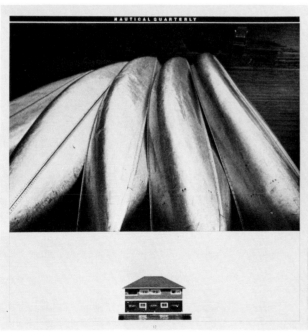

338

339,340

Publication	**L.I. Magazine/Newsday**
Art Director	**Miriam Smith**
Designer	**Miriam Smith**
Photographer	**Don Jacobsen**
Publisher	**Newsday**

339

340

17

PUBLICATION DESIGN
AWARDS

Silver 1

1,2

Publication   **Destinations**
Art Director   **Shelley Williams**
Designer   **Shelley Williams, Michael Freeman, Janine Orr, Michael Marcum**
Publisher   **13-30 Corporation**

Waiters at Michel Rostang urge patrons to indulge—take one, two, even three from the rolling dessert cart.

Where Parisians Dine

The French, of course, know where
to find the finest in French food. That's why
these spots maintain a faithful patronage
among Parisians.

by Patricia Wells

For Parisians, dining out is a way of life. In this city of corner bistros and three-star temples, one could make the rounds for years and never repeat a restaurant.

Food is, of course, taken seriously here, but for Parisians restaurants are more than a place to take a meal. Eating out is a social affair. Frenchmen rarely dine alone but in groups, bringing along their dogs and making themselves right at home. Restaurants become living rooms, where people spend entire afternoons or evenings, always in nonstop, animated conversation. A business lunch will last at least two hours; dinner may be stretched from nine till midnight, when the owner often settles down with the regulars for a warming glass of cognac or a fine cigar.

Although the city is full of places that are exotique—Russian buffets, pizza parlors, Belgian beer bars, even American-style restaurants—the French, who are chauvinistic about French food, they have a love for bargains and keep the best little bistros very busy, dining on such traditional fare as blanquette de veau or ragoût à la moutarde and drinking an expensive country wines but, firstly the patron's family. They like to eat heartily, too. Watching the well-coiffed petite Parisian women down platters of fruits de mer—including half a dozen briny oysters, mussels, clams and crab claws—one wonders how they do it night after night.

For all these reasons, it is well to dine where the Parisians dine in Paris. Here is a selection of restaurants—small and large, formal and informal, serving country cooking and nouvelle cuisine—that bring Parisians back time after time. And as Parisian waiters like to say as they pour out the rough red wine—bon appétit. ▶

Bistros such as this one are neighborhood hangouts.

Silver 2

169

3,4

Publication	**Nautical Quarterly**
Art Director	**B. Martin Pedersen**
Designer	**B. Martin Pedersen**
Illustrator	**Daniel Maffia**
Photographer	**Benjamin Mendlowitz**
Publisher	**Jonson Pedersen Hinrichs & Shakery**

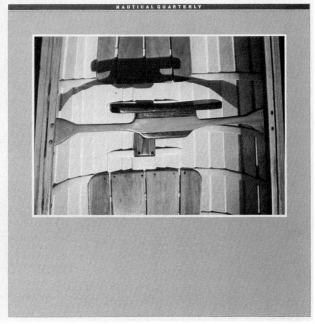

Gold 3

PAINTINGS BY MIHANOVIC

HARD AND SOFT

Marine paintings—whether of clipper ships, yachts or fishboats—tend to be action-packed—a Gloucester schooner rail down on the race to market, a 12 Meter on a spinnaker run, *Taeping* in the Trades with her studding sails out. The paintings on these six pages are different. They are serene and mysterious, their principal action the soft breathing of the Adriatic on the bright coast of Yugoslavia.

It is subtle action to capture, subtler still when a cobbled bottom as precise and intricate as a mosaic slides off under a lambent surface. The artist is Zvonimir Mihanovic (pronounced Ma-han-o-vitch), a Croatian born in Yugoslavia in 1946, whose first painting brought him First Prize in Yugoslavia's Salon of Young Artists in 1962. He studied subsequently at the Academy of Fine Arts in Zagreb and the Brera Academy of Fine Arts in Milan, and traveled in 1972 and 1973 to museums in London, Boston, New York and Washington to study paintings of classical realism.

His own realism is an old tradition of meticulous detail and compelling moodiness, although there is a suggestion of the "hard-edge" realism of recent decades. These paintings have very solid reality—all the heavy essence of the concrete with few distractions. Even the light has a weighty, stone-slab quality.

It is the light of the eastern Med, the almost-physical light that travelers in the Greek islands have so often remarked. The boats are the typical double-enders of the Adriatic's fisheries, full-bodied carvel types with lines that go back to Homer's time, along with dinghies and tenders of the same chunky build. Solid, serene boats on solid, serene water, but with an odd softness of mood and weather.

Mihanovic has done other types of paintings in his two decades of major work, but marine paintings like these are now his preoccupation, indeed his passion. A man at the Wally Findlay Gallery in New York, where Mihanovic paintings were first shown in the U.S. in January and February of 1981, describes him as "absolutely in love with the Adriatic." Mihanovic has a home and studio in Paris, but he spends the long Yugoslavian summer aboard a houseboat in the Adriatic. His paintings are oils on large canvases, and each represents a month to six weeks of work. There were 30-odd paintings in his recent show in New York—two years of work—and it is expected that there will be as many paintings about a year from now when his new work is shown at Wally Findlay's Beverly Hills gallery. He is on the Adriatic as this is written, seeing and wonderfully putting on canvas the hard surfaces and softer depths of coastal images like these.

Gold 4

5
Publication   **American Preservation**
Art Director   **Peter Bradford, Byron Taylor**
Designer   **Peter Bradford**
Publisher   **Briggs Associates, Inc.**

Silver 5

6,7

Publication **Foremost-McKesson Annual Report**
Art Director **Neil Shakery**
Designer **Neil Shakery, Barbara Vick**
Illustrator **Jean Michel Folon**
Publisher **Foremost-McKesson**

8,9

Publication **The E.F. Hutton Group Annual Report**
Art Director **Robin Davis**
Designer **Robin Davis**
Illustrator **Robin Davis**
Photographer **Cheryl Rossum**
Publisher **E.F. Hutton & Company, Inc.**

Gold 6

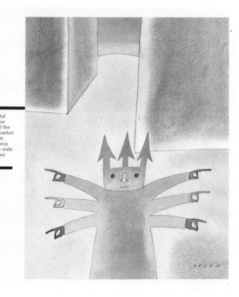

Gold 7

Silver 8

Silver 9

Silver 10

10
Publication	**Docket Call**
Art Director	**David Carothers**
Designer	**David Carothers**
Photographer	**Black Star/Taylor & Dull**
Publisher	**American Bar Association Press**

11
Publication	**Industrial Launderer**
Art Director	**Jack Lefkowitz**
Designer	**Jack Lefkowitz**
Illustrator	**Jack Lefkowitz**
Publisher	**Institute of Industrial Launderers**

12
Publication	**The New York Times Magazine**
Art Director	**Ruth Ansel**
Designer	**Michael Valenti**
Publisher	**The New York Times**

Silver 11

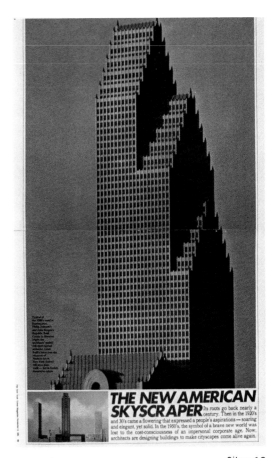

Silver 12

13
Publication   **Emergency Medicine**
Art Director   **Tom Lennon**
Designer   **James T. Walsh**
Illustrator   **Joan Hall**
Publisher   **Fischer Medical Publications**

14
Publication   **Emergency Medicine**
Art Director   **Tom Lennon**
Designer   **Sara Rominek**
Illustrator   **Robert Goldstrom**
Publisher   **Fischer Medical Publications**

Silver 13

Silver 14

15
Publication **MD**
Art Director **Al Foti, Merrill Cason**
Designer **Merrill Cason**
Photographer **S.C. Bisseroot/**
Bruce Coleman, Inc.
Publisher **MD Publications, Inc.**

16
Publication **Cal Today**
Art Director **Howard Shintaku**
Designer **Howard Shintaku**
Illustrator **Mitchell H. Anthony**
Publisher **San Jose Mercury News**

MYSTERIES WITHIN MYSTERIES

BATS

It has hair like a mammal and suckles its young. It flies like a bird, though usually only at night. Looking sometimes like a fox and sometimes like a gargoyle, it lurks in the shadows until twilight, then stretches out its webbed wings attached to elongated fingers and swoops eerily into the night sky in search of prey.

The only mammal that flies, the bat occupies the large *Chiroptera* order, second only to *Rondentia*. It has been estimated that one out of every 10 mammals is a bat. Although there are tens of billions in the

world, many people claim never to have seen one, probably because when it flies in the dark it moves faster than a human's night-blind eye can follow.

Nocturnal and elusive, the bat has been linked in folklore with evil and death. The devil has bat wings. The shades of the dead that pursue Ulysses in Homer's underworld fly on bats' wings. In the Bible the bat is an unclean bird. The Mayans' Bat God presided over the Kingdom of Darkness and Death. Legions of bat-like souls trail mournfully behind

Silver 15

DIVORCE
HERS ❦ HIS

George and I were married for 11 years. Seven of them were very happy. Then I got itchy. There was a big void in my life, something was missing. I wanted to be in love with my husband. It would have been a hell of a lot easier if I had enjoyed making home to him at night. But I didn't.

I loved him—I still do—but I wasn't in love with him anymore. I cared about him. I wanted him to be well and happy, but I no longer craved him. I was so jealous of his well-being, but not desirous of his body.

He was such a klutz, he wasn't any fun. There wasn't any romance in our marriage. One night, he told me that he loved me. I said, "I love you, too—I think."

We met in a roller rink, and were married in San Diego in 1969. I was 18, George was 21. He was in the Navy, and he was exactly what my mother would have picked for me. He was sincere, patient, kind, intelligent and easygoing...

My big mistake, I guess, was thinking that you could just break through marriage. Our marriage wasn't stormy; it simply died of boredom.

Susie's red hair and Southern accent were the initial attractions. She was smart, friendly and cute. I probably could have settled on anyone with those qualities.

Like many men, I was raised to believe that you got married as soon as you had a respectable job. Susie was my first love; neither of us shopped around to find out what we really wanted. At the time, all I wanted was a wife—someone to be at home, wash the dishes, do the laundry, cook and raise the kids, while I watched football games on TV. That's what I thought marriage was about.

We were both virgins when we met, and that was part of the problem. I certainly was influenced by the sexual attraction. In fact, in a mild sense, I was confusing marriage with sex. Maybe if we had gone...

In Santa Clara County, divorces consistently outnumber weddings year after year. These frank first-person stories, as told to staff writer Marsha Kay Seff, offer a revealing portrait of the events that led to the breakup of a typical South Bay couple. To protect their privacy, their names have been changed.

Gold 16

17,18
Publication **Life**
Art Director **Bob Ciano**
Designer **Bob Ciano**
Calligrapher **Tim Girvin**
Photographer **Dennis Waugh**
Publisher **Time Inc.**

19
Publication **Life**
Art Director **Bob Ciano**
Designer **Mary K. Baumann**
Photographer **Bruno Barbey**
Publisher **Time, Inc.**

Silver 17

Silver 18

Silver 19

20–22

Publication **Nautical Quarterly**
Art Director **B. Martin Pedersen**
Designer **B. Martin Pedersen**
Photographer **Jim Brown**
Publisher **Jonson, Pedersen, Hinrichs & Shakery, Inc.**

Silver 20

Silver 21

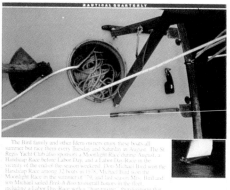

Silver 22

23
Publication **Penthouse**
Art Director **Joe Brooks**
Designer **Claire Victor**
Illustrator **Cristobal Toral**
Publisher **Penthouse International**

24
Publication **Penthouse**
Art Director **Joe Brooks**
Designer **Claire Victor**
Illustrator **Marvin Mattelson**
Publisher **Penthouse International**

Silver 23

Gold 24

25
Publication **Postgraduate Medicine**
Art Director **Tina Adamek**
Designer **Tina Adamek**
Illustrator **John Jude Palencar**
Publisher **McGraw-Hill, Inc.**

26
Publication **Postgraduate Medicine**
Art Director **Tina Adamek**
Designer **Tina Adamek**
Illustrator **Eugene Mihaesco**
Publisher **McGraw-Hill, Inc.**

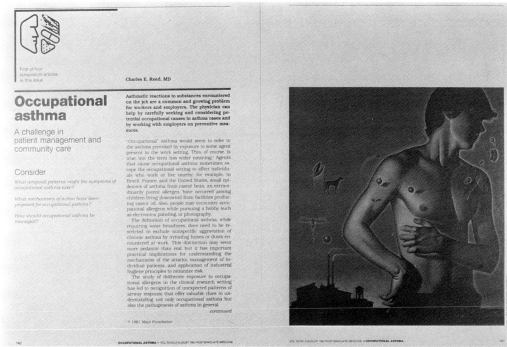

Gold 25

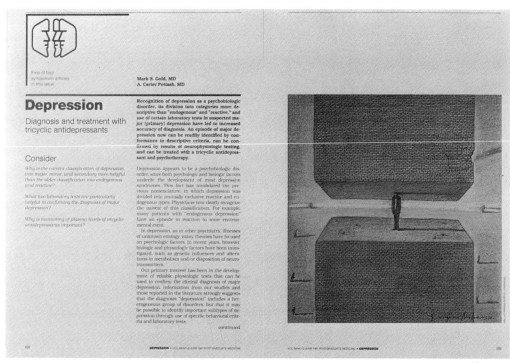

Silver 26

27

Publication **Playboy**
Art Director **Tom Staebler**
Designer **Kerig Pope**
Illustrator **Mel Odom**
Publisher **Playboy Enterprises, Inc.**

28

Publication **The Plain Dealer Magazine**
Art Director **Greg Paul**
Illustrator **Brad Holland**
Publisher **The Plain Dealer Publishing Company**

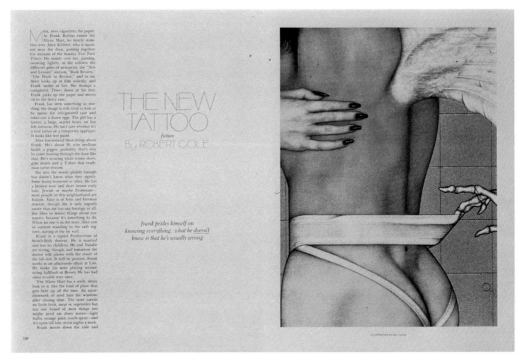

Silver 27

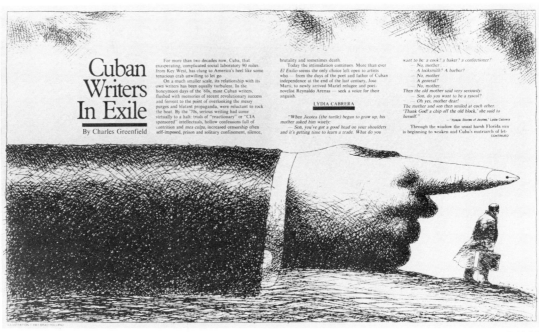

Gold 28

	29		**30**
Publication	**Esquire**	Publication	**L.I. Magazine**
Art Director	**Robert Priest**	Art Director	**Miriam Smith**
Designer	**Stephen Doyle**	Designer	**Lee Hill**
Illustrator	**Gottfried Helnwein**	Illustrator	**Bob Newman**
Publisher	**Esquire Publishing**	Publisher	**Newsday**

Living in the Coronary Culture

BY Michael Halberstam

Try too hard,
worry too much,
lift too strenuously,
and *bim-bam!*
you're dead of a
heart attack.
This brutal possibility
affects not only
the victim himself
but also our society,
our literature,
our commerce, and
what we laughingly call
our living patterns

WHEN NINETEENTH-CENTURY AU-
DIENCES WAITED EAGERLY FOR
THE NEXT BURST OF GENIUS FROM
the likes of Byron, Dumas, and Puccini,
they were unaware that they were participating in an enormous exercise in medical epidemiology. Rather, they celebrated
such authors and composers because
their works were a distillation of life,
and an overwhelming fact of the lives
depicted by artists in the last century
was the slow, painful wasting away of
talented, artistically sensitive young
men and women. These charming
youths lived poetic, bohemian lives.
They died romantic deaths.

The truth is, they died of pulmonary
tuberculosis. So many fictional heroes and
heroines—as well as their authors—died
of TB that disease and creativity became
almost synonymous. The poetic look

Gold 29

Here's why—maybe.
Research has found
that there may be ba-
sic differences in how
men's and women's
brains work—differ-
ences that give each
special skills.

Why Can't a Woman Think More Like a Man (And Vice Versa)?

By Patricia McBroom Illustration by Bob Newman

hat are you think-
ing?" she asked
lazily after a long
silence. The wind
skipped lightly
over the bay,
curling the water
into tiny waves at
their feet. She
stirred. "See that
wave? I'm wondering why it curls. I
think it's because surface tension
makes the top layer of water move
faster than the bottom layers."

"Hmm," she said, jolted. She had
been musing about the sunlight on
the trees, about the laughter of children, about the distance between
them.

"I bet you're surprised," he said,
amused by her reaction. "We think
so differently."

Usually, the differences are stated
more bluntly: "Women talk too
much." "Men have no feelings."
"Women's heads are full of cotton."
"Men miss the forest for the trees."
"This is a man's business." "That's
just women's intuition." "Must have
been a woman driver." "Isn't that
just like a man?"

These days, the old stereotypes are
viewed as bad form. But suppose
there is a nugget of truth in all that?

Sit down. Prepare yourself. We're
in dangerous territory. As most people of goodwill would agree, such
sexual clichés allow their users to
treat other people like cartoon characters (Dagwood and Daisy Mae
come to mind); they help deny
women—and men, too—the opportunity to prove their own merit; they
confine us all within cultural molds.
For someone who wishes to play fair
with the opposite sex, the easiest
thing to do with these old stereotypes is to ignore them. They have
no basis in biological reality (or so if

Patricia McBroom is a freelance writer.

is widely believed), and they certainly do contribute to social prejudice.

But wait. After 30 years of walking a
wide path around sex differences, scientists are discovering that there
may, indeed, be a kernel of truth in
the stereotypes. Men and women
may have different kinds of minds.

But the differences—far from being an excuse to deprive women of
executive power, or men of emotional freedom—show that each sex
has a strength that can be of immense value to society as a whole.
In fact, whatever sex you are, it is
safe to predict that, after reading
this story, you'll be jealous of what
the opposite sex can do.

The new information is based on
studies of the structure and capabili-
ties of the brain. It has been a long
time coming, largely for two reasons: Scientists didn't want to contribute to anybody's prejudices, and
they didn't want to monkey with
their own long-established theories.
So, until a few years ago, an imagi-
nary conversation with the scientific
community would have gone something like this:

Question: Is there any physical difference between men's and wom-
en's brains?

Answer: Yes, a man's brain is larger on the average because of body
size, but that wouldn't affect intelligence. Many geniuses have had
small brains.

Q: Other than size, are there any
differences in structure?

A: No.

Q: Have you looked?

A: No.

Q: Do men and women recover
differently from brain damage?

A: Not that we know of, but it
hasn't been studied.

Q: Why not?

A: We haven't had many female
patients.

Q: What! Don't women suffer

from brain disease, epilepsy and ac-
cidents?

A: Yes, but most of our neurologi-
cal studies have been done on sol-
diers in veterans' hospitals.

Q: Do men and women differ on
intelligence tests?

A: No, the IQs are the same overall.

Q: You say "overall." Do they differ on parts of the tests?

A: Yes, as a matter of fact. Women
excel in some verbal areas, and men
do better in spatial performance.

Q: How long have you known
that?

A: Oh, for about 30 years, since
the IQ tests were first invented.

Q: Why didn't you ever say anything?

A: We didn't think it was important. Anyway, the tests were equal-
ized a long time ago so the sex
difference wouldn't show.

Times have changed. In the past
decade, a growing number of scientists—including many women—have
begun to look at sex differences in
mentality. What they say they are
finding is fascinating in its implica-
tions.

Be warned right now that the results can be confusing, even contra-
dictory. They are based on such a
bewildering variety of medical, psychological and intellectual tests that
even scientists have trouble trying to
correlate them. And one of the biggest problems is that hardly anyone
can form a theory to explain them
without appearing to support some
kind of sexual stereotype. That is because when you're talking about
sex, all the words are loaded—and it
has kept some researchers from
even approaching the subject.

One woman, a neurologist who
has some of the most extensive records anywhere on brain patients,
who have been tested before and
after surgery, hung up the tele-

phone at the first mention of sex differences. Just before the line went
dead, she said she hadn't found any
differences. Colleagues believe she
hasn't looked.

Other researchers also bring personal prejudices to bear on the subject—indeed, they can't help it,
being human. Some women are ex-
cited; others are fearful. Some are
smug, others denying. But when all
the dust has settled, there is general
agreement that something is there,
some difference in the ways the
halves of the brain are organized, or
perhaps in the way they communi-
cate. Men and women are intellectu-
ally different.

The new findings explain and con-
firm some facts that had puzzled scientists for years: Why it is, for
instance, that intelligence tests have
always shown men are superior to
women in spatial ability, while wom-
en consistently are best in verbal
ability. These differences had long
been explained away as cultural programming, but now it begins to appear that they may also have to do
with genetic factors.

Moreover, in finding out just what
it is that makes women, in general,
superior at language and men, in
general, better at math, scientists
are finding that there are some in-
triguing differences in the way the
sexes see the world.

Imagine a line running from between your eyes over the top of
your head to the back of your neck.
That line traces a division in your
brain between the right and left
halves, or hemispheres. Much of the
research centers on what each half
of the brain can do.

Both hemispheres, of course, are
able to control muscles and to receive information from the sense or-
gans. And both have a role in
"thinking"—but not the same role.
Scientists have come to that conclu-

Silver 30

31,32

Publication **Ambassador**
Art Director **Alfred Zelcer**
Designer **Alfred Zelcer**
Illustrator **Stephen Rydberg, Robert Andrew Parker, David Levine, Will Northerner, John Collier**
Publisher **The Webb Co.**

Silver 31

Silver 32

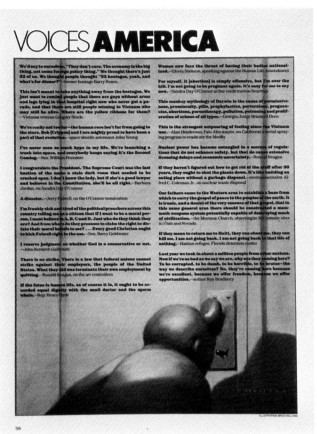

Gold 33

33–35
Publication **Life**
Art Director **Bob Ciano**
Designer **Bob Ciano**
Illustrator **Brad Holland**
Publisher **Time Inc.**

Gold 34

Gold 35

36–38

Publication   **On Campus**
Art Director   **Virginia Murphy-Hamill**
Designer   **Virginia Murphy-Hamill**
Photographer   **Rene Gelpi**
Publisher   **Hearst Publications/
UTP Division**

Documents

An Interview With
René Gelpi
By Jack Neubart

36

37

38

PUBLICATION DESIGN 17

POINT SIZE

13 15

1 — 1

2 — 2

3 — 3

INCHES

	39,40
Publication	**National Geographic**
Art Director	**Howard E. Paine, Jan Adkins**
Designer	**H. Edward Kim, Constance Phelps, Betty Clayman DeAtley,** **Charles C. Uhl, William Douthitt**
Illustrator	**William H. Bond, Ned Seidler, Davis Meltzer**
Photographer	**Kerby Smith, Jonathan Blair, William Curtsinger,** **James A. Sugar, Victor Boswell, Chris Newbert**
Publisher	**National Geographic Society**

39

40

41–43

Publication   **Texas Monthly**
Art Director   **Jim Darilek**
Designer   **Jim Darilek**
Publisher   **Mediatex Communications Corporation**

41

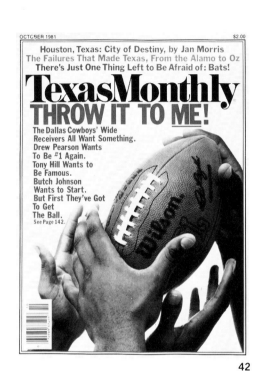

42

43

44,45
Publication **Science Digest**
Art Director **Mary Zisk**
Design Director **Frank Rothmann**
Designer **Frank Rothmann, Mary Zisk,
Russell Zolan, Nancy Oatts,
Connie Williams**
Publisher **Hearst Magazines**

44

Most people have experienced those unsolicited mental pictures that appear in the drowsy but still awake period as they slide into sleep. But Dr. Elmer Green can do better than most. His unconscious mind feeds him images that help him solve difficult problems—and he can help others do the same. During the mid-1960s, while Green was a research assistant in the department of medicine at the University of Chicago, he used these hypnagogic or "twilight" images to help settle a 100-year-old debate about visual brightness and its dependence on stimulus intensity. Forty or 50 times over a period of 16 weeks, he sat quietly in his office, waiting for the solutions that would complete 45 pages of mathematical equations to float into his awareness from his unconscious mind. "I remember once getting an image of two saw blades with their teeth facing each other, fitting perfectly," recalls the biopsychologist, now director of the voluntary controls center at the Menninger Foundation in Topeka, Kansas. "What was that? I asked. Then I perceived that the image of the interlocking saw blades represented the fact that I couldn't go from the equation I was working with to the next continuously, even though the two were a perfect fit." Some of humankind's truly epic creative breakthroughs and insights can be traced to minds that were extraordinarily receptive to such unsolicited imagery. A twilight image enabled the nineteenth-century chemist Friedrich Kekulé to solve one of organic chemistry's most difficult quandaries, the structure of the benzene molecule. The solution came to him in a flash as he dozed, watching images of atoms cavort snakelike in his mind. As he later described it, "One of the snakes had seized hold of its own tail, and the form whirled mockingly before my eyes." Benzene, his unconscious mind was informing him, has a "closed chain" or ringlike structure. The journals of the creative are jammed with such anecdotes. Einstein saw his understanding of relativity take a great leap while he drowsily contemplated walking on a sunbeam. Van Gogh said that "pictures come to me as in a dream." Mozart was once suddenly suffused with the awareness of an entire new musical composition while he dozed in the

You're fully awake. Your brain hums with theta waves and the portals of your unconscious open.

CREATIVE
FLASHES
F R O M   T H E
TWILIGHT
ZONE

BY DUDLEY LYNCH

45

190

46

46,47

Publication **Four Winds**
Art Director **Larry Smitherman**
Publisher **Smitherman Graphic Design**

Polychrome
Water Jar
Ca. 1900–1920.
10" × 12"
School of American Research.
IAF 513

Acoma pottery and text from
"Sky City Salute: Pottery of
Acoma Pueblo." Courtesy of
The Wheelwright Museum of the
American Indian, Santa Fe. All
photographs by Herb Lotz.

SKY CITY SALUTE:
Pottery of Acoma Pueblo

Wheelwright Museum of the American Indian, Santa Fe, New Mexico

Acoma, the westernmost Pueblo of
the Keresan language group, is called
"Sky City" because of its dramatic lo-
cation on top of a large mesa. At the
bottom of the mesa, a map indicates
visitors that the site was inhabited c.
600 A.D. Thus, Acoma is one of the
oldest, continuously inhabited villages in North America. Acoma experienced the pressures of early Spanish
colonialism, participated in the Pueblo Revolt of 1680, and gradually ac-
commodated to a changing world.
The current population is estimated at
slightly over 2,000 persons, making Acoma the largest Keres-speaking
Pueblo. While most people now live
year-round in the summer villages
of Acomita and McCartys, the mountain top Pueblo remains the ceremonial
center, and many families maintain a
home there also. The movement away
from mesa top to neighboring valleys
was the result of several factors: the
absence of a permanent water supply
in the traditional village, the need to
be closer to farm and grazing lands
and, in recent years, the desire to be
nearer the highway, Inter-city and
shopping centers. During the earlier
decades, the traditional agriculturally-
based economy has gradually been re-
placed by some form of wage work.
Revenues from pottery sales provide
an additional source of income for
many families. While the people of
Acoma have entered the 20th century
in many ways, the cultural and spiritual traditions of the Pueblo remain a
vital source of continuity with the past
and enrichment for the present.
    Acoma has a distinguished history
as a prominent pottery-making Pueblo. From A.D. 1300–1700, Acoma
pottery was characterized by a succes-
sion of glaze-painted wares. Material

47

48,49

Publication   **Destinations**
Art Director   **Shelley Williams**
Designer   **Shelley Williams, Michael Freeman,**
Janine Orr, Michael Marcum
Publisher   **13-30 Corporation**

48

On Foot in North Yemen

WANDERING THE ARABIAN HEIGHTS

by Michael Winn

Carved into a craggy desert mountain range is an ancient kingdom of tall mud castles and terraced gardens. Isolated for millenniums, it is the last nation in the Arab world to be opened to Westerners. It is not an easy place to reach. Yet this tiny country is a magnet for adventure-seekers, in a medieval setting that has all but vanished from the earth.

49

50
Publication **Esquire**
Art Director **Robert Priest**
Designer **April Silver**
Photographer **Michael Geiger**
Publisher **Esquire Publishing**

51,52
Publication **Skyline**
Art Director **Massimo Vignelli**
Designer **Michael Bierut**
Publisher **Rizzoli Communications, Inc.**

WorldlyWanderings *FASHION BY VINCENT BOUCHER* You've already begun to long
for spring; maybe you're even chasing the sun to a tropical paradise. Here's a
sophisticated and spirited sampling
of clothes to see you on your way.

WHEREVER YOU GO, let your shirttails fly. Pack the kind of clothes you are
used to wearing in the gym or on the track—a rugby shirt and drawstring
pants. Out of the locker room and on the street, these clothes have been cut
a little trimmer and have been recast
in unexpected colors and icy pastels.

50

51

Skyline   October·1981

The Architecture and Design Review

**Vidler on Jencks:
Cooking up the Classics
Eisenman and Wolfe:
Our House and Bauhaus
Stern on Frampton:
Giedion's Ghost
Peter Brooks:
Prostitution and Paris
Scully and Meier:
Remembering Breuer
Plus: Buildings, Books,
Exhibits, Events, and
The Insider's Guide to
Architects' Offices**

52

53

Publication **Science Digest**
Art Director **Mary Zisk**
Design Director **Frank Rothmann**
Designer **Frank Rothmann, Mary Zisk, Russell Zolan, Nancy Oatts, Connie Williams**
Publisher **Hearst Magazines**

54,55

Publication **Picture Magazine**
Art Director **David Boss**
Designer **Carol Seltzer/Cross Associates**
Publisher **Gardner/Fulmer Lithograph**

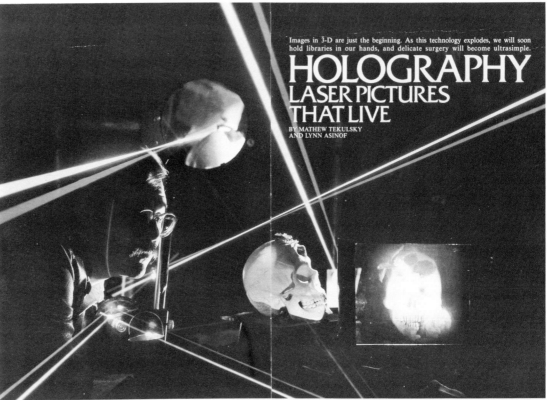

53

54

55

56,57

Publication **Four Winds**
Art Director **Larry Smitherman**
Publisher **Smitherman Graphic Design**

Maynard Dixon   Francisco Zuniga   Navajo Codetalkers
Harry Fonseca   Indian Running   Katalin Ehling
Feather Preservation

56

THE WORLD OF
INDIAN RUNNING

by Peter Nabokov

Bear Clan Racer. Painting by Arlo Nasvamana.
Courtesy of Museum of the American Indian,
Heye Foundation, N.Y.

Couriers of the 1680 Pueblo Revolt

In late spring of 1680, messengers assembled at Red Willow (Taos Pueblo) in what is today northern New Mexico. Speaking to them was a middle-aged man born in the nearby village of

Peter Nabokov, a doctoral candidate in Anthropology at the University of California, Berkeley, writes on a broad range of Native American subjects. (See the Winter Spring 1981 issue of FOUR WINDS for Nabokov's article "Native American Architecture: Preserving Social and Religious Life.") He is collaborating with Robert Easton on a major survey of American Indian architectural traditions to be published by Oxford University Press in 1982.

From Indian Running. Copyright 1981 by Peter Nabokov. Reprinted by permission of Capra Press, P.O. Box 2068, Santa Barbara, CA 93120

Grinding Stone (San Juan Pueblo). Spaniards would record him only as Pope, and revile him as a magician, the devil incarnate. His native name, Pa pay, possibly meant "ripe squash," which could identify him as a religious leader of his village's summer moiety. With him were probably other Pueblo Indian leaders: Luis Tupatu of Picuris, Antonio Malacate of Tesuque and his host, El Saca of Taos. They were conspiring to overthrow Spanish rule in the Southwest.

Deerskins with pictographs were handed to the runners. Po pay told them that the uprising would come upon the new August moon, with the ripening of corn. The runners were rehearsed in the plan behind the pictographs. They went to forewarn all the seventy-odd Pueblos the Spanish had been persecuting for nearly a century.

even to the Hopi villages over 300 miles away.

Word flew on foot and August drew near. They were brought together for a second mission. Given a bundle of knotted yucca-fiber cords as countdown devices, the runners were to repeat the itinerary of Pueblos. Every village was to untie a knot each day until the cords were clear. That day they should grab hidden weapons and burn the temples, break up the bells.

We know that information leaked out, requiring a last-minute runner countermarper to push the date ahead. Two runners from Tesuque were intercepted and hanged. The revised target date, August 10. There is no descrip tion of those couriers at work, but Willa Cather's Death Comes for the Archbishop offers this picture of Pueblo

Winter 1981 Four Winds 19

58
Publication   **American Preservation**
Art Director   **Peter Bradford, Byron Taylor**
Designer   **Peter Bradford**
Publisher   **Briggs Associates, Inc.**

58

59–61

Publication   **New York Magazine**
Art Director   **Robert Best**
Designer   **Patricia Bradbury, Don Morris**
Publisher   **New Group Publication**

59

60

61

62
Publication **Progressive Architecture**
Art Director **George Coderre**
Designer **George Coderre**
Illustrator **April Greiman**
Publisher **Reinhold Publishing**

63,64
Publication **Contact—President's Report/1980**
Art Director **Dennis and David Barnett**
Designer **Dennis and David Barnett**
Illustrator **Harry Wilks, Roger Tully**
Publisher **American International Group**

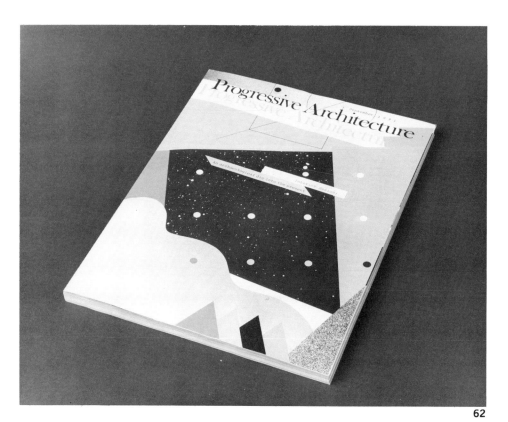

62

63

64

65,66

Publication **Interiors**
Art Director **Paul Hardy**
Illustrator **William Work**
Publisher **Billboard Publications, Inc.**

67,68

Publication **Technology**
Art Director **Noel Werrett**
Designer **Noel Werrett, Joanne Goodfellow**
Publisher **Technology Information Corporation**

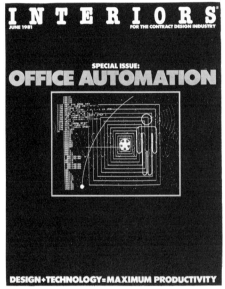

65

66

67

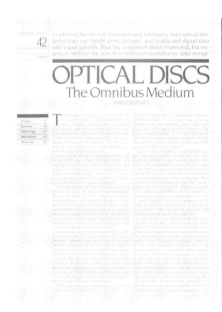

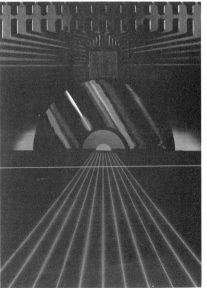

68

69,70

Publication   **Oil & Gas Investor**
Art Director   **Neil Shakery**
Designer   **Neil Shakery**
Publisher   **Investor Publishing Company**

Williston Basin wildcat successes three times national average.

69

A NEW TWIST ON OIL/STOCK SWAPS

Wall Street woos limited partners. Integrated Energy and
Ensource put together first two offers; more will follow.
Is swap a boon . . . or a boondoggle?

ARTICLE BY
RONALD G. COOPER

A brassy new idea apparently has captured the fancy of many an oil and gas limited partner all over the country. If you haven't run across it yet, don't worry. You will.

The idea? New corporations formed to snap up a slew of limited partner interests in public or private oil and gas programs operating all around the U.S. In exchange, the limited partner gets common stock in the new, publicly-traded corporation — virtually tax-free.

But the new corporations have taken their idea a step further. They haven't turned up their noses at everyone save limited partners. In fact, they will horsetrade for general partner interests, working interests in proved oil and gas reserves, and even undeveloped leasehold interests.

Their idea, for all classes of investors, is similar to a tender offer. You choose whether or not to swap your interests for common stock in a new corporation.

Two corporations championing this idea recently have emerged. Both are backed by big hitters in the financial community. One is Integrated Energy Inc., sponsored by Bache Halsey Stuart Shields Inc. The other is Ensource Inc., underwritten by E.F. Hutton & Co. and First Boston Corp.

One of the new firms already is off and winging. Integrated Energy, which plans to apply for listing on the American Stock Exchange, expects its stock to begin trading in late July or early August.

Integrated Energy made a blanket offer to nearly every limited partner, and most interest holders, in the U.S. The offer was for a minimum five million shares at $10 per share. It became effective March 24. Promptly, "hundreds of millions of dollars" worth of valuation requests came pouring in, according to Howard Phillips, a director of Integrated Energy and chairman of its finance committee. (Of the $450 million to $500 million received by mid-April, another source close to the offering said, perhaps half were of questionable value.) The offering sparked such interest, Phillips says, that the original cut off date of May 6 definitely will be extended.

With all those potential subscribers hovering in the background, Integrated obviously can afford to be a little choosy. Further, notes Phillips, Integrated will boost its number of authorized shares, perhaps to 25 million or more.

The other new firm, Ensource, also is about to lift off the runway. In one respect, Ensource will be far more snobbish than Integrated Energy. Ensource will buy out only complete partnership interests it already has solicited, plus some private companies and leasehold interests "of substantial size." In short, if you weren't invited aboard in the first place, you can't buy a ticket.

According to Thomas Edelman, vice president-corporate finance for First Boston, Ensource has accumulated a stable of some 200 limited partnerships who have expressed interest in being bought out. Also, Ensource apparently will have a larger capital base than Integrated Energy. It plans on issuing up to 50 million shares at $20 a pop. Total capitalization, estimates Edelman, will be $700 million to $900 million. Edelman says he sees "no problem" with listing on the Big Board. "My best guess is that we will be out and trading in July," he adds.

Both companies, it should be stressed, are making their offers only once. Limited partners and others won't get a second chance to hop aboard these particular flights. However, should these corporations succeed — and their chances certainly seem rosy now — expect to see a rash of imitators. Edelman of First Boston admits: "This will certainly not be the last deal of this nature we take public." At least six other corporations or brokers reportedly have plans on the board to launch similar ventures.

W hat is the grand appeal of these ventures for the limited partner? Flatly stated: access to cash. Partnership units are long-term investments; they are highly illiquid. For many a year, general partners have had a stranglehold on the limited partner who wants to cash in his units. The discount, even to future proven revenue, has been staggering.

Under these new deals, limited partners who

26

70

71–73

Publication   **Colorado Heritage**
Art Director   **Richard Foy**
Designer   **Julie Herblick, Cathryne Johnson**
Publisher   **Colorado Historical Society**

THE JOURNAL OF THE
COLORADO HISTORICAL SOCIETY

71

72

73

74,75

Publication **Nautical Quarterly**
Art Director **B. Martin Pedersen**
Designer **B. Martin Pedersen**
Illustrator **Daniel Maffia**
Photographer **Benjamin Mendlowitz**
Publisher **Jonson Pedersen Hinrichs & Shakery**

74

NAUTICAL QUARTERLY
PAINTINGS BY MIHANOVIC
HARD AND SOFT

Marine paintings—whether of clipper ships, yachts or fishboats—tend to be action-packed—a Gloucester schooner rail down on the race to market, a 12 Meter on a spinnaker run, *Twegoing* in the Trades with her studding sails out. The paintings on these six pages are different. They are serene and mysterious, their principal action the soft breathing of the Adriatic on the bright coast of Yugoslavia.

It is subtle action to capture, subtler still when a cobbled bottom as precise and intricate as a mosaic slides off under a lambent surface. The artist is Zvonimir Mihanovic (pronounced Ma-han-o-vitch), a Croatian born in Yugoslavia in 1946, whose first painting brought him First Prize in Yugoslavia's Salon of Young Artists in 1962. He studied subsequently at the Academy of Fine Arts in Zagreb and the Brera Academy of Fine Arts in Milan, and traveled in 1972 and 1973 to museums in London, Boston, New York and Washington to study paintings of classical realism.

His own realism is an old tradition of meticulous detail and compelling moodiness, although there is a suggestion of the "hard-edge" realism of recent decades. These paintings have very solid reality—all the heavy essence of the concrete with few distractions. Even the light has a weighty, stone-slab quality.

It is the light of the eastern Med, the almost-physical light that travelers in the Greek islands have so often remarked. The boats are the typical double-enders of the Adriatic's fisheries, full-bodied carvel types with lines that go back to Homer's time, along with dinghies and tenders of the same chunky build. Solid, serene boats on solid, serene water, but with an odd softness of mood and weather.

Mihanovic has done other types of paintings in his two decades of major work, but marine paintings like these are now his preoccupation, indeed his passion. A man at the Wally Findlay Gallery in New York, where Mihanovic paintings were first shown in the U.S. in January and February of 1981, describes him as "absolutely in love with the Adriatic." Mihanovic has a home and studio in Paris, but he spends the long Yugoslavian summer aboard a houseboat in the Adriatic. His paintings are oils on large canvases, and each represents a month to six weeks of work. There were 30-odd paintings in his recent show in New York—two years of work—and it is expected that there will be as many paintings about a year from now when his new work is shown at Wally Findlay's Beverly Hills gallery. He is on the Adriatic as this is written, seeing and wonderfully putting on canvas the hard surfaces and softer depths of coastal images like these.

75

Dedication
S.I. Newhouse Center for Law and Justice
October 17, 1979

RUTGERS

76

76,77

Publication   Dedication; S.I. Newhouse
               Center for Law and Justice
Art Director   Leonard Lee Ringel
Designer   Leonard Lee Ringel
Publisher   Rutgers, The State University of
               New Jersey

Introduction

Peter Simmons
Dean, Rutgers University
School of Law-Newark

October 17, 1979, was a great day in the history of Rutgers School of Law-Newark, for on that date we dedicated its new home, the S.I. Newhouse Center for Law and Justice. At a dedication luncheon, and at the ceremony itself, leading figures of New Jersey's bench and bar, government leaders, law school community members, and its friends and alumniae gathered to celebrate this event, and to pay tribute to the late S.I. Newhouse, whose gift made it all possible. We were honored by the presence of William J. Brennan, Jr., Associate Justice of the U.S. Supreme Court, whose dedication address was the highlight of the ceremony.

The building that became the Newhouse Center—a commanding seventeen-story structure of rose-red brick and limestone—has long been considered one of Newark's most graceful and impressive skyscrapers. Erected in 1930 as the Fireman's Fund Building, it was donated to Rutgers University in August 1976 by the American Express Company. Soon thereafter, the university received a grant of $1.5 million from the S.I. Newhouse Foundation, $475,000 of which was designated for renovation of the building, and the balance to establish an endowment to support research in law and criminal justice, to acquire specialized law books, and to

provide research assistance to professors.

Samuel I. Newhouse was a 1916 graduate of the law school's parent institution, New Jersey Law School, and a newspaper publisher with longstanding ties to Newark. He remarked on making the gift, "We are extremely proud to contribute to the further development of legal education at Rutgers—which boasts one of the finest institutions in the country for the study of law. At the same time, I sincerely hope and expect that this contribution to the center will aid in continuing to build the city of Newark as one of the most outstanding centers for higher education."

In June 1978, in recognition of this gift, the Rutgers University Board of Governors named the building the S.I. Newhouse Center for Law and Justice. Extensive interior remodeling was soon underway, and by 1979 it was sufficiently completed to warrant the official dedication ceremony. In addition to its major function as a base for the law school, the center houses the Graduate School of Criminal Justice, the New Jersey Institute for Continuing Legal Education, administrative offices of the Newark Provost, and several campus administrative offices.

We at the law school are extraordinarily proud of our new home. In commemoration of the dedication, and with gratitude to the Newhouse family and to all our friends and supporters, the school presents this book. In the years to come, we will be working hard to make S.I. Newhouse's prophecy a reality.

77

78,79

Publication	**The Donnelly Record**
Art Director	**Robert J. O'Dell Inc.**
Designer	**Robert O'Dell**
Illustrator	**Edward Odell**
Photographer	**Bill Aller**
Publisher	**Reuben H. Donnelly Corporation**

78

79

80

80,81

Publication   **Scarves for Summer—**
                   The Metropolitan Museum of Art
Art Director   **Alvin Grossman**
Designer   **Alvin Grossman**
Publisher   **The Metropolitan Museum of Art**

A Manchurian roundel from a 19th-century woman's ceremonial coat of silk plain weave, embroidered with silks.

Among the things in Chinese culture which come in fives are the blessings of life. Longevity, one of the Five Blessings, is symbolized by the crane which, like other white beasts, was deemed auspicious because it was thought to inhabit the realm of the immortals and live to the great age of 10,000 years. The other four of life's blessings are riches, health, love of virtue, and a good end.

The color red evokes the summer of life for the Chinese and is associated with family celebrations such as weddings and births. This striking red scarf is made of pure silk *crêpe-de-chine*, cut on the bias. 12" x 52". Regular price $35.00 PREVIEW PRICE (L1897) $30.00

CRANE SCARF

81

82,83

Publication **Assets**
Art Director **Kit Hinrichs**
Designer **Kit Hinrichs, Barbara Vick**
Illustrator **Steve Gerber, Tim Lewis, John Mattos, Hank Osuna**
Photographer **John Blaustein**
Publisher **Crocker National Corporation**

82

83

84

84,85
Publication   **The Potlatch Story**
Art Director   **Linda Hinrichs**
Designer   **Linda Hinrichs**
Illustrator   **John Hyatt, Paul Fusco,**
Ward Schumaker, Philipe Weisbecker
Publisher   **The Potlatch Corporation**

85

86,87

Publication   **Nabisco Brands, Inc.**
Art Director   **Don Johnson**
Designer   **Bonnie Berish**
Photographer   **George Mattei, Robert Schlegel**
Publisher   **Johnson & Simpson Graphic Designers**

86

From the beginning, N.B.C. used its own vehicles to deliver its products to retailers and to advertise those products to passersby.

There were eight employees, including the two partners.

In less than a year, the company had outgrown its quarters and taken over an entire four-story building. Its product line had expanded to include peanut bars, chocolate nut bars, peanut rolls and walnut bars.

By 1913, not even a four-story building could handle the demand, and another move was necessary — this one directly into the heart of peanut country. A processing plant for raw peanuts was established in Suffolk, Virginia. The unit was enlarged several times until eventually it covered seventy-six acres and Suffolk had become truly the peanut capital of the world.

A Monocle and Top Hat
Throughout the company's formative years, partners Obici and Peruzzi were constantly looking for new ways to enhance the popularity of the peanut and to burnish the Planters image. Toward these ends in 1916 they offered a prize for the best sketch suitable for adoption as the company trademark.

The winning design, submitted by a schoolboy, was an animated peanut. Later a commercial artist took the peanut figure, added a top hat, monocle and cane, and Mr. Peanut was born.

The debonair gentleman, usually depicted leaning on his cane, legs crossed nonchalantly, soon became the universal emblem for Planters products — and one of the world's most familiar commercial symbols. But Planters wasn't the only company developing new taste sensations from peanuts and chocolate in the period just preceding America's entry into World War I. In Chicago, a twenty-five-year-old, self-styled entrepreneur named Otto

20

It was a schoolboy in pursuit of a contest prize who originated the dapper character now known as "Mr. Peanut," the symbol for Planters products.

Schnering leased a small room over a plumber's shop, installed a five-gallon kettle and a rented stove and, having hired four employees, grandly announced the formation of the Curtiss Candy Company.

Like Planters, Curtiss, too, was destined to become a member of the Standard Brands family.

For several years after its birth, Curtiss just managed to get by as Schnering and his associates tried out one candy recipe after another. Among the confections they marketed were Curtiss Ostrich Eggs, Curtiss PETERPAN, Curtiss Milk Nut Loaf and Curtiss COCOANUT GROVE — all of them tasty and wholesome but none of them an instantaneous bonanza at the cash register.

A President's Daughter
Then in 1920, Curtiss hit the jackpot. Almost overnight it sprouted from low-volume obscurity to huge-volume industry leadership. The change was reflected in its magazine advertisements, all of them signed by Schnering himself, which now listed five factory cities — New York, Boston, San Francisco, Los Angeles and Chicago — instead of Chicago alone.

The miracle that made the difference: a round, log-shaped candy bar named BABY RUTH. Contrary to rumors that began to circulate, the name was derived not from that of ballplayer Babe Ruth, who in 1920 had just joined the New York Yankees and had not yet become a full-fledged star, but from that of the daughter of former President Grover Cleveland. As an infant she had been the nation's pet, and though she was now a grown woman, the memories lingered.

Even the advertisements for BABY RUTH Candy Bars were mouth-watering. A 1926 ad described it as containing "the finest peanuts from the South — roasted then toasted — the richest chocolate from the East — the choicest milk from the prize herds of the North — the best

butter from the dairy centers of the West — the first grade of sugar from the cane fields of the Tropics."

Another point made in that ad: just six years after its introduction, BABY RUTH was "the world's most popular candy," with over five million bars sold daily.

In the years to come Curtiss would add to its product roster such superstars as BUTTERFINGER Candy Bar, JUMBO BLOCK Peanut Butter Cups, CRACKERJACK Caramel Corn, SUN MAID Raisins and CAMP FIRE Marshmallows.

Snack Time for Fido
In 1917, just one year after the founding of Curtiss in Chicago, F. H. Bennett, a New York City baker, incorporated his business as the F. H. Bennett Biscuit Company. It was an event that was to have a substantial impact on America's dogs and their owners — and a not inconsiderable effect on the National Biscuit Company.

Bennett had been operating a small shop on New York's Lower

21

87

208

RECENT COLOR

88,89
Publication **The Archive**
Designer **Nancy Solomon**
Publisher **Center for Creative Photography/University of Arizona**

RECENT COLOR: A Portfolio

90,91

Publication **Chase Manhattan Corporation Annual Report**
Art Director **Bennett Robinson**
Designer **Bennett Robinson**
Illustrator **Pierre Le Tan**
Photographer **Farrell Grehan, Charles Harbutt,**
Matthew Klein, Arthur Lavine
Publisher **Corporate Graphics, Inc.**

92,93

Publication **Sohio Annual Report**
Art Director **Bennett Robinson**
Designer **Bennett Robinson**
Photographer **Jay Maisel**
Publisher **Corporate Graphics, Inc.**

90

91

92

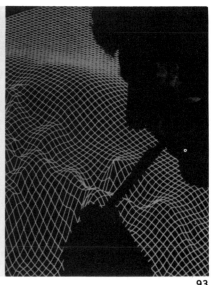

93

94,95
Publication   **The E.F. Hutton Group Annual Report**
Art Director   **Robin Davis**
Designer   **Robin Davis**
Illustrator   **Robin Davis**
Photographer   **Cheryl Rossum**
Publisher   **E.F. Hutton & Company, Inc.**

94

95

96,97

Publication **Beverly Hills Savings & Loan Association**
Art Director **Thomas D. Ohmer**
Designer **Bruce Dobson**
Illustrator **Bruce Dobson**
Photographer **Mark Coppos**
Publisher **Advertising Designers, Inc.**

96

These operations have helped make Beverly Hills Savings a high volume lender compared with associations of similar size. The most recent available data shows that home loans sold by savings associations across the nation averaged about 18% of loans originated in 1979, at Beverly Hills Savings, that figure was 70% in 1980.

In 1980, loan sales were $138 million compared with $205 million in 1979 and $104 million in 1978. Our loan servicing portfolio, which generates substantial revenues, rose to $717 million in 1980, compared with $612 million in 1979 and $353 million in 1978.

Mortgage Instruments
In view of the increasing and volatile cost of savings deposits, federal and state regulatory agencies are considering approval of mortgage instruments more flexible than the traditional fixed rate mortgage or even the more recent variable rate mortgage. This is of critical importance if savings associations are to achieve a yield on mortgage portfolios that will keep pace with changes in the cost of funds.

Fortunately, Beverly Hills Savings' approach to lending has reduced dependence on long-term fixed rate mortgages from 79% of our portfolio in 1975 to less than 45% in 1980. When mortgage instruments which are responsive to market conditions and which can be sold profitably become available, the association stands ready to implement them as an integral part of our lending and mortgage banking activities.

Real Estate Development
Since 1975, the association has actively sought joint ventures with successful residential and commercial developers. Beverly Hills Savings is now engaged in ten residential joint ventures and two commercial joint ventures involving a combined investment of $14.6 million as of year end 1980, compared with $4.2 million in 1979. In the next six years, we expect these residential joint ventures to produce approximately 3,000 new housing units.

In a typical joint venture, Beverly Hills Savings provides equity for a project and receives a percentage of the profits. The association normally does not provide the construction financing on such projects and it may or may not finance the mortgage loans which result from the sale of the housing. Income from joint ventures remained at low levels in 1980 as in 1979, because of the extended project lead times necessary in today's building climate

and because of the overall economic environment. However, with many projects now well underway, management believes that profits from real estate development are likely to increase as economic conditions improve.

Construction Loans
Our construction loan program adds to our portfolio a truly variable rate component, since the interest rate on construction loans varies with changes in the commercial bank prime lending rate. In addition, these loans return higher fees than permanent residential loans and generally have maturities of two to three years—far shorter than the traditional 30-year home loan.

Construction lending continued to be a strong performer for the association in 1980. Construction loan volume was $60 million for 1980, compared with $64 million in 1979. This generated $11 million in revenue, or 21.0% of the total, as compared with $7 million and 16.1% in 1979. The yield on this portfolio was a healthy 16.7% in 1980, compared with 14.5% in 1979. Construction loans as a percentage of assets rose to 23% in 1980 from 20% in 1979.

New Loan Activity

For the Year (Thousands)

	1980		1979	
Single Family (1 to 4 units)				
Existing	$157,485	64.5%	$322,571	73.1%
Construction	25,210	10.3	14,195	3.2
Apartments				
Existing	1,270	.5	5,081	1.2
Construction	185	.1	—	—
Commercial-Industrial				
Existing	4,713	1.9	10,781	2.5
Construction	34,708	14.2	50,090	11.5
Other Loans	20,693	8.5	38,396	8.7
	$244,244	100.0%	$441,317	100.0%

Real Estate Activity

For the Year

	1980	1979
Gross Sales	$11,872,000	$4,693,000
Cost of Sales & Co-Venturer's Share of Profits (Losses)	12,451,000	4,657,000
Association's Share of Profits (Losses)	$ (579,000)	$ 36,000

97

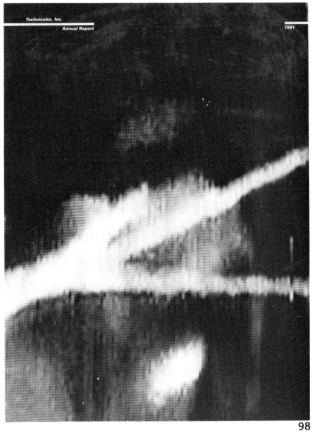

98

98,99
Publication   **Technicolor Incorporated Annual Report**
Art Director   **Jim Berte**
Designer   **Jim Berte**
Photographer   **Steve Kahn**
Publisher   **Robert Miles Runyan & Associates**

The Vidtronics
Company, Inc.

Technicolor's videotape subsidiary showed a gain of 12% in sales during the last fiscal year; however, the thirteen week strike by the Screen Actors Guild and start-up costs related to our new videocassette duplicating operation caused profits to remain relatively flat for 1981.

Vidtronics' post-production division has commitments for eleven prime-time network television programs to use our services during this production year and we anticipate satisfactory increases in sales and profits.

The Vidtronics videocassette duplicating division commenced operations in July, 1981 with an initial capacity of more than 2,000,000 videocassettes per year. The facility has been constructed and equipped to offer "state-of-the-art" capability, unrivaled in the industry. We are pleased to announce that Warner Bros. has signed an exclusive three year agreement with Vidtronics for the Company to supply all of their videocassette duplicating needs for the United States home market. We are actively seeking additional customers for this division and we expect that Vidtronics will become a significant factor in this rapidly developing business.

The Gold Key Division of Vidtronics recorded a significant increase in sales in the last fiscal year due primarily to the success of our new "first run sponsored programming" operation—Gold Key Media. While earnings of Gold Key were down slightly for fiscal 1981 due to the start-up costs of Gold Key Media, we anticipate significant sales and profit improvements in this fiscal year.

Vidtronics

Vidtronics "state-of-the-art" technology and Emmy Award winning editors help bring visual excitement to many television specials and series.

8

99

100,101
Publication **Brooklyn Academy of Music Annual Report**
Art Director **Ellen Shapiro**
Designer **Ellen Shapiro**
Illustrator **Jules Feiffer**
Publisher **Brooklyn Academy of Music**

Brooklyn Academy
of Music
Annual Report
1980-81 Season

A DANCE TO
BAM BAM
BABAM
BAM
BAM

100

Ballet America
A National Celebration
of Dance
Sponsored by
Exxon Corporation

San Francisco Ballet
October 14-19, 1980
Directors:
Lew Christensen
Michael Smuin

Los Angeles Ballet
November 15-20, 1980
Artistic Director
John Clifford

Cleveland Ballet
January 20-25, 1981
Artistic Director
Ian Horvath
Associate Director
Dennis Nahat

Ohio Ballet
March 12-15, 1981
Artistic Director
Heinz Poll

Houston Ballet
April 7-12, 1981
Artistic Director
Ben Stevenson

Pennsylvania Ballet
May 5-10, 1981
Artistic Director
Benjamin Harkarvy
Director
Barbara Weisberger

DANCE

During the 1980-81 season, the Brooklyn Academy of Music emerged center-stage as one of the most important and visible dance presenters in the United States. "Ballet America," a season-long festival, gave six major ballet companies from across the country the opportunity to perform in New York City, many for the first time.

The widely-acclaimed series featured the New York debuts of the Cleveland, Houston and Los Angeles Ballets; only the second New York seasons in recent years by the Ohio and San Francisco Ballets; and the return of the Pennsylvania Ballet, an "old friend" of the Academy's.

BAM's fourth annual DanceAfrica festival also took on national proportions. The spring celebration brought companies from five American cities together for the country's first national celebration of African-American dance.

In all, the Academy presented a total of 66 performances, engaging 15 different dance companies from all over the country, in a season more broadly national in scope than ever before.

The Ballet America festival was made possible by major grants from the Exxon Corporation, the National Endowment for the Arts and the New York State Council on the Arts. The series offered 36 performances—including 24 New York or world premieres—to more than 50,000 people, the largest dance audience at the Academy in many years.

The audiences and critics alike were delighted. Anna Kisselgoff in *The New York Times* wrote: "one of New York's most important dance events...which BAM rightly calls 'a national celebration of dance.'" *New York Post* critic Clive Barnes added: "Manhattan may be the

dance capital of the world, but this season, in a very special sense, Brooklyn has become the dance capital of the United States."

The festival was unique in many respects. It provided a national showcase for American choreographs developed outside of New York City by the artistic directors and collaborators associated with many of America's most important ballet companies. The work of these creative individuals was, until now, too little seen in New York City.

Ballet America also provided New York seasons (in several cases debuts) for companies that are among the best the U.S. has to offer. The festival concept, and its subscription marketing campaign, attracted a large and enthusiastic audience for all of the participating companies. The Theater Development Fund also was instrumental in making tickets available to dance-lovers throughout the New York area. The success of Ballet America not only had impact in New York, but also in each company's home city, where New York recognition enhanced its stature locally.

DanceAfrica '81 included participants from all over the U.S. for the first time: Milwaukee's Ko-Thi Dance Company; Chicago's Muntu Dance Theatre; and The Art of Black Dance and Music from Boston joined such New York companies as Dinizulu and his African Dancers, Drummers and Singers; the Chuck Davis Dance Company; the Charles Moore Dance Theatre; the International Afrikan American Ballet and Welcome Msomi's Izulu Theatre.

The Jamaica National Dance Theatre Company was a highlight of the fall, performing pieces based on the traditional rituals and folk customs of the Caribbean. Under the direction of dancer-choreographer Rex Nettleford, this marked the third appearance of the Company at BAM.

As part of BAM's Ballet America Festival, Andrea Vodehnal, principal dancer in the Houston Ballet, dances in "Four Last Songs." Photo by Geoff Winningham.

3

101

102

102–104
Publication   **The Charles Stark Draper Laboratory, Inc.**
Art Director   **Robert Cipriani**
Designer   **Robert Cipriani**
Photographer   **Gary Koepke, Al Fisher, Pete Turner**
Publisher   **Robert Cipriani Associates**

103

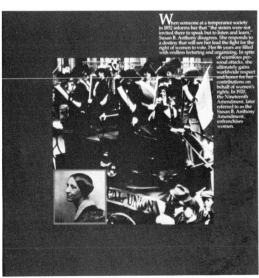

104

105,106
Publication **Electro Rent Corporation Annual**
Art Director **Robert Miles Runyan**
Designer **Rik Besser**
Illustrator **Paul Bice, Kenji Matsumoto**
Publisher **Robert Miles Runyan & Associates**

105

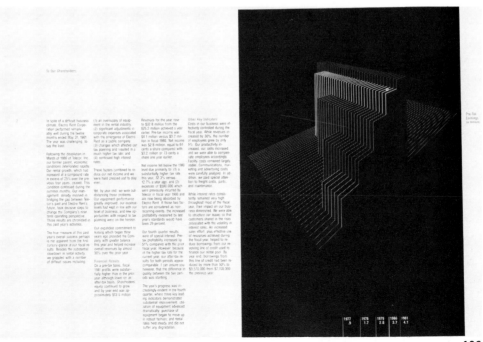

106

107–109

Publication   **Early California Industries Inc., Annual Report**
Art Director   **Robert Miles Runyan**
Designer   **Dennis Tanni**
Illustrator   **Warren Hile**
Publisher   **Robert Miles Runyan & Associates**

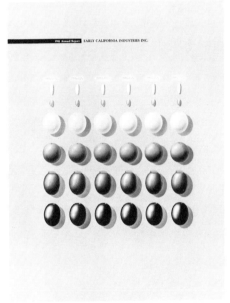

107

108

109

	110,111		112,113
Publication	French American Banking Corporation Annual Report	Publication	Potlatch Annual Report
Art Director	Victor Gialleonardo	Art Director	Kit Hinrichs
Designer	Patricia Allen	Designer	Kit Hinrich, Arlene Finger
Illustrator	Frank Bozzo	Photographer	Tom Tracy
Photographer	Bill Rivelli, Bob Colton	Publisher	Potlatch Corporation
Publisher	Doremus Design		

110

111

112

Skills:

113

114,115

Publication **Transamerica Annual Report**
Art Director **Linda Hinrichs**
Designer **Linda Hinrichs, Lenore Bartz**
Photographer **Tom Tracy, John McDermott**
Publisher **Transamerica**

116,117

Publication **Citicorps Reports/Brazil**
Art Director **Jack Odette**
Designer **Mike Focar**
Publisher **Citibank**

114

115

116

117

	118,119		**120,121**
Publication	**The SFSCA Quarterly**	Publication	**Crocker National Corporation Annual Report**
Art Director	**Kit Hinrichs**	Art Director	**Kit Hinrichs**
Designer	**Kit Hinrichs, Nancy Garrott**	Designer	**Kit Hinrichs, Lenore Bartz**
Illustrator	**Bruce Wolfe, Ward Schumaker**	Photographer	**John Blaustein**
Publisher	**The San Francisco Society of Communication Arts**	Publisher	**Crocker National Corporation**

118

119

120

121

122

Publication   **Fiberglas Canada, Inc., Annual Report**
Art Director   **Roslyn Eskind**
Designer   **Malcolm Waddell**
Photographer   **Rudi Christl, Freeman Paterson,**
               Wayne Barret, Sherman Hines,
               John de Visser, J.A. Krauls, Eberhard Otto,
               Karl Sliva, Michael Proux
Publisher   **Fiberglas Canada, Inc.**

123,124

Publication   **Class Edition**
Art Director   **Michael Richards**
Designer   **Michael Richards, Bill Swensen**
Illustrator   **Bill Swensen**
Publisher   **University of Utah Graphic Design Group**

122

123

124

125

Publication	Musician—Player & Listener
Art Director	Sam Holdsworth
Designer	Sam Holdsworth
Photographer	Deborah Feingold
Publisher	Billboard Publications, Inc.

126

Publication	Pittsburgh Magazine
Art Director	Dennis Ritchey
Photographer	John Lokmer
Publisher	Metropolitan Pittsburgh Public Broadcasting, Inc.

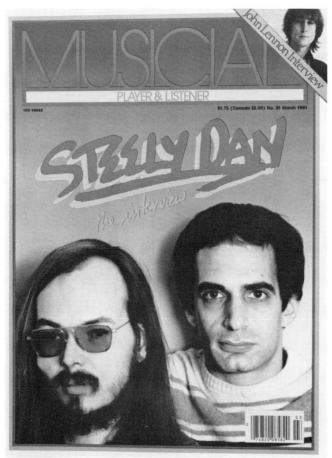

125

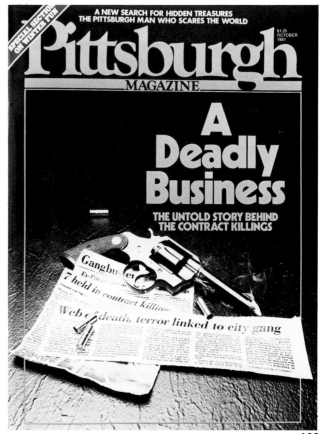

126

127

Publication **Newsweek**
Art Director **Bob Engle, Ron Meyerson**
Designer **Steve Phillips**
Photographer **George Hausman**
Publisher **Newsweek, Inc.**

128

Publication **Time**
Art Director **Rudolph Hoglund**
Illustrator **Jean Michel Folon**
Publisher **Time, Inc.**

127

128

129
Publication — **TV Guide**
Art Director — **Jerry Alten**
Designer — **Jerry Alten**
Illustrator — **David Wilcox**
Publisher — **Triangle Publications**

130
Publication — **Natural History**
Designer — **Tom Page**
Photographer — **Henri Bancaud**
Publisher — **American Museum of Natural History**

129

130

131
Publication **Express**
Art Director **Mika Kyprianides**
Designer **Vigon/Nahas**
Illustrator **Vigon/Nahas**
Publisher **East/West Network**

132
Publication **Fortune**
Art Director **Ron Campbell**
Publisher **Time, Inc.**

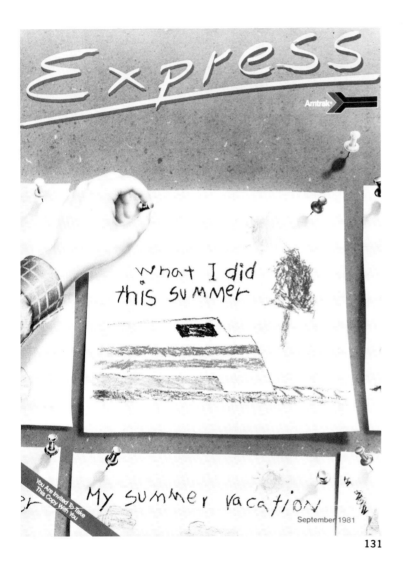

131

132

133
Publication **Chicago**
Art Director **Charles A. Thomas**
Designer **Charles A. Thomas**
Photographer **Tim Schultz**
Publisher **WFMT, Inc.**

134
Publication **Four Winds**
Art Director **Larry Smitherman**
Publisher **Smitherman Graphic Design**

133

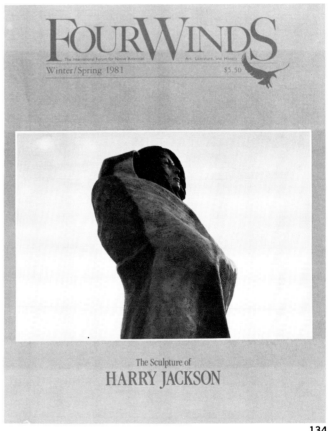

134

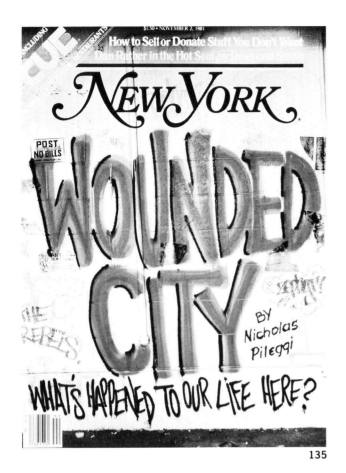

135

136

137

139

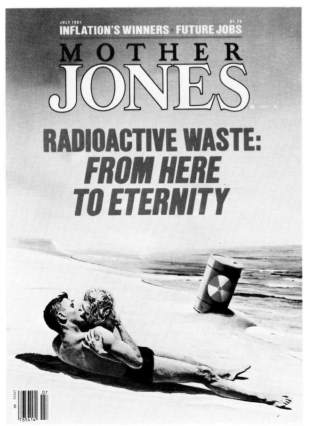

138

140

141

142

141
Publication | Interiors
Art Director | Paul Hardy
Photographer | Michael Datoli
Publisher | Billboard Publications, Inc.

142
Publication | Progressive Architecture
Art Director | George Coderre
Designer | George Coderre
Photographer | Deidi van Schaewen
Publisher | Reinhold Publishing

143
Publication   **Emergency Medicine**
Art Director   **Tom Lennon**
Designer   **Tom Lennon**
Illustrator   **Nick Aristovulos**
Photographer   **Shig Ikeda**
Publisher   **Fischer Medical Publications**

144
Publication   **Nikon World**
Art Director   **Thomas Schwartz**
Designer   **Thomas Schwartz**
Photographer   **Bruno Zehnder**
Publisher   **Nikon, Inc.**

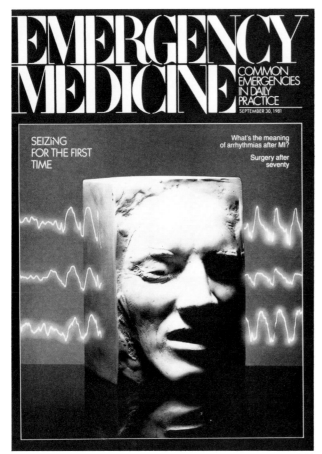

143

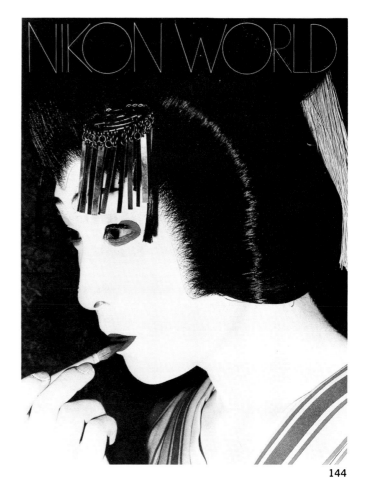

144

145
Publication   **Footwear News**
Art Director   **Traci Churchill**
Designer   **Ann Beckerman**
Photographer   **Anita Butensky, Brian Kosoff**
Publisher   **Fairchild Publications**

146
Publication   **Industrial Launderer**
Art Director   **Jack Lefkowitz**
Designer   **Jack Lefkowitz**
Illustrator   **Jack Lefkowitz**
Publisher   **Institute of Industrial Launderers**

145

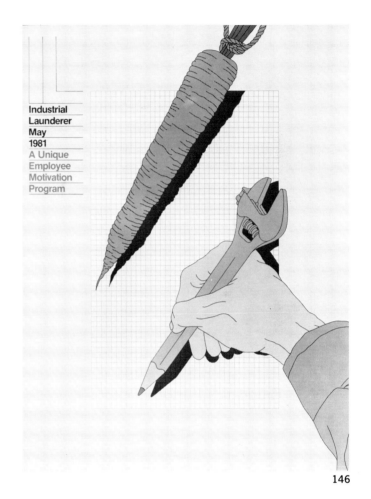

146

147
Publication **Student Lawyer**
Art Director **David N. Carothers**
Designer **David N. Carothers**
Photographer **Herbert Jackson**
Publisher **American Bar Association Press**

148
Publication **Progressive Grocer**
Art Director **Mitch Shostak**
Designer **Mitch Shostak**
Illustrator **Michael Kanarek**
Publisher **Maclean Hunter Media**

149
Publication **The Wharton Magazine**
Art Director **Mitch Shostak**
Designer **Mitch Shostak**
Illustrator **Mick McGinty**
Publisher **The University of Pennsylvania**

148

147

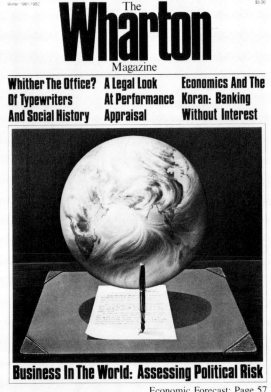

149

150

150
Publication   **Medical Economics**
Art Director   **William J. Kuhn**
Designer   **William J. Kuhn**
Illustrator   **Janice Conklin**
Photographer   **Stephen E. Munz**
Publisher   **Medical Economics
Company, Inc.**

151
Publication   **The Associates**
Art Director   **Robert Mynster**
Designer   **Robert Mynster**
Illustrator   **Tom Taber**
Photographer   **John Hines, Butch Hale**
Publisher   **The Associates Corporation
of North America**

152
Publication   **Nautical Quarterly**
Art Director   **B. Martin Pedersen**
Designer   **B. Martin Pedersen**
Photographer   **Jim Brown**
Publisher   **Jonson, Pedersen,
Hinrichs & Shakery, Inc.**

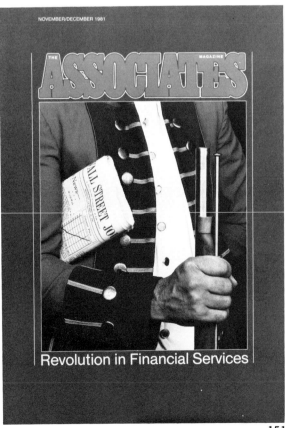

151

152

154

153

155

156
Publication **The New York Times Book Review**
Art Director **Steven Heller**
Designer **Steven Heller**
Illustrator **Seymour Chwast**
Publisher **The New York Times**

157
Publication **The New York Times Magazine**
Art Director **Ruth Ansel**
Designer **Michael Valenti**
Photographer **A.M. Rosenthal**
Publisher **The New York Times**

158
Publication **The Boston Globe Magazine**
Art Director **Ronn Campisi**
Designer **Ronn Campisi**
Illustrator **Jon McIntosh**
Publisher **The Boston Globe**

156

157

158

159
Publication   The Plain Dealer Magazine
Art Director Greg Paul
Illustrator   Victor Juhasz
Publisher   The Plain Dealer
              Publishing Company

160
Publication   Sportscape
Art Director John Kane
Designer   John Kane
Illustrator   Terry Swack
Publisher   Sportscape, Inc.

161
Publication   Raposa
Art Director Oswaldo Miranda
Designer   Oswaldo Miranda
Publisher   Fundacao Cultural
              de Curitaba

160

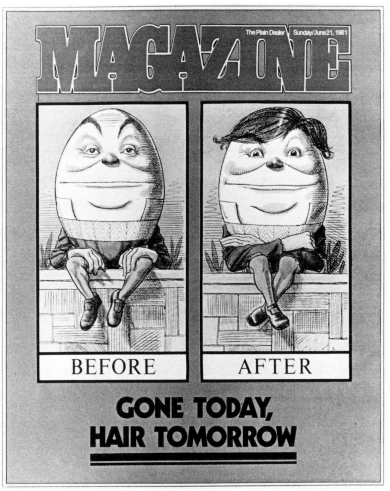

159

161

162
Publication **Cal Today**
Art Director **Howard Shintaku**
Designer **Howard Shintaku**
Illustrator **Charles Waller**
Publisher **San Jose Mercury News**

163
Publication **L.I. Magazine**
Art Director **Miriam Smith**
Designer **Miriam Smith**
Photographer **Ken Spencer**
Publisher **Newsday**

164
Publication **Raposa**
Art Director **Oswaldo Miranda**
Designer **Oswaldo Miranda**
Illustrator **Lew Myers**
Publisher **Fundacao Cultural
de Curitaba**

162

163

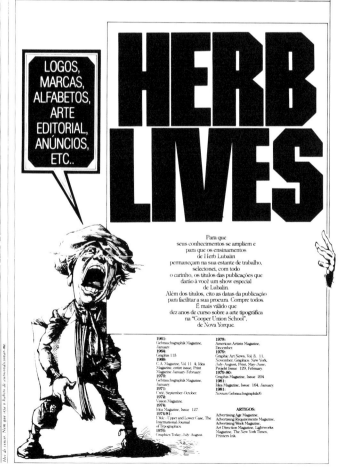

164

165

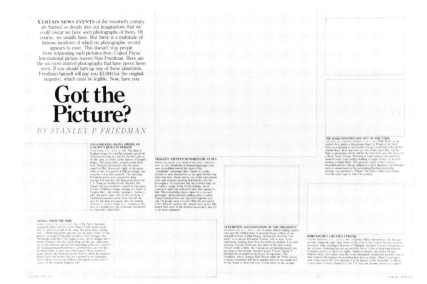

166

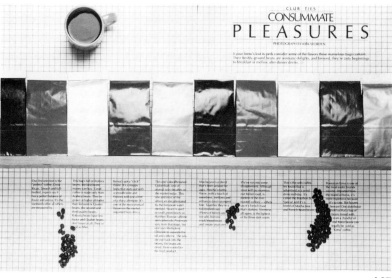

167

168

169

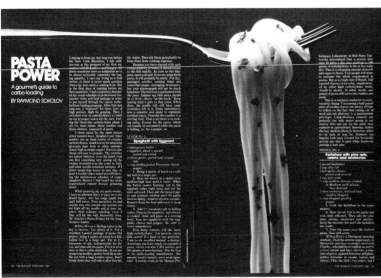

170

171

Publication **Town & Country**
Art Director **Melissa Tardiff**
Designer **Bridget DeSocio**
Photographer **Michel Tcherevkoff**
Publisher **The Hearst Corporation**

172

Publication **Town & Country**
Art Director **Melissa Tardiff**
Designer **Mary Rosen**
Photographer **Cy Gross**
Publisher **The Hearst Corporation**

After a hundred years—
it's back again and wonderful!

American Caviar
BY JAMES VILLAS

Golden caviar from the whitefish,
red from the salmon, and precious
black from the sturgeon—a salute
to American caviar. All, and the
very proper horn spoon, from New
York's Caviarteria. Mikasa plate.
Photograph by Michel Tcherevkoff

171

THE MYSTERIOUS GEM OF GASTRONOMY By James Villas

TRUFFLES

The fresh truffle, "the
underground precious,"
is exceedingly rare and
becoming rarer. Balsamic
and gnarled, earthy and
pungent, it's the most
exquisite delicacy in the
world. Knife: James II.

172

173,174
Publication **Cuisine**
Art Director **David J. Talbot**
Designer **Nina Ovryn**
Photographer **John Paul Endress**
Publisher **Cuisine Magazine, Inc.**

173

174

175

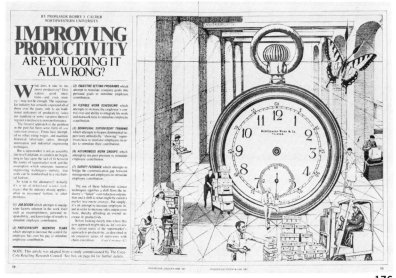

176

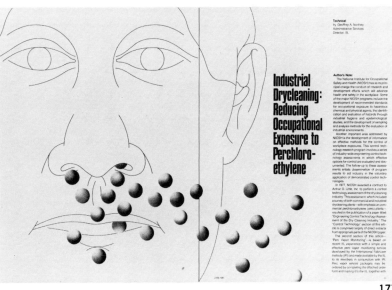

177

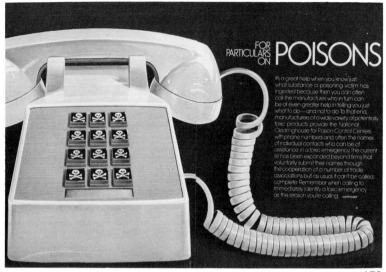

178

179

180

178

Publication   **Emergency Medicine**
Art Director   **Tom Lennon**
Designer   **Sara Rominek**
Illustrator   **Paul Blakey**
Publisher   **Fischer Medical Publications**

179

Publication   **Emergency Medicine**
Art Director   **Tom Lennon**
Designer   **Tom Lennon**
Illustrator   **Sonja Lamut,**
    Nenad Jakesavic
Publisher   **Fischer Medical Publications**

180

Publication   **Restaurant Design**
Art Director   **Jaye Medalia**
Designer   **Jaye Medalia**
Photographer   **Christopher Baker**
Publisher   **Bill Communications**

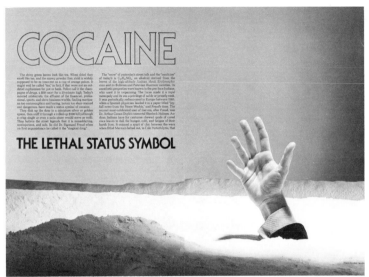

181

182

183

181

Publication	**MD**
Art Director	**Al Foti**
Designer	**Al Foti**
Photographer	**Joel Gordon**
Publisher	**MD Publications, Inc.**

182

Publication	**MD**
Art Director	**Al Foti**
Designer	**Al Foti**
Photographer	**The Cowboy Artist of America**
Publisher	**MD Publications, Inc.**

183

Publication	**Medical Economics**
Art Director	**Barbara Groenteman**
Designer	**John Newcomb**
Illustrator	**Janice Conklin**
Photographer	**Stephen E. Munz**
Publisher	**Medical Economics Company, Inc.**

184

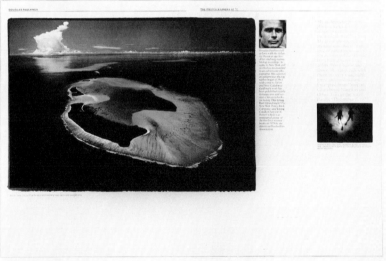

185

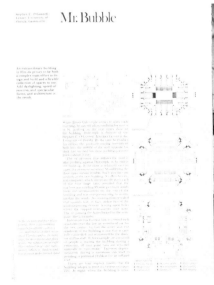

186

	184
Publication	**Nikon World**
Art Director	**Tom Schwartz**
Designer	**Tom Schwartz**
Photographer	**John Shaw**
Publisher	**Nikon, Inc.**

	185
Publication	**Nikon World**
Art Director	**Tom Schwartz**
Designer	**Tom Schwartz**
Photographer	**Douglas Faulkner**
Publisher	**Nikon, Inc.**

	186
Publication	**Progressive Architecture**
Art Director	**George Coderre**
Photographer	**Balthazar Korab**
Publisher	**Reinhold Publishing**

187
Publication — **Medical Laboratory Observer**
Art Director — **Thomas Darnsteadt**
Designer — **John Newcomb**
Illustrator — **Janice Conklin**
Photographer — **Stephen E. Munz**
Publisher — **Medical Economics Company, Inc.**

188
Publication — **Raposa**
Art Director — **Oswaldo Miranda**
Designer — **Oswaldo Miranda**
Illustrator — **Oswaldo Miranda**
Publisher — **Fundacao Cultural de Curitiba**

187

188

	189		**190**		**191**
Publication	**Nameless—Art Directors Club of Indiana**	Publication	**The Plain Dealer Magazine**	Publication	**Nautical Quarterly**
Art Director	**David Walters**	Art Director	**Greg Paul**	Art Director	**B. Martin Pedersen**
Designer	**David Walters**	Illustrator	**Brad Holland**	Designer	**B. Martin Pedersen**
Illustrator	**David Young**	Publisher	**The Plain Dealer Publishing Company**	Photographer	**Alan Weitz**
Publisher	**Shohet/Walters Design Group**			Publisher	**Jonson, Pedersen, Hinrichs & Shakery, Inc.**

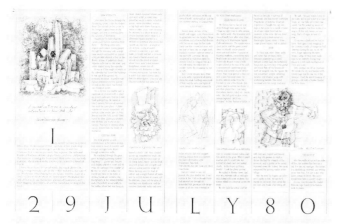

189

190

191

192

Publication — **The Washington Post/Arts & Entertainment**
Art Director — **Robert Barkin**
Designer — **Alice M. Kresse**
Illustrator — **Alice M. Kresse**
Publisher — **The Washington Post Company**

193

Publication — **The New York Times/Op-Ed**
Art Director — **Jerelle Kraus**
Designer — **Jerelle Kraus**
Illustrator — **David Suter**
Publisher — **The New York Times**

194

Publication — **The Plain Dealer Magazine**
Art Director — **Greg Paul**
Illustrator — **Bob Brown**
Publisher — **The Plain Dealer Publishing Company**

192

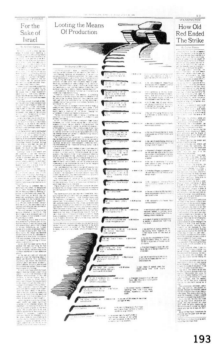

193

194

195

Publication **Raposa**
Art Director **Oswaldo Miranda**
Designer **Oswaldo Miranda**
Illustrator **Saul Steinberg**
Publisher **Fundacao Cultural de Curitaba**

196

Publication **The Boston Globe Magazine**
Art Director **Ronn Campisi**
Designer **Ronn Campisi**
Illustrator **Andrzej Dudzinski**
Publisher **The Boston Globe**

195

WHO WRITES THE BOOKS OF LOVE?

By Jill Bloom Mooradian

She descended the staircase to the ballroom, her heart thumping against the white eyelet of her summer dress. One hand clutched the banister, the other clung tightly to the package of promotional material printed with elegant flourishes on glossy paper. Both palms were damp.

For a moment, the sea of faces below her made her want to turn and run back up to her hotel room. What was she, an unassuming writer from Cambridge with a 2-year-old daughter and a thirty-year mortgage, doing at a gathering like this? What perverse curiosity had impelled her to venture into the hinterlands to search for

196

249

197,198

Publication **Texas Monthly**
Art Director **Jim Darilek**
Designer **Jim Darilek**
Photographer **George Oliver**
Publisher **Mediatex Communications Corporation**

197

198

199,200
Publication **McCall's**
Art Director **Alvin Grossman**
Designer **Alvin Grossman**
Photographer **Roger Prigent**
Publisher **The McCall Publishing Company**

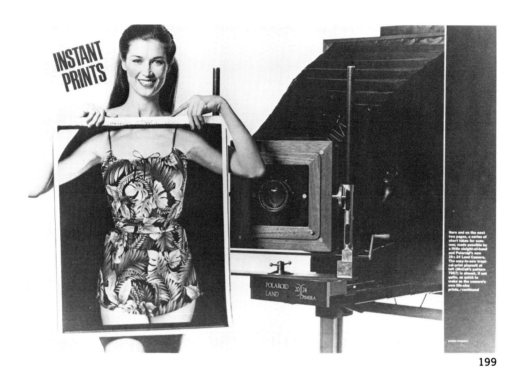

199

200

201
Publication **Esquire**
Art Director **Robert Priest**
Designer **April Silver**
Publisher **Esquire Publishing**

202
Publication **Town & Country**
Art Director **Melissa Tardiff**
Designer **Bridget DeSocio**
Photographer **Cy Gross**
Publisher **The Hearst Corporation**

201

202

203,204
Publication **Geo**
Art Director **Greg Leeds**
Designer **Greg Leeds**
Publisher **Knapp Communications, Inc.**

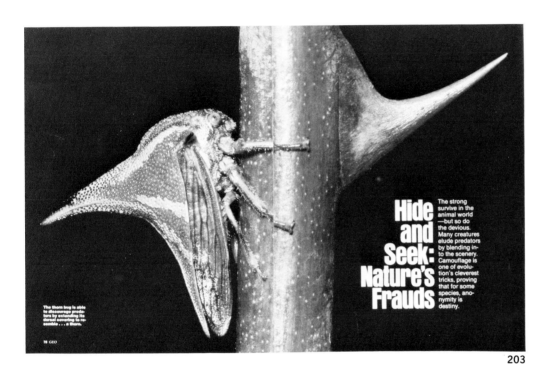

The thorn bug is able to discourage predators by extending its dorsal covering to resemble . . . a thorn.

Hide and Seek: Nature's Frauds

The strong survive in the animal world —but so do the devious. Many creatures elude predators by blending into the scenery. Camouflage is one of evolution's cleverest tricks, proving that for some species, anonymity is destiny.

78 GEO

203

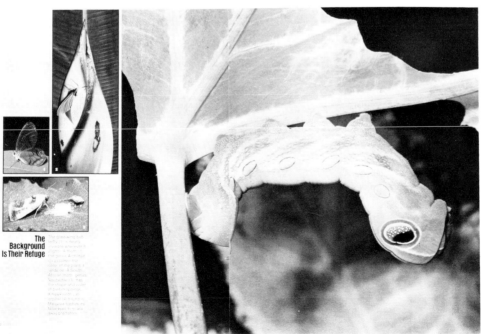

The Background Is Their Refuge

204

205,206

Publication   **Musician—Player and Listener**
Art Director   **Sam Holdsworth**
Designer   **Sam Holdsworth**
Photographer   **Allan Tannenbaum**
Publisher   **Billboard Publications, Inc.**

205

206

207

208

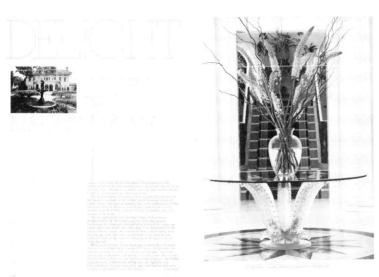

209

207,208
Publication   **Harper's Bazaar**
Art Director   **Robert Flora**
Designer   **Robert Flora**
Photographer   **Deborah Turbeville,
Sharon Schuster**
Publisher   **The Hearst
Corporation**

209
Publication   **House & Garden**
Art Director   **Lloyd Ziff**
Designer   **Lloyd Ziff**
Photographer   **Karen Radkai,
Edward Oleksak,
David Massey**
Publisher   **Conde Nast
Publications, Inc.**

210,211

Publication   **Restaurants & Institutions**
Art Director   **Queenie Burns**
Designer   **Queenie Burns**
Photographer   **Bob Vuksanovich**
Publisher   **Cahners Publishing Company**

'400' SALES CLIMB 10.7% TO $61.8 BILLION

The uncertain conditions that shaped all business in 1980 also threatened to shake the "400's" confidence. Higher inflation rates, lower discretionary incomes and reduced customer counts cut into the notion that foodservice is "counter-cyclical," and reminded the "400" that automatic real growth is not necessarily a God-given right. To be sure, there were bright spots. But most remained on the horizon as the "400" struggled to put the woes of 1980 behind and move briskly into the future.

17th ANNUAL'400' ISSUE
REPORT I

210

INCREASED PROFITS AND CREATIVITY FOR MASTER FILE '500'

If rising profits and productivity are measures of success, 1980 was not a bad year for the 500 operators of million-dollar units in all industry segments who make up the *Restaurants & Institutions* Master File.

More than 50% of the restaurateurs in this year's compilation of individual-unit operators reported an increase in after-tax profits. In Florida and Texas, several operators reported increases in excess of 100%, even after adjustment for 1980's 9.9% inflation rate.

Among noncommercial operators, productivity was a topic of increased interest, although many Master File institutions put out twice as many meals per employee per day as even the most efficient fast-food operations. Hospitals and colleges lead the nation in automation and streamlining food preparation and delivery techniques.

For the individual operator, however, fine tuning for the future is just as crucial and constant an activity as monitoring current sales. Here, too, the Master File "500" measure up.

A spaghetti bar, an in-house bakery, a solar hot-water heater and programs for increased employee involvement in the decision-making process are among the innovations this year's Master File operators instituted to ensure profitability and productivity in the years to come.

211

1981 HFBL WINNERS

Just about every type of housing is represented among the 20 First-Honor and Award-of-Merit winners in this year's Homes for Better Living program. There are, for example, tightly sited urban infill projects, units that step up and down steep hillsides, homes, and apartments recycled from non-res structures, sprawling and moderate-size custom homes and remodelings.

Having so diversified a group of winners exemplifies the growth of the HFBL program since its inception 26 years ago. Then, production housing as we know it today was in its infancy—and only one-of-a-kind homes were accepted for judging. Now it takes two juries*—one devoted to production housing, the other to custom homes—to select winners. Site of the two-day judging is the Washington, D.C. headquarters of the American Institute of Architects, which co-sponsors the program with HOUSING. —JUNE R. VOLLMAN and BARBARA BEHRENS GERS

* Production-housing jury: Howard J. Barker AIA, chairman; James F. Culpepper, associate member, AIA; Remert Huygens AIA; Yvonne Kearney, architectural student; Peter Sampton FAIA; Philip Sheridan, builder; June R. Vollman, senior editor, HOUSING. Custom-home jury: Don Hisaka AIA, chairman; John Field AIA; Barbara Neski FAIA; Linda A. Pinto, associate member AIA; Matthew Eric Poe, architectural student; Jefferson Riley AIA; Walter F. Wagner, editor, Architectural Record.

58
Eight varied multifamily winners: for-sale housing on tight or steep sites; rental units for the elderly; an urban mixed-use project.

64
Eight custom winners are drawn from the East, Midwest, South, and West. Included: six new homes, a restoration and a remodeling.

70
Four rehabilitations—all recyclings from non-res—provide for-sale and rental units. Locations: New York, Pennsylvania, Maine, Illinois.

212,213
Publication **Housing**
Art Director **Joseph Davis**
Designer **Joseph Davis**
Illustrator **Dyke Fledderus**
Publisher **McGraw Hill**

212

MULTIFAMILY

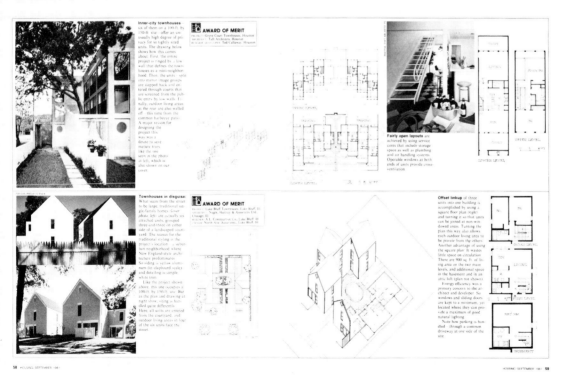

213

257

214,215

Publication **Progressive Architecture**
Art Director **George Coderre**
Designer **George Coderre**
Photographer **Cervin Robinson**
Publisher **Reinhold Publishing**

Americana Hotel,
Ft. Worth, Tx.

Nature's way

In some rooms at the new Americana Hotel in Ft. Worth, motifs from nature became the design inspiration.

When Benjamin Baldwin was commissioned to do the interiors for the new Americana Hotel designed by SD/international in Ft. Worth, Tx, he asked Roger Ferri to join the design team, which also included assistant Jonathan Warwick. The reasons Ferri was asked were that the job was too big, given the time constraints, for Baldwin and his assistant alone, and also because Baldwin had seen, and been impressed by, Ferri's exhibit of a hypothetical "Pedestrian City" at New York's Museum of Modern Art in 1978.

The responsibilities for the hotel's interior were divided up, but the three worked together as a team in constant consultation with each other throughout the entire design process. Consequently, it is not possible to say that any one person was totally responsible for any particular part of the design. However, Baldwin and his assistant were primarily responsible for all guest rooms, the coffee shop, a lounge, and the furniture and fabrics for the two main lobbies. These are done in the impeccable and refined style that has now become his well-known hallmark. Ferri took charge of the architectural redesign of the main lobbies, the design of the meeting rooms and Junior Ballroom, and the other portions shown here, the Main Ballroom and its prefunction area, and the gourmet restaurant.

A combination of three interests makes Ferri somewhat unique among that group of young designers now considered to be in the avant-garde. Whereas he makes considerable use of applied decoration, he never uses it simply for its own sake or for the sake of form alone. Rather, the design is always related psychologically or symbolically to the use of the space to the people who will be in it. The design inspiration always comes, sometimes quite directly, from motifs found in nature. To carry out these ideas physically, Ferri has developed an intense interest in the crafts of decorative arts, including mosaics, tapestry weaving and dying, plaster and metalwork, and upholstery, all of which are represented at the Americana Hotel.

Prefunction area

The main focus of the ballroom lobby, or prefunction area as it is now called, is a series of three identical wool tapestries, each measuring 30' x 20', and illuminated from above by wells of natural light. Ferri's design for these is based on turbulence patterns, such as found in air or water masses in nature. Besides their purely decorative function of enlivening large expanses of wall space, their purpose in the lobby is also to establish an iconographic link to or "anticipation" of the

For the ballroom prefunction area, Roger Ferri designed three huge tapestries that were woven at the V'Soske mills in Puerto Rico. The design of these hangings was inspired by turbulence patterns found in nature, as when different air or water masses meet each other. Natural motifs are also used in other parts of the hotel, as shown on the following pages.

Progressive Architecture 9:81

184

Americana Hotel,
Ft. Worth, Tx.

The turbulence pattern introduced in the prefunction area is repeated inside the main ballroom (these pages), but in a more formalized manner. The scheme fits both the suspended acoustical ceiling and the upholstered walls. (Drawings above) was worked out on a 2-ft planning grid.

same theme found inside the ballroom, where it is interpreted in a much less naturalistic manner.

The ballroom

Because, as Ferri explains it, the ballroom is the setting for dance—for the rhythmic pattern of body movement in space—rhythmic patterns in nature became the departure point for an architectural design to subtle but constant harmonic motion. Inside the ballroom, the turbulence patterns of the lobby tapestries become highly formalized and ordered. Here, the design is worked out through a 2' x 2' planning grid in which the curves are rotated and flipped in relation to each other to achieve an unusual richness and complexity for the ceiling and walls. The ceiling is a deep grille of free-floating acoustic baffles that swirl around suspended light fixtures. Their undersides, Ferri explains, are cut to trochoid curves in the mathematical equation of ocean waves to suggest a sea in motion.

The ballroom can be divided into four distinct rooms, and to maintain the integrity of the space in any configuration, both the permanent and movable walls have been given the same treatment. The pattern of curves seen in the ceiling is here extended, but still planned on a 2-ft module, to form a three-tiered "screen" around the room from light tones at the bottom to dark tones where it meets the ceiling. The walls are padded, or upholstered, and white piping and roundels outline the design motif. At the entries, the pattern becomes three-dimensional and is formed into graceful, scalloped plaster frames around the doorways. The richness of all of these elements together compensates for the neutral tones, which are surely unusual for a ballroom. The absence of color, however, was the clients wish; they wanted the guests to bring their own colors into the room.

Gourmet restaurant

Like the other rooms, the gourmet restaurant (page 186) also uses motifs from nature as a basis for design, but in this case the refer-

ences are to botanical forms. In this respect, the restaurant represents a continuation of ideas Ferri had been developing earlier, as seen in the drawings for the MoMA show (page 186) and in those for the dining room of Lutèce restaurant in New York in 1976 (not shown). This space differs from those, however, in that the architect had to deal with some existing massive columns that could not be radically altered. Ferri turned these into huge lotus forms, but as the MoMA drawings show, they are not characteristic of the more lyrical quality of his other work.

The lotus columns rise from or next to a shallow reflecting pool surfaced in colored glass mosaic. Around this, small floor areas rise in terraces to create intimate dining spaces that seem to have been placed in a private little amphitheatre. Thus, the sense of theatricality—of entering and leaving, of seeing and being seen—is heightened while at the same time the sense of intimacy is maintained.

The end columns, treated as budding flowers, support a dark, low ceiling, but the central column rising out of the pool becomes a full blossom whose six petals extend to support a hexagonal trellis system above. Beyond this rises a higher, illusional night sky. Ferri says the room, which is called "Reflections," is a fictive outdoor room, which utilizes water, masonry, and trellises to both domesticate a benign climate for outdoor living.

Roger Ferri probably could not be considered part of today's group of Post-Modernists mainly because his design inspiration does not come from architecture itself or from historical allusion to it. He is like them, though, in showing considerable interest in the use of decorative elements. But both his decoration

Progressive Architecture 9:81

186

216,217

Publication **Nautical Quarterly**
Art Director **B. Martin Pedersen**
Designer **B. Martin Pedersen**
Photographer **Andrew Unangst**
Publisher **Jonson, Pedersen, Hinrichs & Shakery, Inc.**

GEAR

BY PETER SPECTRE

216

217

218,219

Publication **American Heritage Magazine**
Art Director **Murray Belsky**
Designer **Beth Whitaker**
Illustrator **Nick Fasciano**
Publisher **American Heritage Publishing Company, Inc.**

218

219

220

221

222

223–225

Publication   **The New York Times Magazine Section**

Art Director   **Ruth Ansel**

Designer   **Diana LaGuardia**

Publisher   **The New York Times**

223

224

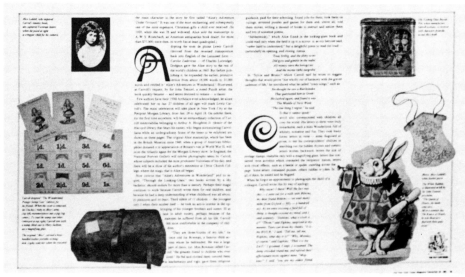

226

227

226

Publication	**Life**
Art Director	**Bob Ciano**
Designer	**Mary Kate Baumann**
Photographer	**Harald Sund**
Publisher	**Time, Inc.**

227

Publication	**Life**
Art Director	**Bob Ciano**
Designer	**Carla Barr**
Photographer	**Terry O'Neill**
Publisher	**Time, Inc.**

228

Publication	**Life**
Art Director	**Bob Ciano**
Designer	**Bob Ciano**
Photographer	**Stephen Green-Armitage**
Publisher	**Time, Inc.**

228

229

Publication — **The Dial**
Art Director — **Susan Reinhardt**
Designer — **Susan Reinhardt**
Illustrator — **R.O. Blechman**
Publisher — **Public Broadcasting Communications, Inc.**

230

Publication — **Newsweek**
Art Director — **Bob Engle, Ron Meyerson**
Designer — **Steve Phillips**
Illustrator — **Marvin Mattelson**
Publisher — **Newsweek, Inc.**

229

230

231

Publication	TV Guide
Art Director	Jerry Alten
Designer	Jerry Alten
Illustrator	Richard Hess
Publisher	Triangle Publications

232

Publication	Science Digest
Art Director	Mary Zisk
Design Director	Frank Rothmann
Designer	Frank Rothmann, Mary Zisk
Illustrator	Alex Ebel
Publisher	Hearst Magazines

233

Publication	National Lampoon
Art Director	Skip Johnson
Designer	Skip Johnson
Illustrator	Kinuko Craft
Publisher	NL Communications, Inc.

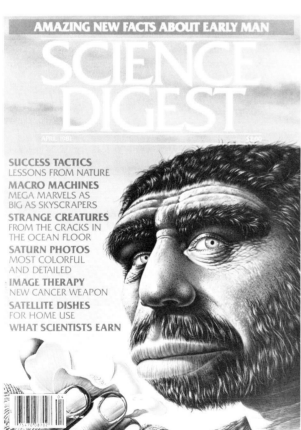

232

233

234
Publication **The Atlantic Monthly**
Art Director **Judy Garlan**
Designer **Judy Garlan**
Illustrator **Andre Francois**
Publisher **The Atlantic Monthly Company**

235
Publication **Ambassador**
Art Director **Alfred Zelcer**
Designer **Mark Simonson**
Illustrator **Kinuko Craft**
Publisher **The Webb Company**

234

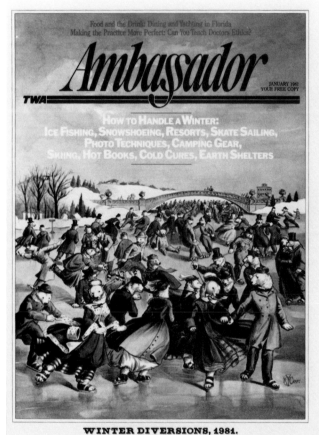

235

236

Publication   **Psychology Today**
Art Director   **Carveth Kramer**
Designer   **Carveth Kramer**
Illustrator   **Jean-Francois Allaux**
Publisher   **Ziff-Davis Publishing Company**

237

Publication   **New York Magazine**
Art Director   **Robert Best**
Designer   **Patricia Bradbury, Don Morris**
Illustrator   **Richard Sparks**
Publisher   **News Group Publications**

236

237

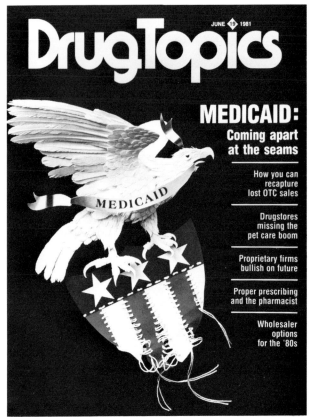

239

238

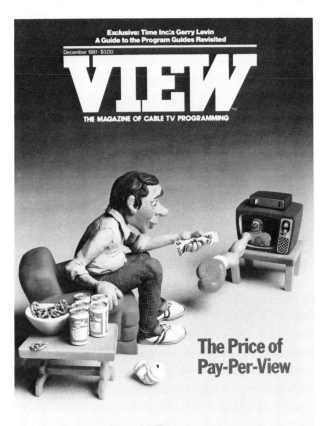

240

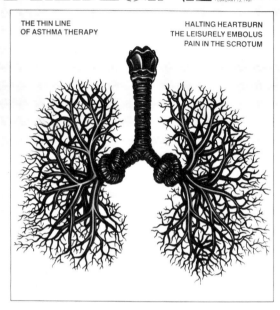

241

Publication   **Emergency Medicine**
Art Director   **Tom Lennon**
Designer   **James T. Walsh**
Illustrator   **Houik Dilakian**
Publisher   **Fischer Medical Publications**

242

Publication   **Food Management**
Art Director   **Donna L. Boss**
Designer   **Andrew Ross**
Illustrator   **Judy Clifford**
Publisher   **Harcourt Brace Jovanovich**

241

242

243
Publication   **American Bar Association Journal**
Art Director   **David Jendras**
Illustrator   **Chuck Slack**
Publisher   **American Bar Association**

244
Publication   **The Plain Dealer Magazine**
Art Director   **Greg Paul**
Illustrator   **Daniel Maffia**
Publisher   **The Plain Dealer Publishing Company**

243

244

245
Publication   **Monthly Detroit**
Art Director   **Eric Keller**
Designer   **Eric Keller**
Illustrator   **John Benson**
Publisher   **City Magazines, Inc.**

246
Publication   **Chicago**
Art Director   **Charles A. Thomas**
Designer   **Charles A. Thomas**
Illustrator   **John Zielinski**
Publisher   **WFMT, Inc.**

245

*The competition is fierce, and the faces change every week.
Courtesy is important. But the tour is definitely not a sorority.*

246

247
Publication **Playboy**
Art Director **Tom Staebler**
Designer **Bob Post**
Illustrator **Parviz Sadighian**
Publisher **Playboy Enterprises, Inc.**

248
Publication **Playboy**
Art Director **Tom Staebler**
Designer **Bruce Hansen**
Illustrator **Martin Hoffman**
Publisher **Playboy Enterprises, Inc.**

247

248

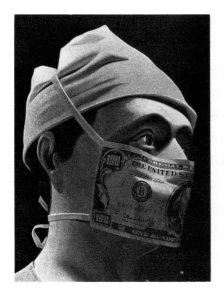

249

250

251

252
Publication **Time**
Art Director **Rudolph Hoglund**
Designer **Rudolph Hoglund**
Illustrator **Robert Grossman**
Publisher **Time, Inc.**

253
Publication **Best of Business**
Art Director **Shelley Williams**
Designer **Ken Smith**
Illustrator **John Cayea**
Publisher **13-30 Corporation**

254
Publication **Esquire**
Art Director **Robert Priest**
Designer **Ellen Rongstad**
Illustrator **Teresa Fasolino**
Publisher **Esquire Publishing**

252

253

254

255

Publication **Science Digest**
Art Director **Mary Zisk**
Design Director **Frank Rothmann**
Designer **Frank Rothmann**
Illustrator **Braldt Bralds**
Publisher **Hearst Magazines**

256

Publication **McCall's Working Mother**
Art Director **Nina Scerbo**
Illustrator **Brian Ajhar**
Publisher **McCall's Publishing Company**

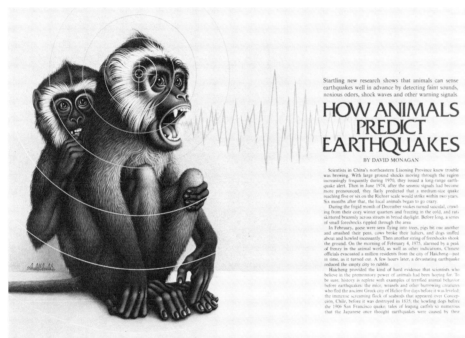

Startling new research shows that animals can sense earthquakes well in advance by detecting faint sounds, noxious odors, shock waves and other warning signals.

HOW ANIMALS PREDICT EARTHQUAKES

BY DAVID MONAGAN

Scientists in China's northeastern Liaoning Province knew trouble was brewing. With large ground shocks moving through the region increasingly frequently during 1970, they issued a long-range earthquake alert. Then in June 1974, after the seismic signals had become more pronounced, they flatly predicted that a medium-size quake reaching five or six on the Richter scale would strike within two years. Six months after that, the local animals began to go crazy.

During the frigid month of December snakes turned suicidal, crawling from their cozy winter quarters and freezing in the cold, and rats skittered brazenly across streets in broad daylight. Before long, a series of small foreshocks rippled through the area.

In February, geese were seen flying into trees, pigs bit one another and smashed their pens, cows broke their halters, and dogs sniffed about and howled incessantly. Then another string of foreshocks shook the ground. On the morning of February 4, 1975, alarmed by a peak of frenzy in the animal world, as well as other indications, Chinese officials evacuated a million residents from the city of Haicheng—just in time, as it turned out. A few hours later, a devastating earthquake reduced the empty city to rubble.

Haicheng provided the kind of hard evidence that scientists who believe in the premonitory power of animals had been hoping for. To be sure, history is replete with examples of terrified animal behavior before earthquakes: the mice, weasels and other burrowing creatures who fled the ancient Greek city of Helice five days before it was leveled; the immense screaming flock of seabirds that appeared over Concepción, Chile, before it was destroyed in 1835; the howling dogs before the 1906 San Francisco quake; tales of leaping catfish so numerous that the Japanese once thought earthquakes were caused by their

255

"Where is the pain, Mrs. Mundis?"

"In the neck, Doctor"

BY HESTER MUNDIS

There are more misconceptions about doctors than there are about the gross national product, yogurt or the mating habits of Sumi wrestlers. For instance, most people are completely unaware of it, but the worst time to try to see a doctor is when you're ill. If you need a checkup for a job or insurance purposes, or your kid needs a routine lookover for camp, there's no difficulty. The nurse is pleasant and courteous, delighted to fit you in at a convenient time on a mutually agreeable day ("Of course, Mrs. Mundis. Would you prefer Monday or Tuesday? Morning or afternoon?"). This is because nurses, not unlike pilots, plumbers and politicians, find it easy to be pleasant and courteous when they don't have to face a problem. But just say that you have a pain in your left side and

256

257

Publication — **Mother Jones**
Art Director — **Louise Kollenbaum**
Designer — **Dian-Aziza Ooka**
Illustrator — **Braldt Bralds**
Publisher — **Foundation for National Progress**

258

Publication — **The Atlantic Monthly**
Art Director — **Judy Garlan**
Designer — **Judy Garlan**
Illustrator — **Guy Billout**
Publisher — **The Atlantic Monthly Company**

The Crucifixion Of Evolution

What Your Kids Will Be Unlearning This Fall

By Frank Viviano

Illustration by Braldt Bralds

257

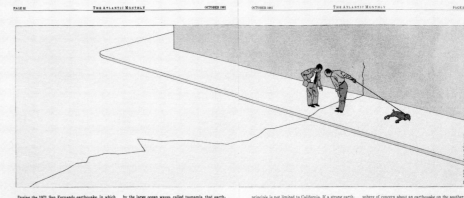

258

259

Publication **Science Digest**
Art Director **Mary Zisk**
Design Director **Frank Rothmann**
Designer **Mary Zisk, Nancy Oatts**
Illustrator **Thomas Leonard**
Publisher **Hearst Magazines**

260

Publication **McCall's**
Art Director **Alvin Grossman**
Designer **Alvin Grossman**
Illustrator **Robert Giusti**
Publisher **The McCall's Publishing Company**

THE
POWER
OF THE
EMPTY PILL

BY LAURENCE CHERRY

The mysterious placebo, long scorned, is now having a rebirth. Doctors know it can alter heart rates, heal ulcers, even eliminate psychiatric symptoms. They are now exploring the relation between the placebo and the brain's chemistry.

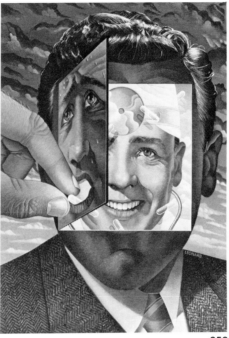

259

The cow with the come-hither look

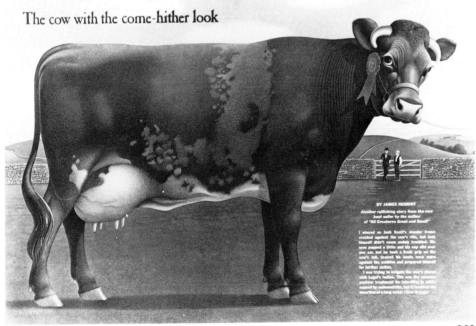

260

261
Publication **Florida Trend**
Art Director **Steve Duckett**
Designer **Steve Duckett**
Photographer **Richard Riley**
Publisher **Florida Trend, Inc.**

262
Publication **Emergency Medicine**
Art Director **Tom Lennon**
Designer **James T. Walsh**
Illustrator **Roger Roth**
Publisher **Fischer Medical Publications**

263
Publication **Emergency Medicine**
Art Director **Tom Lennon**
Designer **James T. Walsh**
Illustrator **Joan Hall**
Publisher **Fischer Medical Publications**

261

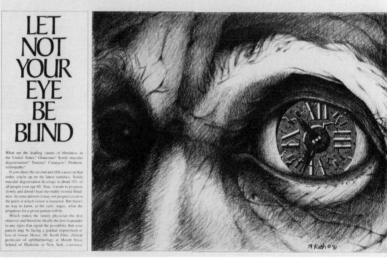

262

263

FREE ENTERPRISE AND THE GHETTO FAMILY
BY JAGNA WOJCICKA SHARFF

For Hispanics on New York's Lower East Side, the large family is an insurance policy against poverty, a weapon for self-defense, an investment portfolio for the future. An anthropological team studied how family members develop the specialized roles most useful for survival—including street representative, child-reproducer, and scholar/advocate.

264

The firm's attitude toward innovation is essentially passive, because it is effectively a ward of its ministry.

265

Managing The Arts

It's a lot like other kinds of management, according to New York City's commissioner of cultural affairs. He recommends command unity, intelligent marketing, and a clear sense of goals.

266

264

Publication   **Psychology Today**
Art Director   **Carveth Kramer**
Designer   **Carveth Kramer**
Illustrator   **Burt Silverman**
Publisher   **Ziff-Davis Publishing Company**

265

Publication   **The Wharton Magazine**
Art Director   **Mitch Shostak**
Designer   **Mitch Shostak**
Illustrator   **David Pelavin**
Publisher   **The University of Pennsylvania**

266

Publication   **The Wharton Magazine**
Art Director   **Mitch Shostak**
Designer   **Mitch Shostak**
Illustrator   **David Hockney**
Publisher   **The University of Pennsylvania**

267
Publication **Diagnostic Medicine**
Art Director **Cristine Hafner**
Designer **Cristine Hafner**
Illustrator **Alan E. Cober**
Publisher **Medical Economics Company, Inc.**

268
Publication **Postgraduate Medicine**
Art Director **Tina Adamek**
Designer **Tina Adamek**
Illustrator **Geoffrey Moss**
Publisher **McGraw-Hill, Inc.**

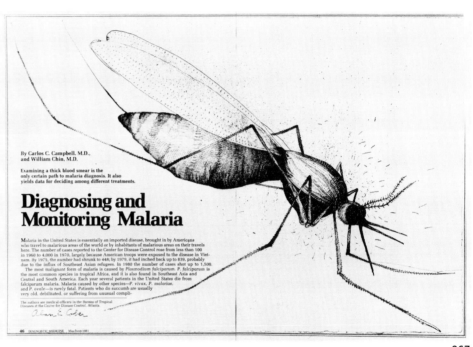

267

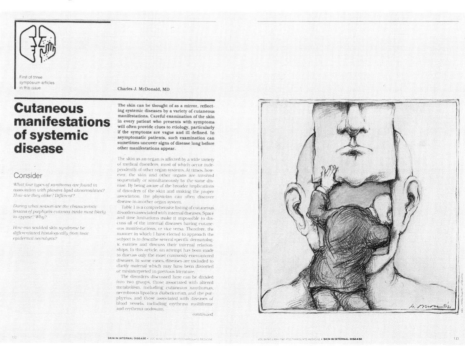

268

	269			**270**
Publication	Animal Kingdom		Publication	Patient Care
Art Director	Brigid Quinn		Art Director	Elizabeth R. Cash
Designer	Brigid Quinn		Designer	Suzanne Winchell, Robert Glaser
Illustrator	Geoffrey Moss, Jim O'Connell, Salvatore Catalano,		Illustrator	Paul J. Singh-Roy
Photographer	Jen & Des Bartlett, Georg Gerster, Masud Quraishy		Publisher	Patient Care Communications, Inc.
Publisher	The New York Zoological Society			

271

Publication	Quest
Art Director	Noel Werrett
Illustrator	Ken Dallison
Publisher	Ambassador International Foundation

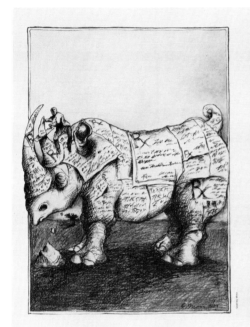

269

270

271

272
Publication **The Plain Dealer Magazine**
Art Director **Greg Paul**
Designer **Sam Capuano**
Illustrator **Linda Crockett-Hanzel**
Publisher **The Plain Dealer Publishing Company**

273
Publication **The New York Times Book Review**
Art Director **Steven Heller**
Designer **Steven Heller**
Illustrator **Elliott Banfield**
Publisher **The New York Times**

A Ringside Seat for Life

*Normand Poirier was a newspaperman because he
loved the business. And he was a drinker because he had
so much murder and violence in his head that
he was afraid to sleep with the lights out.*

BY PETE HAMILL

One humid summer night long ago, a man named Normand Poirier walked into the city room of the old New York Post to try out for a job as a rewrite man. That same night, I began my own career as a newspaperman. We formed the instant bond of new arrivals, and when the shift ended at 8 in the morning, we retired to a local saloon called the Page One.

There, as the beer trucks made their deliveries, and the stockbrokers belted down morning martinis as protection against the day, my truest education started. Normand Poirier was one of the principal instructors.

"You never worked in a newspaper before?" he said, his gray, pouched face taking on color with the first brandy. "Really? Well, listen: You'll learn it. It's not so hard. Never use a long word if you can use a short word. Never use two words of one will do.

"Remember that every story has a beginning, a middle and an end, even if it's three paragraphs long. Just don't leave the important stuff for the end, or some printer will chop it off on the stone in the composing room. Bartender? Hit us again here, will you?"

The routine started that way, and lasted all summer. We would work through the night, in the old Post building across the street from the United Fruit Co. piers; there was no air conditioning, and fruit flies arrived through the open windows in dense swarms.

We would type and smack, type and smack, and then, finished for the night, the paper locked up, the stories all gone, we'd head for the Page One.

"You're the eyes and ears of the reader, not the brain," Poirier would say. "See, hear, don't think."

Others joined us: boomers from the Midwest, trying out one last shot on a New York paper; reformed drunks sipping ginger ale; copy boys, divorced guys — the infantry of the newspaper business.

The printers would bring in the first edition, and Poirier would sit on a stool, his legs crossed, pushing back his tortoise-rimmed glasses, and analyze all of the stories in the paper. There were seven newspapers in New York then, and after a while someone would show up with the competition, and there would be more analysis.

All of us who were on summer trial were convinced that we were a hell of a lot better than the people who had the permanent jobs and in some cases, we were right. Late in the morning we would move on, emerging into the plump largess of the New York summer, heading uptown to the Village.

Through all of this, Poirier revealed very little of himself. I knew he was from Worcester, Mass., had worked on newspapers in New England, and then done a long stint at the Pottstown (Pa.) Mercury.

He was living at the seedy Hotel Earle; there might once have been a wife; certainly there was a chubby barmaid at a joint called the Jericho. Nobody pressed him about his past. He would talk about women, and the smoke-colored eyes would brighten, but there was also a strange note of grieving about him, even then, two decades ago.

We knew only one thing with absolute certainty: He was a professional. And about newspapers, he was a thorough romantic.

"You've got a ringside seat for life," he said to me one booze-hazy morning. "Don't blow it."

The summer faded. We were both hired. I plunged into the great dangerous city, chasing fires and homicides and robberies, learning the craft of the newspaper trade; Normand became one of the horses of the rewrite staff, writing concocted features, hard news, obits, captions for photographs.

I changed shifts, going "on the town" to cover Broadway from a photographer's radio car that parked each night outside Lindy's; Walter Winchell came around one night and rode with us. We knew cops, press agents, wise guys, hoodlums, pimps, whores. It was one of the most delicious times of my life.

CONTINUED ON PAGE 47

ILLUSTRATION/LINDA CROCKETT-HANZEL

272

Book Review

OCTOBER 4, 1981

The Poet Himself

W. H. AUDEN
A Biography.
By Humphrey Carpenter.
*Illustrated. 495 pp. Boston:
Houghton Mifflin Co. $19.95.*

By Paul Fussell

WITH Stephen Spender's "W. H. Auden: A Tribute," Charles Osborne's "W. H. Auden: The Life of a Poet" and Edward Mendelson's recent "Early Auden," it's clear that Auden has been superbly served by memory and criticism. This new full biography by Humphrey Carpenter, who wrote the life of J. R. R. Tolkien a few years back, is the best yet, so interesting, indeed, that it may have the effect of shifting attention from Auden's poems to his character and personality. More people may soon be enjoying anecdotes about Auden than reading his work.

In that respect, as a literary character he may come to resemble Samuel Johnson. And our fascination with his life, his wit aside, arises from a characteristic he shares not just with Johnson but with the subjects of most remarkable biographies of his contradictoriness. Auden was a moralist who drank too much, a homosexual who thought

| Ronald Reagan: a report on his record so far | **7** | Donald Barthelme: a collection of sixty stories | **9** | Field Marshal Montgomery: the making of a general | **14** |

273

274

274
Publication   San Jose Mercury News
Art Director   David Miller
Illustrator   Sidney Fischer
Publisher   San Jose Mercury News

275
Publication   Cal Today
Art Director   Howard Shintaku
Designer   Howard Shintaku
Illustrator   Mitchell H. Anthony
Publisher   San Jose Mercury News

275

276
Publication **Playboy**
Art Director **Tom Staebler**
Designer **Kerig Pope**
Illustrator **Brad Holland**
Publisher **Playboy Enterprises, Inc.**

ROSALIE'S GOOD EATS CAFE

By Shel Silverstein

ILLUSTRATIONS BY BRAD HOLLAND

It's two in the mornin' on Saturday night
At Rosalie's Good Eats Café.
The onions are fryin', the neon is bright
And the jukebox is startin' to play.
And the sign on the wall says, IN GOD WE TRUST,
ALL OTHERS HAVE TO PAY.
And it's two in the mornin' on Saturday night
At Rosalie's Good Eats Café.

The short-order cook with the MOMMA tattoo,
He's turnin' them hamburgers slow,
Eggs over easy, whole wheat down.
"D' y'all want that coffee to go?"
He never once dreamed as a rodeo star
That he'd wind up here today
At two in the mornin' on Saturday night
At Rosalie's Good Eats Café.

There's a tall, skinny girl in the very back booth
Wearin' jeans and a secondhand fur.
She's been to the doctor, then called up a man
And now wonders just where she can turn.
She stares at her coffee, then looks toward the ceiling,
And, Lord, it's a strange place to pray
At two in the mornin' on Saturday night
At Rosalie's Good Eats Café.

There's a guy in a tux and he stands in the corner,
Feedin' the jukebox his dimes.
He just had a woman and thought that he'd bought her
But found he'd just rented some time.
And he just couldn't sleep, so he come back to see
If anyone else wants to play
At two in the mornin' on Saturday night
At Rosalie's Good Eats Café.

There's an old dollar bill in a frame on the wall,
The first one that Rose ever made.
It was once worth a dollar a long time ago,
But, like Rose, it's beginnin' to fade.
She's back of the register, dreamin' of someone,
And how things'd be if he'd stayed,
But it's two in the mornin' on Saturday night
At Rosalie's Good Eats Café.

251

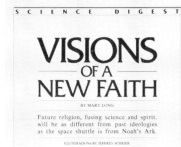

277

277,278
Publication   **Science Digest**
Art Director   **Mary Zisk**
Designer   **Mary Zisk**
Illustrator   **Jeffrey Schrier**
Publisher   **Hearst Magazines**

279
Publication   **People**
Art Director   **Robert N. Essman**
Designer   **Robert N. Essman**
Photographer   **Evelyn Floret**
Publisher   **Time, Inc.**

278

279

280,281

Publication **Newsweek**
Art Director **Thomas R. Lunde**
Illustrator **Alan E. Cober**
Publisher **Newsweek, Inc.**

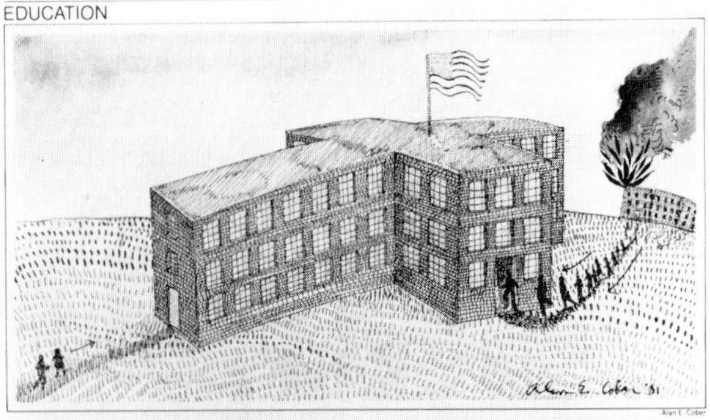

Alan E. Cober

Especially in the South, fundamentalist academies are spreading like kudzu, and teaching grammar according to the Gospel

The Bright Flight

There are no drugs, no jeans and not much adolescent sass at the Sheridan Road Christian School outside Saginaw, Mich. Most classes begin and end with a prayer. Students attend chapel once a week, and those who misbehave are not spared the rod. They learn, in no uncertain terms, that God created man and that history is really *his* story. Sheridan Road teachers believe that they were called to a special mission, and in a way so do Sheridan Road parents. "In my job I see the violence and the result of drugs in public schools," says James Cross, a police officer and father of a senior. "I just don't want my kids involved with that. I'm trying to do the best I can for them, so they'll grow up to be Christians and raise Christian kids themselves."

It used to be that private schools were luxuries for the rich or the Roman Catholic. But now middle-class families that can barely meet their mortgage payments are helping to turn the academies into educational necessities. Some parents, like the Crosses, want a clear moral framework for their children. Others are fleeing declining academic standards and disciplinary problems in the public schools. The exodus cuts across political lines to include conservatives who oppose busing and liberals who support integration. And despite tuition that can top $6,000 a year, the applications keep coming. Some private academies have bought empty public-school buildings to teach the overflow; all seem to be profiting from the panic—from venerable Phillips Academy in Andover, Mass., which turned 203 years old this year, to the Jesus Only Tabernacle, a fundamentalist school that began seven months ago in a Nashville, Tenn., basement. Says Gerald Grant of Syracuse University: "Only private schools now have a public."

Private schools are booming—drawing the brightest pupils from public schools beset with problems.

Worried public-school officials have coined a new term to define the phenomenon: bright flight. The private-school boom is skimming off many of the nation's most gifted and motivated students—and what's even worse, the drain is occurring during one of the biggest baby-busts of this century. In the last ten years public enrollment dipped 11 per cent in the West while private enrollment climbed 19 per cent. In the South the number of students in public schools declined by 6 per cent while private enrollment increased by 31 per cent. Some educators are afraid that if the defections continue unchecked, they could erode financial and political support for public education. The NEWSWEEK Poll seems to support their fear: 54 per cent of parents with children in public school say they have considered the private alternative; 23 per cent say they would be likely to switch to private schools if Congress approved tuition tax credits of $250 to $500 a year.

James Coleman's new study argues that minority students may have the most to gain if the government helps foot the private-school bill. And the Rev. Andrew Greeley, a sociologist and Catholic priest, made common cause with Coleman by releasing his own study showing that blacks and Hispanics perform better in Catholic schools than in public schools. A lot of parents already know that. Blacks and Hispanics together make up one-sixth of Catholic-school enrollment today, up from one-tenth a decade ago; California Catholic schools enroll a higher percentage of minorities than do the public schools. And if Catholic schools are the biggest draw for minorities, they are not the only alternative. There are all-black Christian academies too, and a relative handful of minorities manage to infiltrate the main-line prep schools. Moernike Irvin, girls' senior class president at Choate, is one of 6,000 black

66

NEWSWEEK/APRIL 20, 1981

280

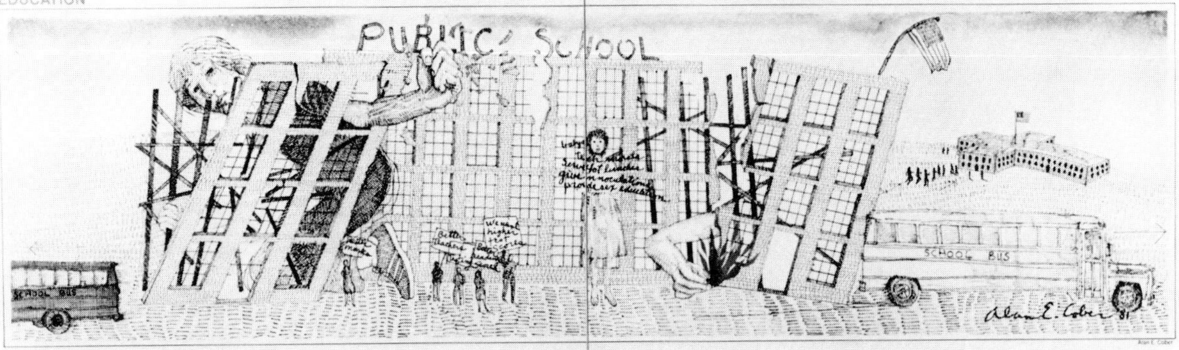

Alan E. Cober

Why Public Schools Fail

The odd thing is that the public schools are probably getting better. But try telling that to Dorothy Tillman, whose son Jimmy marched off to kindergarten in Chicago already reading at second-grade level and, after seven years, now reads at fourth-grade level. Mention it to Basil Huffman, the San Jose high-school principal who had to fire half his teachers in a fiscal pinch—including all but one of his math teachers. Tell Jody Krieger, who was driven from her Maryland classroom by abusive 13-year-olds and is now in real estate. Or pass the word to all the parents who have given up on public education and begun paying private schools to give their kids a better chance.

There are good schools, even model schools: Little Rock's Central High, a paradigm of racial confrontation in 1957, now lures students back from the private sector. The long slide in SAT scores that started in 1963 shows signs of slowing down. The trendy pendulum that swung toward "relevant" classes and open classrooms in the 1960s and '70s is swinging back toward basics these days. Best of all, more kids than ever are making it through school. As recently as 1950, less than 60 per cent of the nation's children graduated from high school. The figure is now 75 per cent, and nearly half of the graduates go on to college—including unprecedented numbers of blacks and Hispanics.

Never mind. In the sweeping public verdict of 1981, the schools are failing. In a NEWSWEEK Poll conducted by The Gallup Organization, nearly half the respondents say schools are doing a poor or only fair job—a verdict that would have been unthinkable just seven years ago, when two-thirds in a similar poll rated schools excellent or good. Fifty-nine per cent believe teachers should be better trained; more than 60 per cent want their children taught in a more orderly atmosphere; almost 70 per cent call for more stress on academic basics.

That public verdict is increasingly shared by professional educators. Last week, in a comprehensive study of public and private high schools made for the National Center for Education Statistics, sociologist James S. Coleman concluded that the private schools not only give better academic training, but are in some respects less segregated than public schools. He argued that there is a good case for public support in the form of tuition tax credits or vouchers for parents who choose private education. Even without it, private schools are the healthiest segment of the educational system these days. In an era of dwindling enrollments, demographers predict a 12 per cent increase in private pupils by 1988 (following story).

The roll call of problems is almost as familiar as the ABC's. Academic standards seem to get flimsier by the year. Costs per pupil are rising at the same time enrollments are falling and budgets shrinking. Administrators are overwhelmed with paperwork; teachers have to contend with drugs and alcohol, truancy and vandalism, apathy and ignorance. Some have plainly given up, victims of a classroom epidemic called teacher burnout. Others are plainly incompetent, unable to cope with their problem students or teach their normal ones. Schools sometimes seem more like detention halls than the groves of academe. Back talk is routine and felonious assault more common than anyone wants to admit. "There are things going on in my class that I can't seem to control," says Martha DeSue, who teaches at the Rainbow Park Elementary School in North Miami. "How can you teach when students won't sit down long enough to listen?"

Big-city schools have been trying—unsuccessfully—to answer such questions for years. What gives the current crisis urgency is that the inner-city blues now echo across suburban communities and rural glens as well. Highly regarded New Trier High School, which educates the affluent children of Chicago's North Shore suburbs, faces many of the same economic pressures and disciplinary problems that the blackboard jungles do downtown. Students in the farm community of Mt. Orab, Ohio, unconvinced that book learning will help buy a Grand Prix, are smoking pot, playing hooky, dropping out. When Robert Kitchen asked one of his sophomore English students why he hadn't read the four-page homework assignment, the student responded matter-of-factly: "I don't think we're going to need this stuff."

In growing numbers, parents in turn are yanking their kids out. The elite private schools are turning away applicants despite collegelike tuition. After a long decline, Roman Catholic schools are returning to health. Christian fundamentalist schools are spreading like kudzu from Atlanta to Anaheim. What concerns public-school educators even more than the number of defections is who's leaving: the middle-class backbone of the system, kids whose parents once would never have considered private schools. The danger is that the public schools could eventually become the last resort—an educational scrapheap for the poorest and least motivated children of the nation's underclass.

Beginning a three-part Special Report on the crisis of confidence in the American public-school system, the flight from public education —and how faith can be restored.

The American way of education is, in some respects, a victim of a more general loss of faith in the American way itself. In his first major address as Secretary of Education earlier this year, Terrel H. Bell suggested that pessimism about the public schools is inevitable, given the national mood. "When we lack confidence in ourselves, when we are troubled and when we are not prospering," he said, "it reflects in the nation's attitude, respect and support for schools."

But U.S. schools have chronically been in crisis, whether they were struggling to teach the three R's to pioneers or American ways to immigrant children. The problem now is also a very real increase in the need for education. In a culture that constantly demands more sophisticated knowledge just to hold a job, an educational system that isn't getting better fast is by definition getting worse. "What passed for competency in 1960 wouldn't pass for it in 1980 and cannot hope to pass for it in the year 2000," says Graham Down of the Council for Basic Education.

And until recently, the trend in U.S. schools has been to undercut, not enrich, the academic menu—in large part because the schools are expected to provide so many nonacademic services. They are asked to feed, inoculate, integrate, baby-sit and counsel the young. They are expected to teach driver ed, sex ed, phys ed and special ed, and still find time for regular ed besides. To be sure, the need is real. Twenty per cent of all students now have only one parent at home, and that number is growing by more than 300,000 each year. Half have no one at home during the day. Miami art teacher Peggy Rudolph was so moved by the sight of her students wearing house keys around their necks and waiting for school to open in the morning that she began showing up at 6:45. "My class has become home to them," she says. "I have to force myself not to go in on weekends." But the result is an educational tragedy, says former Chicago school superintendent Angeline Caruso. "We've gotten so far afield from education that we have little time or energy left to do what we're supposed to do."

Much of the pressure on the schools comes from Washington. The predominant symbol of Federal interference is the school bus; after years of forced busing, even families committed to integration have ambivalent feelings about the value of busing—and opponents consider it tantamount to abducting their children into hostile territory. But judicially mandated integration was only a beginning. The Elementary and Secondary Education Act of 1965 marked the government's first major effort to target Federal aid to needy students. Public Law 94-142, passed in 1975, provided

62

NEWSWEEK/APRIL 20, 1981

NEWSWEEK/APRIL 20, 1981

63

281

286

282

283

284

282–284
Publication **Life**
Art Director **Bob Ciano, Carla Barr, Mary Kate Baumann**
Designer **Carla Barr**
Illustrator **Guy Billout**
Publisher **Time, Inc.**

287

285, 286
Publication   **Fortune**
Art Director   **Ron Campbell**
Designer   **Leo McCarthy**
Illustrator   **Barry Brothers**
Publisher   **Time, Inc.**

REFINERIES REFINED

A FORTUNE PORTFOLIO

There is more than one way to view an oil refinery. To the accountant it is simply an economic unit, swallowing barrels of crude oil at one end and spewing out greenbacks at the other. To the car lover it may be a symbol of pleasure, helping to sustain old-fashioned notions of the good life. To environmentalists, and often to people who live nearby, a refinery can seem a hideous and infernal monster, a tangled mass of steel and fire that pollutes the air and water and belches forth intolerable odors. To people concerned about regulation of business, a refinery is a pawn in a gigantic and erratic chess game between the bureaucrats and the refiners—a theme discussed in the preceding article.

But to some, strange as it may seem, a refinery can be a work of art—or at least the inspiration for one. The paintings on these pages and on the cover express the singular vision of a 26-year-old New York artist named Barry Brothers. Brothers traveled to Pennsylvania, Texas, and Wyoming, to explore, photograph, and ultimately paint the nation's oldest, largest, and smallest oil refineries. As a comparing glance at the photos and paintings will show, Brothers did not attempt to be starkly realistic. As he explains: "By reducing the visual to its essential form, ridding it of obscuring detail, one can see the true relations, the patterns, more clearly."
—ARTHUR M. LOUIS

THE SMALLEST

The smallest refinery in the U.S., at Lusk, Wyoming, is called C&H, after its two late founders, Ray Chamberlain and Jim Habit. It processes just 190 barrels of crude oil a day, and sells gasoline directly to retail customers from a service station partly visible at the left of the picture. The fuel oil tanks in the foreground hold 500 barrels each. The building at the rear is used to house materials.

THE OLDEST

America's oldest refinery is found, appropriately enough, in western Pennsylvania, where the oil boom began. Built in 1869, and rebuilt many times since, it is Ashland Oil's Freedom Refinery, so named for the town on the Allegheny River where it is located. Its capacity is only 6,800 barrels a day. The storage tanks on this page contain stocks of high-quality lubricants. The center building in the picture on the facing page houses machinery used to produce rust preventives, which are stored in the tanks towering overhead.

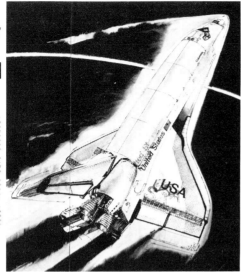

Columbia's Astronauts' Own Story: Our Phenomenal First Flight

WE WERE 40 MILES above Midway and coming home. Crip and I, when we saw the reddish pink glow. The space shuttle *Columbia* was dropping through deep black night during the last half hour of our phenomenal first flight. Our nose was pointed 40 degrees up so that the heat-shielding silica tiles on *Columbia*'s underbelly would bear the brunt of the scorching temperatures as it broke into the upper reaches of earth's atmosphere.

People had worried a lot about this reentry heat. Even our own engineers had told us that at least one of the critical tiles on the underside would probably come off. If enough did, they said, the hot plasma outside could burn right through *Columbia*.

But we had faith in those tiles, and that tenuous glow proved they were out there doing what they were made to do. They were taking 2300°F and lighting up the sky around us. Outside our windows that glow was light red, but it turned reddish orange near the superhot nose right. I felt as if we were flying through a neon tube.

I grabbed my camera, but the film was too slow to record the glow. Then the sun lit up the far horizon. For a moment that bright band of dawn streaked through, then the full burst of sunrise washed the glow away. It was so beautiful, I hated to see it go. *(Continued on page 485)*

By JOHN W. YOUNG and
ROBERT L. CRIPPEN
Paintings by KEN DALLISON

287

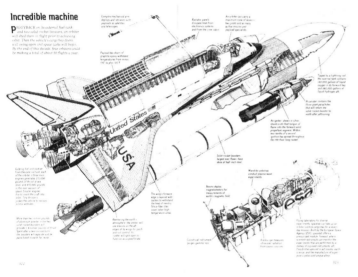

Incredible machine

PIGGYBACK on its external fuel tank and two solid rocket boosters, an orbiter will shed them in flight prior to achieving orbit. Then the vehicle's cargo bay doors will swing open and space tasks will begin. By the end of this decade, four orbiters could be making a total of about 50 flights a year.

288

289

287, 288

Publication **National Geographic**
Art Director **Howard E. Paine**
Illustrator **Ken Dallison**
Publisher **National Geographic Society**

289

Publication **Ambassador**
Art Director **Alfred Zelcer**
Designer **Alfred Zelcer**
Illustrators **Stephen Rydberg, Robert Andrew Parker, David Levine, Will Northerner, John Collier**
Publisher **The Webb Co.**

290,291

Publication   **Nautical Quarterly**
Art Director   **B. Martin Pedersen**
Designer   **B. Martin Pedersen**
Illustrator   **Daniel Maffia**
Publisher   **Jonson, Pedersen, Hinrichs & Shakery, Inc.**

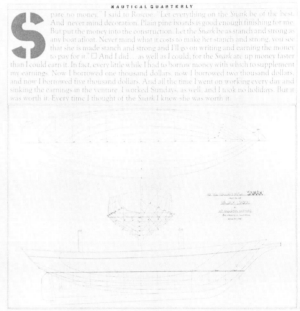

290

291

292

292

Publication	**American Film**
Art Director	**Victoria Valentine**
Designer	**Victoria Valentine**
Photographer	**Maureen Lambray**
Publisher	**The American Film Institute**

293

Publication	**Texas Monthly**
Art Director	**Jim Darilek**
Designer	**Jim Darilek**
Photographer	**Will van Overbeek**
Publisher	**Mediatex Communications Corp.**

294

Publication	**Americana**
Art Director	**Mervyn E. Clay**
Photographer	**Peter Lemon**
Publisher	**Americana, Inc.**

293

294

295
Publication   **Travel & Leisure**
Art Director   **Adrian Taylor**
Designer   **Adrian Taylor**
Photographer   **John Lewis Stage**
Publisher   **American Express Publishing Corporation**

296
Publication   **Cuisine**
Art Director   **David J. Talbot**
Designer   **Nina Ovryn**
Photographer   **John Paul Endress**
Publisher   **Cuisine Magazine, Inc.**

295

296

Questions of
American Life:
Anthropologist
Marvin Harris on

• Why Terror
  Walks the Streets

• Why Products
  Don't Work

• Why Women
  Were Liberated

How Saying No
Helps Define
Our Identity

Conquering
Foreign-Language
Phobia

**Putting Time Limits on Therapy–
Can Deadlines Speed a Cure?**

297

298

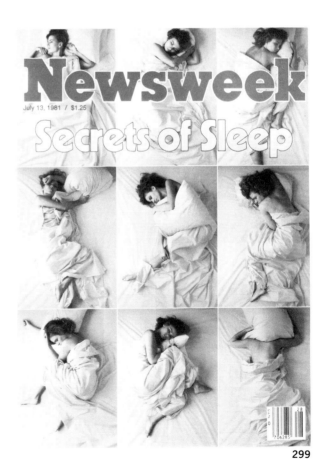

299

300

Publication   **Physician and Sportsmedicine**
Art Director   **Tina Adamek**
Designer   **Steve Blom**
Photographer   **Tim Davis**
Publisher   **McGraw-Hill, Inc.**

301

Publication   **Progressive Architecture**
Art Director   **George Coderre**
Designer   **George Coderre**
Photographer   **Steve Rosenthal**
Publisher   **Reinhold Publishing**

302

Publication   **Emergency Medicine**
Art Director   **Tom Lennon**
Designer   **Tom Lennon**
Illustrator   **Nick Aristovulos**
Photographer   **Shig Ikeda**
Publisher   **Fischer Medical Publications**

301

300

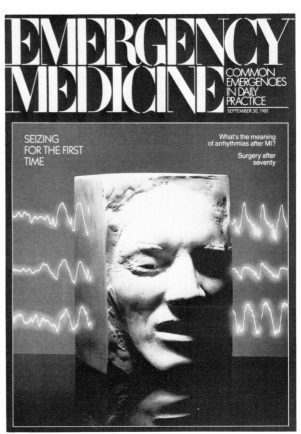

302

303
Publication   **Animal Kingdom**
Art Director **Brigid Quinn**
Designer   **Brigid Quinn**
Photographer **Jeff Rotman**
Publisher   **The New York Zoological Society**

304
Publication   **Animal Kingdom**
Art Director **Brigid Quinn**
Designer   **Brigid Quinn**
Photographer **Bill Frakes**
Publisher   **The New York Zoological Society**

303

304

305
Publication   **The Dial**
Art Director   **Susan Reinhardt**
Designer   **Susan Reinhardt**
Photographer   **Bill King**
Publisher   **Public Broadcasting Communications, Inc.**

306
Publication   **Esquire**
Art Director   **Robert Priest**
Designer   **April Silver**
Photographer   **Jean Moss**
Publisher   **Esquire Publishing**

307
Publication   **Chicago**
Art Director   **Jeff Pilarski**
Designer   **Jeff Pilarski**
Photographer   **E. Michael James**
Publisher   **WFMT, Inc.**

305

306

307

Wolfgang Amadeus Mozart

AFTER TWO CENTURIES, AUSTRIA'S CHILD PRODIGY HAS BECOME THE WORLD'S FAVORITE COMPOSER

As a child, Mozart composed on the clavier or harpsichord, scratching the notes down afterward. Later he began composing for the piano.

CREATING A CALIFORNIA CUISINE

Not long ago California cuisine was defined as any dish garnished with a strawberry and a fresh orange slice. No more. Today a new breed of food-conscious Californians strives to develop a distinct cuisine. In kitchens up and down the state, in restaurants like Chez Panisse in Berkeley and Green's in San Francisco and in food shops such as the Oakville Grocery in San Francisco, the bounty from land and sea is being creatively exploited.

The still-evolving cuisine borrows from others: a dash of spice from the Mexican kitchen, a penchant for unusual combinations of flavors from the nouvelle cuisine and a sense of delicacy from the substantial.

by Patricia Wells

Is Success Killing Greektown?

by MATT BEER

Trappers Alley, a trendy new development, is about to open on Detroit's favorite strip. Some say it's Greektown's horn of plenty. Some say it's the neighborhood's Trojan horse.

308

309

310

311
Publication **Ambassador**
Art Director **Barbara Koster**
Designer **Marcia Wright**
Photographer **Ryuzo**
Publisher **The Webb Company**

312,313
Publication **Travel & Leisure**
Art Director **Adrian Taylor**
Designer **Adrian Taylor**
Photographer **Kelly/Moony**
Publisher **American Express**
Publishing Corporation

311

312

313

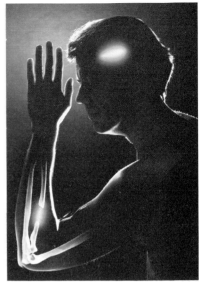

314

315

316

317

318

319

317
Publication   Playboy
Art Director   Tom Staebler
Designer   Tom Staebler
Photographer   Tom Staebler
Publisher   Playboy Enterprises, Inc.

318
Publication   Playboy
Art Director   Tom Staebler
Designer   Tom Staebler
Photographer   Richard Izui
Publisher   Playboy Enterprises, Inc.

319
Publication   Time
Art Director   Rudolph Hoglund
Designer   Irene Ramp
Photographer   Dirck Halstead
Publisher   Time, Inc.

THE GROUND'S THE LIMIT

by Harry Hurt III

When Phil Smith and his friends saw the tallest building in Texas rising up from the streets of Houston, there was only one thing they wanted to do—jump off the top and live to tell the tale.

320

320

Publication	**Texas Monthly**
Art Director	**Jim Darilek**
Designer	**Jim Darilek**
Photographer	**Carl Boenish**
Publisher	**Mediatex Communications, Inc.**

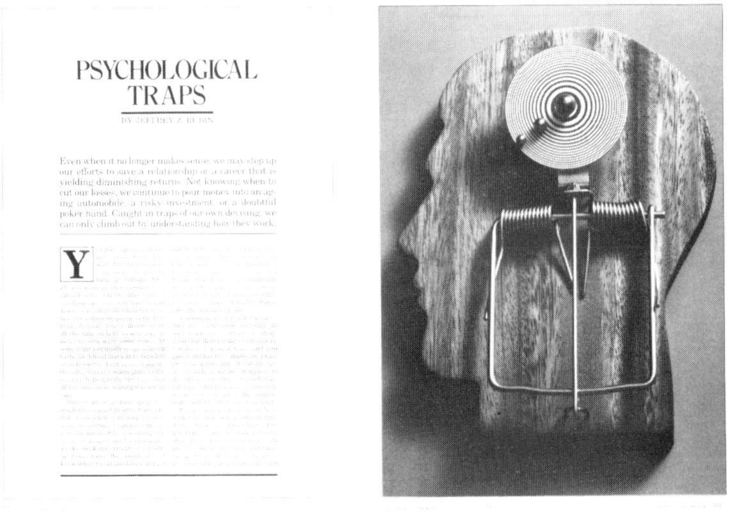
PSYCHOLOGICAL TRAPS

BY JEFFREY Z. RUBIN

Even when it no longer makes sense, we may step up our efforts to save a relationship or a career that is yielding diminishing returns. Not knowing when to cut our losses, we continue to pour money into an aging automobile, a risky investment, or a doubtful poker hand. Caught in traps of our own devising, we can only climb out by understanding how they work.

321

321

Publication	**Psychology Today**
Art Director	**Carveth Kramer**
Designer	**Carveth Kramer**
Photographer	**Fred Burrell**
Publisher	**Ziff-Davis Publishing Company**

psychology today

THE NEW COMPETENCY TESTS:
Matching the Right People to the Right Jobs

BY DANIEL GOLEMAN

What distinguishes the "water walkers" from the mediocre performers in any occupation? Harvard psychologist David C. McClelland says it's an elusive set of motives, traits, and social skills. He and his colleagues say they can identify and train these competencies.

322

322

Publication	**Psychology Today**
Art Director	**Carveth Kramer**
Designer	**Carveth Kramer**
Photographer	**Carl Fischer**
Publisher	**Ziff-Davis Publishing Company**

323

Publication **Emergency Medicine**
Art Director **Tom Lennon**
Designer **James T. Walsh**
Illustrator **John Tenison**
Photographer **John Tenison**
Publisher **Fischer Medical Publications**

324,325

Publication **Florida Trend**
Art Director **Steve Duckett**
Designer **Steve Duckett**
Photographer **Richard Riley**
Publisher **Florida Trend, Inc.**

OVERDOING THE ANTICHOLINERGICS

323

1981 Golden Spoon Awards

By Robert Tolf

Once again, FLORIDA TREND readers have voted for their favorite restaurants. This year newcomers were added to the list of regional winners while several perennial favorites dominated the "Best Restaurants" category.

BEST OF ALL

Bern's Steak House, Tampa
Maison & Jardin, Altamonte Springs
Chalet Suzanne, Lake Wales
La Vieille Maison, Boca Raton
Captain Anderson's, Panama City
Cafe Chauveron, Miami Beach
Siple's Garden Seat, Clearwater
Freddie's Steak House, Fern Park
Piccadilly, Orlando

324

America's little secret

By Erik Calonius

$150 billion changes hands every year in the subterranean economy, where criminals and solid citizens have two things in common. They deal in cash and they cheat the IRS.

325

326
Publication **Mother Jones**
Art Director **Louise Kollenbaum**
Designer **Dian-Aziza Kollenbaum**
Photographer **John Hoaglund**
Publisher **Foundation for National Progress**

327
Publication **New York Magazine**
Art Director **Robert Best**
Designer **Karen Mullarkey, Jordan Schaps**
Photographer **Harry Benson**
Publisher **News Group Publications**

328
Publication **Judges' Journal**
Art Director **Robert Woolley**
Designer **Robert Woolley**
Photographer **Frida Schubert**
Publisher **American Bar Association Press**

326

327

STRESS
What it does to judges, and how it can be lessened

By Isaiah M. Zimmerman

4   5   328

329

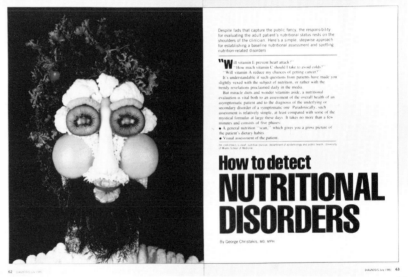

330

331

	332,333
Publication	Four Winds
Art Director	Larry Smitherman
Publisher	Smitherman Graphic Design

	334
Publication	Town & Country
Art Director	Melissa Tardiff
Designer	Mark Borden
Photographer	Paccione
Publisher	The Hearst Corporation

332

333

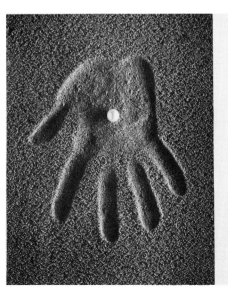

334

335,336
Publication   New York Magazine
Art Director   Robert Best
Designer   Karen Mullarkey
Photographer   Harry Benson
Publisher   News Group Publication

Inside Rikers Island

By Nicholas Pileggi

"...An unofficial truce lets drugs and sex flourish..."

Let out of their cells for fourteen hours a day, inmates are jammed together with guards in crowded corridors.

Photographs by Harry Benson

335

"...'Everybody is conspiring to keep the lid on,' says   the head of the guards' union. 'And we pay the price'..."

With Rikers' brooding population already exceeding the jail's capacity, officials and inmates worry about an explosion during the long, hot summer.

Many inmates spend their leisure time strengthening their muscles for life on the outside. "I want to come out hard," explains one confessed mugger.

336

306

THE GAME WITHIN

PHOTOGRAPHS BY MICHAEL ZAGARIS
HAND-TINTS BY KRISTIN SUNDBOM

Someone plays a tape machine. Someone else walks across a tile floor in cleats that go *clickclickclickclickclick*. Ordinary sound magnifies itself. Ordinary time expands. One of the ironies of pro football, a sport that excites and entertains by way of random collision, is that its pregame ritual demands meditation and solitude. Similarly, the techniques used here, to record the stillness of NFL locker rooms, involved a sort of removal. One artist seizes a moment, another studies and interprets its mood.

Above: Lawrence Pillers, San Francisco 49ers

337

337,338
Publication **Pro!**
Art Director **Cliff Wynne**
Designer **Cliff Wynne**
Illustrator **Kristin Sundbom**
Photographer **Michael Zagaris**
Publisher **NFL Properties, Inc.**

Craig Morton (seated), Denver Broncos

Earl Cooper, San Francisco 49ers

338

339

339–341

Publication	**Passages**
Art Director	**Barbara Koster**
Designer	**Barbara Koster**
Photographer	**Judy Olansen,**
	Chuck Keeler, Jr.
Publisher	**The Webb Company**

340

341

342,343
Publication **Time**
Art Director **Rudolph Hoglund**
Designer **Thomas Bentkowski**
Publisher **Time, Inc.**

342

343

344,345

Publication **Penthouse**
Art Director **Joe Brooks**
Designer **Claire Victor**
Photographer **Pete Turner**
Publisher **Penthouse International**

Dressing from the ground up

FASHION FOOTNOTES

Once upon a time, men's footwear toed the traditional lines of black wing tips, brown loafers, and the occasional sneaker peeking out from beneath blue jeans. Now, propelled by an explosion of new styles, running from fun to formal, shoes have taken a big step out of fashion's forgettable footnotes and into the spotlight. Sleekly styled dress shoes, with pronounced textures and sharp toe treatments, are ideal for high-stepping in the office or on the town. Be footloose and fancy free in casual shoes that can be dressed up or down for the sporting life or just sporting about. Whether you're pounding pavements or prairies, cowboy boots are durable, functional, and good-looking and range in look from the truly Western to the urban. An abundance of choices in shoe styles lays the groundwork, so that whatever your needs, you can be sure of putting your best foot forward.

FASHIONS BY ED EMMERLING
PHOTOGRAPHS BY PETE TURNER

344

345

346,347

Publication **Popular Photography**

Art Director **Shinichiro Tora**

Designer **Shinichiro Tora**

Photographer **Jack Krawczyk**

Publisher **Ziff-Davis Publishing Company**

346

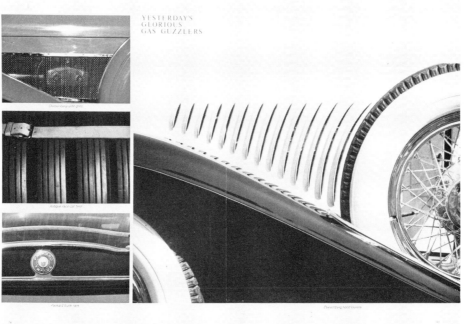

347

348

348,349
Publication   **Mother Jones**
Art Director   **Louise Kollenbaum**
Designer   **Dian-Aziza Ooka**
Photographer   **Susa Meiselas**
Publisher   **Foundation for National Progress**

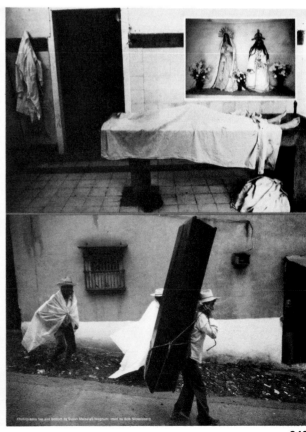

MOTHER JONES

GUATEMALA:
THE MUFFLED SCREAM
A Field Report On The Unthinkable Revolution
By Julia Preston

The Guatemalan government dislikes foreign journalists. It views any reporting on the unending political violence in the country as part of a conspiracy to propagate a chilling image of Guatemala abroad. Today the authorities keep a list at the airport of the correspondents considered undesirable, which seems to include virtually everyone who has filed stories regularly from there in the past decade.

In early May 1980, a veteran CBS television correspondent with a clean middle-of-the-road reputation laid over for a few hours in Guatemala to await a connecting flight to Honduras. He was pulled from an airport immigration line by police and held overnight under heavy guard. Mexico City correspondents for both *The New York Times* and *The Washington Post* no longer venture into the country, having received a string of death threats from the right wing. The telex at the Camino Real Hotel stands idle, for even those reporters who do go into this lush, Central American nation don't dare to file from inside it.

As a result, while neighboring El Salvador is overrun with American newshounds, a silence has fallen over Guatemala, a country that has been called

"the strategic key to Central America" (by recently appointed Ambassador Frederic Chapin) and a nation where a civil conflict as vicious as El Salvador's is gradually coming to a head.

Guatemala, with almost seven million inhabitants, is the region's most populous nation, with its most abundant resources. It has the highest level of American investment: more than 190 firms and affiliates have contributed nearly $300 million to its wealth. Last March, Texaco struck oil in a northern corner of Guatemala and is now busy drilling for more. The American Chamber of Commerce is a laconic but potent political bloc working in close tandem with the Guatemalan private sector.

From the perspective of the Reagan administration, a revolution in Guatemala is not only unacceptable, it is unthinkable. It would bring a hostile regime to the rim of the colossal oil fields of Chiapas, Mexico, considered part of the United States' strategic reserve. It would dismantle the Guatemalan army, the region's largest at 18,000 strong, considered a pillar of the military *ancien régime* in Central America. It would squeeze Honduras between the Sandinistas in Nicaragua and the rebels in El Salvador, tipping the balance of forces

to the left in Central America, perhaps irrevocably.

Within the Reagan administration, discretion has surrounded State Department moves to restore American leverage to the Guatemalan military. The Carter government suspended military assistance to Guatemala in 1977 on the basis of flagrant human rights violations. Reagan's, on the other hand, first granted a commercial license to the nation to purchase $3.2 million in jeeps and trucks, then agreed to train Guatemalan pilots.

The prevailing view in Washington is that Guatemala's military regime, led by General Romeo Lucas Garcia, needs military assistance to fight off a growing Cuban presence in Central America. "Cuba has been systematically creating a machine for the destruction of established institutions and governments [in Latin America]," according to Assistant Secretary of State Thomas Enders. Reagan's State Department also hopes the U.S. military assistance will help the Guatemalan military curb

Since summer, deaths from what officials call "natural Guatemalan causes" are running as high as 26 a day. But to the untutored eye, nothing of this shows.

NOVEMBER 1981
40

349

350,351

Publication **Science Digest**
Art Director **Mary Zisk**
Designer **Mark Zisk**
Photographer **Bruno Zehnder**
Publisher **Hearst Magazines**

LAND
OF A MILLION
KINGS

TEXT BY ROGER TORY PETERSON
PHOTOGRAPHS BY BRUNO ZEHNDER

On a remote Antarctic isle, science
meets a vast flock of the world's
most unusual seabird: the penguin.

I've been a penguin watcher—a penguin addict—for 15 years. In
fact, my bird-watching friends call me King Penguin. I've visited
my totem bird on a dozen Antarctic voyages. But it wasn't until
this year that I fulfilled a longtime dream and visited the land
of a million kings—the world's largest king-penguin colony, on
the Crozet Islands, 2,500 miles south of the Cape of Good Hope.
The sight was staggering: 1 million birds creating a living royal
carpet spread to the horizon. On Crozet, I found myself in a penguin city considerably more populous than Boston or San Francisco and far more congested. Long lines of birds paraded up and
down the slopes to the sea, half a mile away. The trumpeting
of the adults and the whistling of the chicks was deafening. For

350

Before mating, king penguins sometimes nuzzle, but more often they face each other, raise their raised heads and trumpet loudly

centuries, their forebears had used their
same avenues through the tussock grass
until tunnels two or three feet deep had
been worn by the pressure of millions of
leathery feet.

The main colony was an agitated mass
of birds, some on eggs, others squabbling
or simply loafing. Whenever a bird re-
turned to relieve its mate, who was incu-
bating—instead of resting, keeps balance
their eggs on their large feet—there was
a mutual display of head waving, nibbling
and bowing, accompanied by considerable musical trumpeting.

I have observed king penguins in Mac-
quarie Island, south of Australia, and on
South Georgia Island, off South America.
A colony of 30,000, such as the one at
the Bay of Isles, South Georgia, is impressive—but there is nothing that can beat
a million kings.

The second largest species of the penguin family, the king stands three feet
from beak to tail and weighs from 30 to
40 pounds. Its version of the traditional
black-and-white penguin uniform shows

regal touches of color: a blue-gray jacket,
yellow chest and orange collar.

Other sub-Antarctic islands like the
Falklands and Heard once held colonies
as vast as the one at Crozet, but the king
penguin was slaughtered in three places a
century ago by sealers and whalers who
rendered them for oil. They are beginning
to return in small numbers—pioneer re-
cruits from several neighboring islands
whose remoteness somehow enabled
them to survive the slaughter. Someday
they may again see large numbers in the
accessible Falklands, where, it is said, the

That penguins can run as
fast as a man is truly
a remarkable feat, since
the length of their
stride is but six inches.

last colony of king penguins was boiled
down by a shepherd for the sole purpose
of oiling his roof.

Most people are aware of only one kind
of penguin, the Adélie, that "little chap
in the dress suit." Actually, there are 17
species, only 4 or 5 of which are found
as far south as the Antarctic continent
and its offshore islands. Not all penguins
live in icy surroundings. The Galápagos
penguin, the world's rarest, is found in
the sunny subtropical archipelago at the
same name. The biggest and most color-
ful penguins are the king and the emper-
or, which stands four feet tall and weighs
90 pounds. These species are set apart not
only by size but by the fact that they lay
one egg—most penguins lay two—which
they incubate on their feet. The smallest
penguins are the more northerly—the
five-pound Galápagos and the three-
pound little blue of New Zealand and
southern Australia. Penguins of all sizes
and climes feed on fish, squid and krill,
a kind of crustacean.

The king's nesting colonies are not on

the Antarctic continent but on the sub-
Antarctic islands. They are usually found
at the feet of glaciers or snowbanks,
where meltwater turns the earth into a
quagmire. Here the kings gather by the
thousands, spaced evenly, each keeping
its neighbor in place by a jab of the beak
or a whack of the flipper.

As we watched the crowd on Crozet,
an self-training bird sometimes failed to
observe the correct behavioral signals as
it proceeded through the colony. It was
assailed from all sides until a test for all
developed, the silvery breasts of contest-
ants blunted by the bruising flippers of
their opponents.

Our team of scientists, adventurers and
photographers from the *Lindblad Explor-
er*—walked among groups of brown teddy
bearlike young from an earlier nesting
who mingled with unusual. It takes 13 to
14 months for the young to be on their
own, a part of kings can rear only two
young in a three-year period.

At the staging area in the outer beach,
where the birds enter or emerge from the
sea, more than 100,000 birds had gathered, many of them resting before making
the trek to other colonies. Just entering

*Above: Spaced equally on
their breeding ground,
king penguins each guard a
tiny territory by flailing
flippers and jabbing at re-
sharp beaks at neighbors
that come too close. The
crowded colony, usually
located on muddy flats,
become filthy by season's
end. Left: This chin-strap
penguin, aptly named for
the thin black stripe
under its bill, is found
only in the Antarctic.*

Where the Good Life Is Easy

In Mexico's hill towns, a rare blend of culture and comfort draws painters, poets, loungers, and expatriates.

by Ron Hansen

It could be the Sonoma lands of Colorado or southwest country in Nebraska, a broad sun-burned valley of scant-brown earth, scrub brush, and small towns where ranchers in straw cowboy hats linger around a Coke machine and chat about hurricanes and snow. But the state is Guanajuato 150 miles northwest of Mexico City in the scenic agricultural heart of what is called the Bajío.

East are the foothills of the Sierra Madre Oriental mountains and west the Sierra de Pénjamo, each chain a bluish-blue inch on the horizon. Between these hills is a lush basin of wheatfields and wild flowers whose composition scratch out a living with avocados, beans, chili peppers, strawberries, and squash. Girls squat outside orange brick hovels on side roads and clap corn mash into tortillas. Small boys flick stones at cattle that steer them into a corral made of boulders, and four-year-old electrical button-down vendors scamper...

It's a mountain area the Bajío. The climate is salubrious,

never colder than a Savannah April nor warmer than Denver in June. The altitude of the hill towns, over 6,000 feet, is one itself and is exhausting only when you're climbing stairs. Stars are the blue of blankets for baby boys. The clouds are so low you can throw rocks into them. And when the rains come, they come well the rug sheets of a mailman in the afternoon.

You can meticate in the Bajío. You can 'go native' and rent a black-tie 19-a-month and read at night between the large and fetch your water by pail. But in the Bajío, you are 'an Mi-guel de Allende and Guana-juato. Mexicans loosheot full names. Here the calm and curiousness of another era coincide with European culture and expatriates where there are cinema clubs, art institutes, chic restaurants country Sunday concerts with solemn violins and petite ap-plause, cafes where the amel-tigenition can bear about Mars and walk here only cigarette smoke. Orchid gardens and mansions are concealed behind stained divots and blossomed stucco walls. Here, folk cou-tury churches were con-structed and such as addobbe the mortar was mixed with olive root dust and red wine.

The road from Mexico City to the town of San Miguel de Allende cuts between acres of orange and yellow wildflowers that are as flamboyant as sum-mer scarves. Farther (all on sloul-est) glovs and mountains that wear the violet shades of clouds as if they were green. Rowdy forest at the wind and dive after smaller herds on the lone-colored cactus.

Via rented car or hire Casa bus, the ride from the capital's suburbian outbenits takes about three hours. Tracks blur along the nighthard lanes with their canvas covers treating in the wind and black sheet re-lease to low. Muffers have dis-integrated or been removed and the noise is like that of dul-ti slammed garden skillet set strikes to the second. The sec-ond class buses canten with a little less harizone but far more visual effects: spangles, tassels, window fringe, bumper slo-gans, gumball colors. ➤

San Miguel is a city of art galleries and cinema clubs, cafes and Sunday concerts.

The climate is salubrious, never colder than a Savannah April nor warmer than Denver in June.

seasons of the substantial cluster mountains as an extensive English/Spanish being a bizarre class of the hills of Western state San class to Grande than can be found in over 1 test times in are a rightisone radio broadcast of Big Band and string tunes and a slew of anecdotes about some meditation insurers who've lived here. Lawrence Ferlinghetti was Beverly Stricer. I blend to rag you Cherries, and Neal Cassady chilled on the railroad tracks in Celaya.

But the enchantment of San Miguel comes from the na-tives the descendants of the Otomi, Huachichol, and Chichimec Indians. There are the pretty girls in knee-socks who giggle at the dried poster at Casa Allchuca, the stow-peen-die-arti who hunker near the churches and serve us from the town for cent ourselves loud, the stow or young or lotheo clothes and confine hair with-lag on-mra from the 1 to the nose and no moss-air rusk with a dipper. The streets the work and much of the life is the out-long bursces are very much as they were 100 years ago.

The town has changed very little in last anno September 16th, 1810, when the men who reat struck for independence I then the cumulphasia of Queretaro. Della hasty scur-ried to the carpetman and bullfighter's Ignacio Allende that their scheme for Mexican independence which has to start with a skirmish at a Decceber 10th mouth by had been straited for the Spanish in-surgener wrapped in Allende suited in on his home in San Miguel and told at once to the small village of Dolores 25 miles north on the road that is now Highway 51 and the has room to Guanajuato. At 11 o'clock on that Saturday Fa-ther Miguel Hidalgo y Costilla rang the church bells there and called. I rong for the wrgue of Guadalupe Death re-half government of leads in the colonial palace 1 the same pale, as Dolores is accounted as the parish church as it on ones l the parish. Mexican president.

On the following Sunday morning an army of Mexilicha and mestizos murched under the banner of a Virgin of Guadalupe at the sanctuary at adobe mantle that is toppled with purely and crowned ➤

This "Tree of Life" is a familiar sight in the Bajío.

It was a two-hour stroll that es-cort in Guanajuato, and for that reason the Bajío is now called the Cradle of Indepen-dence.

Today the Allendula icons seen that houses pre-Hispanic art, copies of the Mexican state's most resputable dera-doers, documents also nor Diego Rivera and colonial murals by Jose Chavez Mor-ade. Also in evidence are car-ney books that the iounegant Spanish authorities used to hang both ages that held the several heads of Hidalgo, Al-lende, Aldama, and Jimenez after their execution in Chihuahua. South of the mu-seum on the left of the scene, there is a heavily monument to Pipila that winched down on a swank city of more than 50,000 residents in an area that claims to be the geographical pas of Mexico and has once its cultural center. Here child guides hire out for 120 pesos and as tour Spanish or pidgin English continue the purest ague into a fiery roll their eyes watch their riches and rein then discerning.

The overlook here is at least 20 stories up on a landscaped bluff. Naked somehow to the crumbling earth are cliff houses that loom over the can-yon like driving beards. The people park their cars on col-stained roofs and descend into their kitchens Guanajuato is a bizarre city in that was full of death deliance, and look may-no-hands bravado. Some zore ago there was a song about Guanajuato that carried the re-frain: la mala no rude (ando) them life is worth nothing a sinister notion that could have originated with the silz-silver mines of the men den revolu-tions. It is a romantic notion as well.

And there is romance in Guanajuato, Across from the triangular harden de la Unicn is the sumptuous, tree-twined Juarez Theater, the part of Mex-ican late life, the floors are polished marble, the choir cushions are red velvet, the curtain is a rare 19th-century version off communiqués The entire crescent chandelored opera home seems spoken/th gar-landed gilded and braided. Near the Basilica de Nuestra Senoria Guanajuato, which enshrouses a Virgin carved on Spanish 7th chated in a blue mantle that is inggied with pearls and crowned ➤

San Miguel's outdoor market is a combination of barn social and carnival.

352,353
Publication **Destinations**
Art Director **Shelley Williams**
Designer **Michael Freeman**
Photographer **Dan Weaks**
Publisher **13-30 Corporation**

354
Publication **Esquire**
Art Director **Robert Priest**
Designer **April Silver**
Photographer **Michael Geiger**
Publisher **Esquire Publishing**

352

353

Worldly Wanderings
PHOTOGRAPHS BY PASQUALE BALSAMO

You've already begun to long for spring; maybe you're even chasing the sun to a tropical paradise. Here's a sophisticated and spirited sampling of clothes to see you on your way.

WHEREVER YOU GO, let your shirttails fly. Pack the kind of clothes you are used to wearing in the gym or on the track—a rugby shirt and drawstring pants. Out of the locker room and on the street, these clothes have been cut a little trimmer and have been recast in unexpected colors and icy pastels.

354

355

356

357

355–357

Publication **Ambassador**
Art Director **Alfred Zelcer**
Designer **Alfred Zelcer**
Photographer **Bud Lee**
Publisher **The Webb Company**

358,359

Publication   **Travel & Leisure**
Art Director   **Adrian Taylor**
Designer   **Adrian Taylor**
Photographer   **John Lewis Stage**
Publisher   **American Express Publishing Corporation**

Skirt snapping in the breeze, Frances Evans whizzes down Colonial Williamsburg's Duke of Gloucester Street to her job as a glazier at the bootmaker's shop.

358

A few years ago, the Nature Conservancy managed to acquire a group of 13 wild barrier islands that teem with bird life: shore-birds, migratory waterfowl, waders, songbirds. About 30 tours, with six participants each, are scheduled from April through October (\$20 per person). A small boat takes you right up to the breeding grounds, so close you often don't even need binocu-lars. June is the best time. To find Virginia Coast Reserve head-quarters, in an old farmhouse at the dead end of a dirt road, you turn back at Nassawadox for directions; there are no signs. For tour schedule and reservations, contact Rod Hennessey or Barry Truitt, Virginia Coast Reserve, Brownsville, Nassawa-dox, Va. 23413; phone 804-442-3049.

In this area of the Shore, tourist facilities are few and far between. Most convenient to the Virginia Coast Reserve is the **Whispering Pines Motel** on U.S. 13 outside Accomac (\$25 to \$48). Farther south, you'll probably do best overnighting at one of the modern motels at Cape Charles just before you get on the Bridge Tunnel. About a quarter-mile north of its entrance, the **America House Motor Inn** has nice rooms (doubles, \$40) and serves fresh seafood and steaks; there is a pool as well as a pri-vate beach.

For general information on the Shore: Anita H. Conquest, **Eastern Shore of Virginia Chamber of Commerce,** Accomac, Va. 23301; phone 804-787-2460.

A sailboat tranquilly sits at anchor off Corpus's Island (above) at the setting sun softly paints the sky. The bronzed, weather-toughened skin of William Truitt (left) bespeaks his strenuous work as a Chesapeake crab fisherman. Retired farmer Peter B. Taylor and grandson Peter B. Taylor III show off the fruits of their garden at Point Breeze, the family home (right).

359

360,361
Publication   **Nautical Quarterly**
Art Director   **B. Martin Pedersen**
Designer   **B. Martin Pedersen**
Photographer   **Jim Brown**
Publisher   **Jonson, Pedersen, Hinrichs & Shakery, Inc.**

360

Along with eleven of her sisters, the graceful daysailer on
these pages is a survivor from the first summer of this
century, a time when racing sailboats were designed
with long tapering overhangs, skimming-dish bottoms
and an amazing spread of gaff-rigged sail. The Idem
class—called by the Latin word for identical—was
launched in 1900 for a group of summer residents on Upper St. Regis
Lake in the Adirondacks, and it is the oldest surviving one-design
class in the world that consists of the original boats. Twelve boats
were the original fleet—seven built in the spring of 1900 and five
during a few later summers—and all twelve have survived—nine still
on their home lake, one on Lake Champlain, one on Upper Saranac,
and one proudly displayed by the Adirondack Museum in Blue
Mountain Lake, N.Y.

Peek-A-Boo (her original name) was built for Robert W. Stuart as
one of the original seven and passed on to several owners before she
came to Clark J. Lawrence and his family in the 'thirties. Clark
Lawrence's daughter Audrey, now Mrs. Don-Michael Bird of
Winnetka, Illinois, inherited the boat in 1972. Peek-A-Boo has had a
typical Idem history of loving care, occasional unavoidable neglect,
and ownership in the same family or among neighbors on the lake.
She was stored ashore during World War II, came out of retirement
several times in the 'fifties, then went under cover from 1959 to 1968.
The Birds have sailed her every season since, except for the summer
of 1970 when she was loaned to an Upper St. Regis Lake neighbor,
and she was refinished and slightly rebuilt for the 1981 season by
Michael Bird and several friends. She is an heirloom, as are most of
her sisters.

Clinton Crane designed an outstanding little sloop named Momo
for Augustus Durkee in 1897, and that summer Durkee brought the
boat to his vacation house on Upper St. Regis Lake after she won a
Canadian-American challenge on the St. Lawrence. With Crane at the
helm, the 20'-waterline Momo beat every other boat on the lake, and
the idea of a St. Regis one-design class began to be discussed. Crane
studied wind conditions on Upper St. Regis Lake in 1899, especially
the extreme variations in wind strength at different places on a forest
lake full of points, bays and islands, and he came up with a boat that
would sail on its ear with fair control, spill wind when hit by a gust, and
take advantage of light air with a big spread of medium-aspect sail.

361

INDEX

POINT SIZE

13   15

INCHES

1 — 1

2 — 2

3 — 3

Art Directors

Designers

Illustrators

Photographers

Publications

Publishers